In appreciation of your
generosity, friendship and partnership
in helping to sustain and expand
the vital programs and outreach efforts
of the Orthodox Union and NCSY.

צדקה מקרבת את הגאולה

The Aryeh Kaplan Anthology I.

The
Aryeh Kaplan

Published by

ncsy

ORTHODOX UNION · תורה ומצות

Anthology I.

*Illuminating expositions
on Jewish thought and practice
by a revered teacher*

THE ARYEH KAPLAN ANTHOLOGY VOL. I

© *Copyright 1975, 1976, 1981, 1983, 1984, 1985, 1991*
by National Conference of Synagogue Youth /
Union of Orthodox Jewish Congregations of America
333 Seventh Avenue / New York, N.Y. 10001 / (212) 563-4000

Distributed in the U.S.A. and Canada by
MESORAH PUBLICATIONS, Ltd.
4401 Second Avenue
Brooklyn, New York 11232

Distributed in Israel by
MESORAH MAFITZIM / J. GROSSMAN
Rechov Harav Uziel 117
Jerusalem, Israel

Distributed in Australia & New Zealand by
GOLD'S BOOK & GIFT CO.
36 William Street
Balaclava 3183, Vic., Australia

Distributed in Europe by
J. LEHMANN HEBREW BOOKSELLERS
20 Cambridge Terrace
Gateshead, Tyne and Wear
England NE8 1RP

Distributed in South Africa by
KOLLEL BOOKSHOP
22 Muller Street
Yeoville 2198
Johannesburg, South Africa

ISBN: 0-89906-466-9 (hard cover)
0-89906-867-7 (paperback)

Printed In The United States Of America by
Noble Book Press Corp., New York, NY

Contents

As Great as the Message
Is the Man Who Brought the Message

Foreward: An appreciation of the author

by Rabbi Pinchas Stolper

Aryeh Kaplan lives on through the writings he left behind — a living legacy of piercing and penetrating thought.

Who else but Rabbi Aryeh Kaplan possessed the magic touch with which to make complicated, mystical, philosophical and religious concepts come to life with clarity, simplicity and force. Only he was able to lower his pail deep into the wellsprings of our tradition, deeper than had been done in the English language until his time, and bring us refreshing and revealing Torah insights.

Religious concepts are often difficult to understand, and for many are elusive and unattainable. Rabbi Kaplan possessed the rare ability to bring them into focus. He had the special gifts and talents which made it possible to connect science to Torah, philosophy to action, mysticism to logic and clarity of thought. He knew how to take abstract concepts and give them life. He had the talent to restore faith, to bring God's living message to our hearts and minds. Despite the fact that he was a deep and distinguished scholar, a rare *talmid chacham* who had mastered all branches of the Torah and Talmud, he possessed the common touch; he understood how people think and was able to translate deep and complicated concepts into everyday language.

Rabbi Aryeh Kaplan's meteoric rise as one of the most effective, persuasive, scholarly and prolific exponents of Judaism in the English language came to an abrupt end on January 28, 1983, with his sudden death at the age of 48. He was a multi-faceted, uniquely creative and talented author, scholar, thinker, rabbi and educator who touched the lives of thousands. The 52 volumes that were his life's work accounted for a qualitative and quantitative leap in Jewish publishing, making a host of difficult topics and concepts available to the English-reading public.

In the course of a writing career spanning only twelve years, Aryeh Kaplan became known to Jewish youth and adult readers for such books as *Waters of Eden — The Mystery of the Mikvah; Sabbath — Day of Eternity; God, Man and Tefillin; Tzitzit — The Thread of Light; The Light Beyond; Adventures in Chassidic Thought (An Anthology); The Handbook of Jewish Thought; The Bahir — a Commentary and Translation; Meditation and the Bible; Meditation and the Kaballah; Jewish Meditation;* and *Made in Heaven — A Jewish Wedding Guide.*

Rabbi Kaplan was a resourceful and creative translator, as his sweeping and highly readable translation of the Five Books of Moses, *The Living Torah,* attests. Rabbi Kaplan also translated *The Way of God* — Luzzato's *Derech Hashem;* the 17-volume Torah Anthology — a translation of R' Yaakov Culi's *Me'am Loez,* the classic Sephardic commentary on the Torah; the Passover Haggadah, and *Rabbi Nachman's Wisdom,* the writings of Rabbi Nachman of Bratslav.

Many of his books have been translated into Hebrew, Russian, Spanish, and even Dutch.

Rabbi Kaplan was born in New York City and was educated in the Torah Vodaath and Mir Yeshivos in Brooklyn. After years of study at Jerusalem's Mir Yeshiva, he was ordained by some of Israel's foremost rabbinic authorities. He also earned a Master's degree in physics and was the youngest person to be listed in Who's Who in Physics in the United States. "I use my physics background to analyze and systemize data, very much as a physicist would deal with physical reality," Rabbi Kaplan once said.

I first encountered this extraordinary individual when by "chance" I spotted his article on "Immortality in the Soul" in "Intercom," the journal of the Association of Orthodox Jewish Scientists, and was taken by his unusual ability to explain a difficult topic — one usually reserved for advanced scholars, a topic almost untouched previously in English — with such simplicity that it could be understood by any intelligent reader. It was clear to me that his special talent could fill a significant void in English Judaica. I always counted as one of my greatest z'chusim (a spiritual merit granted by God) to have had the privilege of "discovering" Rabbi Kaplan. And once we met, we became lifelong friends.

When I invited Rabbi Kaplan to write on the concept of tefillin for the Orthodox Union's National Conference of Synagogue Youth, he completed the 96-page manuscript of God, Man and Tefillin with sources and footnotes from the Talmud, Midrash and Zohar — in less than 2 weeks. The book — masterful, comprehensive, inspiring yet simple — set a pattern which was to characterize all of his succeeding works.

A soft-spoken, unassuming individual, modest despite his spreading renown and popularity, Aryeh Kaplan was an activist for NCSY, a firm believer in acquainting unaffiliated and alienated Jewish youth with their heritage. He attended numerous events, and was the center of attraction at many national conventions. He truly believed that NCSY possessed the power to bring new spiritual energies to the Jewish community. This confidence has been borne out through the scores of NCSY graduates who became Torah scholars, roshei yeshiva, rabbonim, Torah educators and communal leaders. He was a prime force behind the teshuvah movement, the modern movement of return to Jewish observance. "Throughout history, Jews have always been observant," he noted in an interview. "The teshuvah movement is just a normalization. The Jewish people are sort of getting their act back together again. We are just doing what we are supposed to be doing." Indeed, his books reflect a similar, upbeat philosophy. The message he tried to get across was that "Judaism is a live, growing concern. A person looking for meaning in life need not go anywhere else."

Aryeh Kaplan's unusual warmth, sincerity and total dedication to Torah were an inspiration to the thousands he reached personally. His home was always open, his table crowded with Sabbath guests and students. He traveled far and wide to share his knowledge and commitment with young people at seminars, retreats and college campuses. He helped create an NCSY collegiate organization which, through no fault of his, was short-lived.

Rabbi Aryeh Moshe Eliyahu ben Shmuel Kaplan abandoned a promising career in physics, deciding instead to devote himself totally to the dissemination of Torah. He succeeded in uniting many elements in one personality — he was the Talmudic sage, the man of Halachah, the master of Western civilization, and the scientist, with an uncanny grasp of Kaballah, Jewish mysticism and Chassidic thought.

In the process of bringing Torah to the masses, Rabbi Kaplan revealed much that was previously hidden. His mind contained libraries of books, waiting to be put into writing. It was the will of the Lord that so much be revealed and no more.

I had the pleasure of serving as the editor of the books published in these volumes, so much so that Rabbi Kaplan trusted me to edit without his reviewing the final draft. Since his passing it has been my privilege to continue to serve in this role. His name and memory are for me a sacred trust — a jewel on the crown of the Torah.

Hopefully, they will adorn the reader's crown as well.

MAIMONIDES' PRINCIPLES
The Fundamentals of Jewish Faith

י"ג עקרים של הרמב"ם

Aryeh Kaplan

Preface

by Rabbi Baruch Taub

The very formulation of a system of Jewish discipline is more profound than the discipline itself. In establishing the 13 Principles of Jewish Faith, Rambam (Rabbi Moses Maimonides) is stating that being Jewish itself is an obligation. In so doing, the myth of often-repeated expressions such as "I am a Jew at heart" is put to rest. To be a "Jew at heart" requires the development of a sense of obligation to the heart of Jewishness. Rather than a "do your own thing" system defined by the individual Jew, being Jewish means individual articulation of the established 13 Principles of Faith.

In truth, it is the contemporary Jew himself who has put this myth to rest. We are experiencing what has been popularly termed a generation of *teshuva* (return). It is our contention that young Jews today have moved the "*teshuva* movement" to a new place of development. No longer are contemporary Jews interested in learning about Judaism. There is an eagerness to learn and live Judaism itself. There has been a demand of late for Jewish classical literature in the vernacular as opposed to books "about" Judaism, and the response has been a noble one. In recent years, the great works of traditional Jewish literature have been made available to the layman and have greatly advanced the cause of Torah and mitzvot. Being Jewish is now being approached by young Jews throughout the world with that sense of obligation which lies at the heart of Rambam's Principles of Jewish Faith. The challenge is to oblige this growing sense of obligation.

In this vein, it is instructive to note that RAVAD (Rabbi

Avraham Ben David) takes issue with Rambam with regard to the third of the 13 Principles. This principle, according to Rambam, states that God has no bodily form.

Ravad insists that the non-corporeality of God is not to be considered as one of the 13 Principles of Jewish Faith. To be sure, Ravad's disagreement with Rambam is not based upon a contention that God in fact does exist in bodily form. Clearly, Ravad's concern is that the many anthropomorphic references of the Torah ("hand of God" etc.) will lead the unschooled layman to conclude that He in fact does embody human form. If this then was a fundamental principle of Jewish faith, contends Ravad, many unknowing laymen would be discouraged from living up to Jewish expectation. Ravad's concern therefore is that the spirit of Rambam's fundamental principles should open doors to the searching Jew rather than close them.

This popular version of the 13 Principles of Jewish Faith represents a summarized version of the original work which appears in Rambam's commentary to the *Mishna Sanhedrin*. In presenting the commentary to the popular version, Rabbi Kaplan draws upon the original work as well as other sources utilizing his extensive knowledge of Jewish sources.

This work is an effort to perpetuate what was undoubtedly the intent of Rambam in presenting these fundamentals. To open the doors of the storehcuse of Torah living and learning for the unschooled, as well as to provide a keener understanding of the basic principles of Jewish responsibility to both schooled and unschooled alike, is at the heart of this presentation.

May its dissemination encourage increased sensitivity to the Torah way.

Introduction

One of the clearest statements of Jewish belief is that contained in Maimonides' Thirteen Principles of Faith. These were first enunciated in his commentary on the Mishnah and, in an abbreviated form, are found in virtually every prayer book. They also form the basis of the well-known synagogue hymn, *Yigdal*.

In formulating these principles, Maimonides went through the entire length and breadth of Jewish literature, determining which principles are always taken for granted and are unique to Judaism. In clear, concise language, he then set these down in the well-known Thirteen Principles. These principles have been discussed for the past eight hundred years, and are still accepted by all Jews as the one clear unambiguous creed of Judaism.

For the Jew, however, it was never enough merely to accept a creed. One can believe, but if one does not act on the basis of his belief, then his statement of faith is just so many empty words. On the other hand, however, one cannot practice Judaism in any sense at all unless he understands and believes in the roots from which it stems.

It is important to know something about the compiler of these most important principles. Moses Maimonides is considered the greatest codifier and philosopher in Jewish history. He is often affectionately referred to as the Rambam, after the initials of his name and title, Rabenu Moshe Ben Maimon (Our Rabbi, Moses son of Maimon).

Moses Maimonides was born in the city of Cordova, Spain, on a Sabbath, the day before Passover (14 Nissan 4895, or March 30, 1135), at one o'clock in the afternoon. It is not often that the birth of an ancient Jewish sage is known with such minute accuracy. Usually, we do not even know the year, let alone the day and hour. But so great was his renown, even in his lifetime, that many of the most minute details of Maimonides' life remain preserved.

Maimonides was only thirteen when his native city of Cordova fell into the hands of the Almohades, fanatical zealots from Morocco who renewed the ancient motto of the early Moslem conquerors, "The Koran or the Sword." Under their rule, no Jew dared openly avow his faith, and Maimonides and his family were forced to emigrate.

They wandered from city to city in Spain, and finally, in 1160, settled in Fez, Morocco. It was during these wanderings that Maimonides began working on the first of his major works, his Commentary on the Mishnah.

The Mishnah, the earliest portion of the Talmud, had been complied almost a thousand years earlier by Rabbi Judah the Prince, and details of its development are outlined in detail in the Eighth Principle. Written in extremely concise language, the Mishnah formed the basis of all later Talmudic writings, but by itself, it was most difficult to understand. Maimonides wrote the first clear commentary on this work that was so central to Jewish thought.

It is most interesting to note that this Commentary was written in Arabic, the spoken language of most Mediterranean Jews, rather than in the more scholarly Hebrew. Maimonides was writing for his contemporaries, and was aware of the need to communicate in a language with which they were familiar.

It was in this commentary that Maimonides first enunciated the Thirteen Principles of Faith. In the tenth chapter of the tract of *Sanhedrin*, the Mishnah outlines the beliefs that are basic to Judaism. The Thirteen Principles are basically an elaboration of this Mishnah.

In this volume, we have attempted to present the Principles as they appear in this Commentary in clear, precise English. Whenever we refer to the "Commentary on Mishnah," our reference is to the first enunciation of these principles. We will also refer to other places in the Commentary on the same Mishnah, and will speak of it as "Commentary on Mishnah,

Sanhedrin 10:1."

The Moslem persecutions finally caught up with the Maimonides' family in Fez, and they left for Israel in 1165, where they lived briefly in Jerusalem and Hebron. Finding life in the Holy Land very difficult, they then moved to Egypt and settled in Fostat. Supporting himself as a jewelry merchant in partnership with his brother David, he spent every spare moment working on his Commentary to the Mishnah. It was finally completed in 1168, and was published under the Arabic title *Kitab as-Siraj*, meaning "Book of Illumination."

This work itself would have been enough to establish Maimonides' reputation as a giant of Jewish scholarship. It is included in every edition of the Talmud, and is considered the clearest explanation of the Mishnah ever written. Thus, at the age of 33, Maimonides attained a reputation as one of the leading rabbinical authorities in Egypt, and was soon appointed chief rabbi of Cairo and spiritual leader of all Egyptian Jewry. Besides this, Maimonides also established for himself a considerable reputation as a physician, and in 1170 was appointed physician to Saladin's grand visier, Alfadhil. Although occupied both as court physician and as healer to his own people, he still found time to embark upon another monumental project, the codification of all the laws of the Talmud.

Anyone who has ever studied Talmud is familiar with the *Gemorah*, the second and last part of the Talmud. Written as a commentary on the Mishnah, in many places it assumes the form of minutes of the debates which took place in the great Talmudic academies of Israel and Babylon. Many laws appear in the discussion in places where the main debate centers around a completely different topic. In order to determine a law, one must often track down every place it is mentioned in such debates. This is an extremely difficult task, even for a major Talmudic scholar. Remember, in size the Talmud is approximately the same as the *Encyclopedia Britannica.*

Maimonides spent twelve years extracting every decision and law from the Talmud, and arranging them into 14 systematic volumes. The work was finally completed in 1180, and was called *Mishneh Torah,* or "Code of the Torah." It was also called the *Yad Chazakah* or "Strong Hand." The word *Yad* (hand) in Hebrew is written exactly the same as the number 14, alluding to the 14 volumes of this work. For short, it is often called the *Yad* or simply the "Rambam."

This code established Maimonides as the leading Jewish authority of his generation. In communities such as Spain it became as popular as the Bible, and virtually every family owned a copy. The author's name became a household word in Jewish communities throughout the world.

Although the Thirteen Principles are not discussed explicitly in this Code, they play an important role in a number of areas. This is particularly true of the first section, where the "Foundations of the Torah" are discussed, and later in the section on "Repentance," which speaks of man's condition in general.

Here again, we will bring the pertinent sections of the *Yad* in translation. In many places the style here is more concise and legalistic than in the Commentary on the Mishnah, and the discussion also often involves much greater detail. This is especially true when it involves the interpretation of one of the commandments of the Torah.

At the same time that Maimonides' reputation as a Torah giant was becoming established, he was also attaining renown as a physician. For almost a thousand years, the teachings of the Greek physician Galen were accepted without question, often with disastrous results. Maimonides was the first to challenge these teachings, and, on the basis of his own experiments, developed many new and radical cures. He became renowned for his ability to affect cures after all other doctors had given up hope, and in 1185 was appointed physician to the royal court of Saladin, the sultan of Egypt and Syria.

In this position, Maimonides soon became established as the greatest physician of his generation. His fame even spread to England, where Richard the Lion-Hearted invited him to become his personal physician. The great sage and physician elected, however, to remain in Egypt.

During this period, Maimonides was involved in preparing his third major work. This was also written in Arabic, and was first published in 1190 under the title *Dalalat al Hairin.* It is better known by its Hebrew name, *Moreh Nevuchim*, or "Guide to the Perplexed."

What Maimonides had done was to integrate all the philosophical knowledge of his time, and clearly demonstrate how it all blended in with the teachings of the Torah. This work firmly established Maimonides as the dean of all Jewish philosophers. It not only attained a reputation as the greatest work on Jewish philosophy ever written, but also gained a place among the great classics of world philosophy in general.

Although a considerable amount of the material in the *Guide* deals with the Thirteen Principles, much of it is presented in a manner almost unintelligible to the person not familiar with philosophical terminology. We therefore only bring a single quote from this monumental work, in our discussion of the Fourth Principle.

A fourth major work of Maimonides was his *Sefer HaMitzvos,* or "Book of Commandments," also written in Arabic, in which he clearly enumerates the 613 commandments of the Torah. Besides all this, he also found time to write books on both Medicine and Astronomy.

Maimonides thus achieved the highest eminence as a Talmudist, codifier, philosopher and physician. His accomplishments in any one of these fields would have been enough to assure him a prominent place in history. The fact that he was able to excel in all four fields established him as an individual unique in the annals of history.

Besides his major works, Maimonides also wrote a number of shorter letters and essays, mostly in Arabic. The most famous of these is his *Iggeres Taimon* or "Letter to Yemen," in which he offered his oppressed brethren encouragement and urged them not to despair.

Another important essay is his *Maamar Techiyas HaMeisim* or "Discourse on the Resurrection," which was written in 1911. A short excerpt is included in the Thirteenth Principle.

Maimonides' strength began to fail him in his old age, and he died in his seventieth year on 20 Teveth, 4693 (December 13, 1204) in Fostat. He was mourned by Jews all over the world and eventually buried in Tiberias, where his grave is a shrine to this very day.

About a hundred years after Maimonides' death, Rabbi Daniel bar Yehudah of Rome made the Thirteen Principles into a song. It is known as *Yigdal*, and is included in all prayer books and sung in synagogues around the world.

In presenting Maimonides' writings in English, we are merely following his own example of expressing the truths of Judaism in a language readily accessible to the average man. We will also include a brief discussion guide after each principle, and it is hoped that this will further help make this volume a useful tool for classes and discussion groups.

It is most important that we recognize the central core of principles which the rest of the Torah serves to express. It was for this reason that the Thirteen Principles were originally set forth. In our generation, more than any time in the past, this is needed. We live in an age where we are constantly exposed to principles diametrically opposed to the Torah, and it is vital that we clarify for ourselves, and especially for those whose ignorance makes them vulnerable to confusion, the essential uniqueness of Torah thought.

May it be God's will that this volume make a small contribution in this direction.

Aryeh Kaplan
Rosh Chodesh Sivan, 5733

Translator's Note:
For the sake of clarity, it has occasionally been necessary to add words or phrases not included in the original text. All such additions are indicated by square brackets. The same is true of portions of Biblical verses absent in the original but included in the translation.

Ar. K.

THE THIRTEEN PRINCIPLES

1. I believe with perfect faith that God is the Creator and Ruler of all things. He alone has made, does make, and will make all things.
2. I believe with perfect faith that God is One. There is no unity that is in any way like His. He alone is our God— He was, He is and He will be.
3. I believe with perfect faith that God does not have a body. Physical concepts do not apply to Him. There is nothing whatsoever that resembles Him at all.
4. I believe with perfect faith that God is first and last.
5. I believe with perfect faith that it is only proper to pray to God. One may not pray to anyone or anything else.
6. I believe with perfect faith that all the words of the prophets are true.
7. I believe with perfect faith that the prophecy of Moses is absolutely true. He was the chief of all prophets, both before and after him.
8. I believe with perfect faith that the entire Torah that we now have is that which was given to Moses.
9. I believe with perfect faith that this Torah will not be changed, and that there will never be another Torah given by God.
10. I believe with perfect faith that God knows all of man's deeds and thoughts. It is thus written *(Psalm* 33:15), 'He has molded every heart together, He understands what each one does."
11. I believe with perfect faith that God rewards those who keep His commandments, and punishes those who transgress His commandments.
12. I believe with perfect faith in the coming of the Messiah. No matter how long it takes, I will await his coming every day.
13. I believe with perfect faith that the dead will be brought back to life when God wills it to happen.

YIGDAL

1. Great is the Living God, and praised,
   He exists, yet His existence has no time.

2.   He is One, no unity is like His,
           He is hidden, His unity has no end.

3. He does not have bodily form, He is not a body
   He is beyond compare in His holiness.

4.   He preceded all things that were created,
           He is first, yet without beginning.

5. He is the Lord of the world, and all things created,
   Display His greatness and His majesty.

6.   He has granted the bounty of His prophecy
           To the men of His choice and glory.

7. There has not arisen another like Moses
   A prophet who looked upon His image.

8.   God gave a true Torah to His people,
           Through His prophet, trusted in all His house.

9. God will not replace nor change His Law
   For all time, for anything else.

10.   He sees, He knows our secrets,
           He sees each thing's end at its very beginning.

11. He rewards man with love, as his deeds deserve,
    He gives the wicked evil, according to their wrong.

12.   He will send our Messiah at the End of Days,
           To redeem those who await His final salvation.

13. God will bring the dead to life with His great love;
    May His glorious name be blessed for all time.

אֲנִי מַאֲמִין

בֶּאֱמוּנָה שְׁלֵמָה
שֶׁהַבּוֹרֵא, יִתְבָּרַךְ שְׁמוֹ,
הוּא בּוֹרֵא וּמַנְהִיג
לְכָל־הַבְּרוּאִים,
וְהוּא לְבַדּוֹ
עָשָׂה וְעוֹשֶׂה וְיַעֲשֶׂה
לְכָל־הַמַּעֲשִׂים.

The First Principle

אֲנִי מַאֲמִין בֶּאֱמוּנָה שְׁלֵמָה שֶׁהַבּוֹרֵא, יִתְבָּרַךְ שְׁמוֹ,
הוּא בּוֹרֵא וּמַנְהִיג לְכָל־הַבְּרוּאִים,
וְהוּא לְבַדּוֹ עָשָׂה וְעוֹשֶׂה וְיַעֲשֶׂה לְכָל־הַמַּעֲשִׂים.

*I believe with perfect faith that God
is the Creator and Ruler of all things.
He alone has made, does make,
and will make all things.*

❧ Yigdal

Great is the Living God, and praised,
He exists, yet His existence has no time.

❧ Commentary on Mishnah

The first principle involves belief in the existence of God.

There is a Being, perfect in every possible way, who is the ultimate Cause of all existence.

All existence depends on Him and is derived from Him.

It is inconceivable that He does not exist. If He did not exist, everything else would also cease to exist and nothing would remain.

If, however, we could imagine that nothing else existed, He would not cease to exist. He would not be diminished in any way.

Only God is totally self-sufficient and, therefore, Unity and Mastery belong only to Him. He has everything that He needs in Himself and does not need anything else at all.

Everything else, however, whether it be an angel, a star, or anything associated with them above or below, all depend on Him for their very existence.

The Torah teaches us this first principle in the first of the Ten Commandments (*Exodus* 20:2): "I am the Lord your God."

∗§ Code, Foundations of the Torah
(*Yad, Yesodey HaTorah*)

1:1 The ultimate foundation and pillar of wisdom is the realization that there is a first Being who brought everything else into existence.

Everything else in heaven and earth only exists as a result of the reality of His existence.

1:2 If one could conceive that He did not exist, then neither could anything else exist.

1:3 If, however, one could conceive that nothing else existed, then He alone would still exist.

He would not cease to exist when they did; for all things depend on Him, but He does not depend on them at all.

Therefore, nothing is quite as real as He is.

1:4 The Prophet therefore said (*Jeremiah* 10:10), "The Lord, God, is Real." Only He is real. Nothing else is real in the sense that He is.

The Torah likewise says (*Deuteronomy* 4:35), "There is nothing else besides Him." Nothing else shares His ultimate reality.

1:5 This Being is God of the world, Lord of all the earth. . .His power has neither end nor limit. . .

1:6 To know this is one of the commandments of the Torah. It is thus written (*Exodus* 20:2), "I am the Lord your God."

∗§ Code, Repentance
(*Yad, Tshuvah*)

3:7 Five are in the category of the nonbeliever (*Min*): One who says that there is no God and that the world has no Master. . .

◆§ Points for Discussion

1. How do we define God?

2. Why do we say that God is both Creator and Ruler? Is it possible that He be one without being the other? Are there religions or philosophies that only believe in one of these two facets?

3. What do we mean when we say that God is perfect in every possible way?

4. We say that God does not need His creation. If so, why did He create the world? What do we say of a person when he does something that he is not required to do? How does this relate to God?

5. What do we mean when we say that nothing is as real as God?

6. The first of the Ten Commandments reads, "I am the Lord your God, who took you out of the land of Egypt, from the house of slavery." Why is the Exodus mentioned in this commandment, and not creation itself? That is, why does the first commandment not say, "I am the Lord your God, who created you?"

7. Maimonides (Rambam) counts "I am the Lord" as a commandment to believe in God. How is it possible for God to command us to believe in Him? What purpose does this commandment serve?

8. Nachmanides (Ramban) disputes Maimonides and contends that belief in God is the foundation of our faith and therefore cannot be considered a mere commandment. Discuss both opinions.

9. Discuss the verse in *Yigdal* in light of this principle. Is time also included among the things that depend on God?

אֲנִי מַאֲמִין

בֶּאֱמוּנָה שְׁלֵמָה
שֶׁהַבּוֹרֵא, יִתְבָּרַךְ שְׁמוֹ,
הוּא יָחִיד,
וְאֵין יְחִידוּת כָּמוֹהוּ
בְּשׁוּם פָּנִים,
וְהוּא לְבַדּוֹ אֱלֹהֵינוּ,
הָיָה, הֹוֶה, וְיִהְיֶה.

The Second Principle

אֲנִי מַאֲמִין בֶּאֱמוּנָה שְׁלֵמָה שֶׁהַבּוֹרֵא, יִתְבָּרַךְ שְׁמוֹ,
הוּא יָחִיד, וְאֵין יְחִידוּת כָּמוֹהוּ בְּשׁוּם פָּנִים,
וְהוּא לְבַדּוֹ אֱלֹהֵינוּ, הָיָה, הֹוֶה, וְיִהְיֶה.

I believe with perfect faith that God is One.
There is no unity that is in any way like His.
He alone is our God — He was, He is,
and He will be.

◦§ Yigdal

He is One, no unity is like His,
He is hidden, His unity has no end.

◦§ Commentary on Mishnah

The second principle involves the unity of God. We believe that the Cause of everything is One.

He is not one, however, like a member of a pair or species.

He is therefore not like a single thing, which can be divided into a number of elements.

He is not even like the simplest physical thing, which is still infinitely divisible.

God is One is a unique way. There is no other unity like His.

The Torah teaches us this second principle when it says (*Deuteronomy* 6:4), "Hear O Israel, the Lord is our God, the Lord is One."

◦§ Code, Foundations of the Torah

(*Yad, Yesodey HaTorah*)

1:6 If one even allows himself to think that there is another deity other than God, then he violates the commandment (*Exodus* 20:3), "You shall have no other gods before Me."

Such a person is counted as one who denies the fundamental principle (*Kofer Belkkar*), since this is the great principle upon which everything else depends.

1:7 God is one. He is not two nor more than two, but One.

His unity, however, is like none other in the world.

He is not one like a species, which still encompasses many individuals.

He is not one like a physical thing, which can be divided into parts and dimensions.

He is one with a Unity that is absolutely unique.

If there were many deities, then they would have to have bodies and physical existence. This is because similar things can only be separated through their physical qualities.

If God were physical, then he would have to be finite. This is because it is impossible for anything physical to be infinite. If His body were finite, however, then His power would also be finite.[1]

But we know that God's power is infinite and continuous. . .It is therefore not associated with anything physical. Since He is not physical, however, there can be no physical qualities separating Him from another similar being.

There can therefore only be one God.

To know this is a commandment of the Torah. It is thus written (*Deuteronomy* 6:4), "Hear O Israel, the Lord is our God, the Lord is One."

◄§ Code, Repentance

(*Yad, Tshuvah*)

3:7 Five are in the category of the nonbeliever (*Min*). . . One who admits that the world has a Master, but says that there are two or more.

1. What do we mean when we say that God's unity is unique?

2. Would you describe God as being simple? If so, can you imagine anything as simple as God?

3. Can God exist in space? Can the concept of position apply to Him?

4. The main difference between the physical and the spiritual involves the concept of space. If there is no space in the spiritual realm, then how are things differentiated? Explain the statement, "Equal things can only be separated by their physical qualities." Is position one of these qualities?

5. Can an absolute unity such as God exist in two different times? How then would the concept of time apply to Him? Explain the statement in the second principle, "He was, He is, and He will be." Why is this included in this principle?

6. Can an absolute unity be visible? What would you see? Discuss this in the context of *Yigdal*.

7. Can an absolute unity be bounded? By what would it be bounded? Again, discuss this in the context of *Yigdal*.

8. Discuss the Christian concept of the Trinity in the light of this principle.

בֶּאֱמוּנָה שְׁלֵמָה
שֶׁהַבּוֹרֵא, יִתְבָּרַךְ שְׁמוֹ,
אֵינוֹ גוּף,
וְלֹא יַשִּׂיגוּהוּ
מַשִּׂיגֵי הַגוּף,
וְאֵין לוֹ
שׁוּם דְּמִיוֹן כְּלָל.

The Third Principle

אֲנִי מַאֲמִין בֶּאֱמוּנָה שְׁלֵמָה שֶׁהַבּוֹרֵא, יִתְבָּרַךְ שְׁמוֹ,
אֵינוֹ גוּף, וְלֹא יַשִּׂיגוּהוּ מַשִּׂיגֵי הַגּוּף,
וְאֵין לוֹ שׁוּם דִּמְיוֹן כְּלָל.

I believe with perfect faith
that God does not have a body.
Physical concepts do not apply to Him.
There is nothing whatsoever
that resembles Him at all.

❧ Yigdal

He does not have bodily form, He is not a body.
He is beyond compare in His holiness.

❧ Commentary on Mishnah

The third principle is that God is totally nonphysical.

We believe that this Unity [which we call God] is not a body or a physical force.

Nothing associated with the physical can apply to Him in any way.

We thus cannot say that God moves, rests, or exists in a given place. Things such as this can neither happen to Him, nor be part of His intrinsic nature.

When our sages speak of God, they therefore teach that such concepts as combination and separation do not apply to Him. They say in the Talmud (*Chagigah* 15a), "On high, there is neither sitting nor standing, neither combination nor separation."[2]

The Prophet says (*Isaiah* 40:25), " 'To whom will you liken

Me? To what am I equal?' says the Holy One." If God were physical then He would resemble other physical things.

In many places, however, our holy scriptures do speak of God in physical terms. Thus, we find such concepts as walking, standing, sitting and speaking used in relation to God. In all these cases, though, scripture is only speaking metaphorically. Our sages teach us scripture is only speaking metaphorically. Our sages teach us (*Berachos* 31b), "The Torah speaks in the language of man."

The Torah teaches us this third principle when it says (*Deuteronomy* 4:15), "You have not seen any image." We cannot conceive of God as having any image or form. This is because He is not a physical being or force, as discussed earlier.

◄§ Code, Foundations of the Torah
(*Yad, Yesodey HaTorah*)

1:8 It is clearly expressed in both the Torah and in the Prophets that God has neither a body nor any other physical attributes.

It is thus written (*Joshua 2:* 11)), "The Lord your God is God in the heavens above and on the earth beneath."[3] A physical body, however, cannot be in two places at the same time.

The Torah likewise says (*Deuteronomy* 4:15), "You have not seen any image."

God furthermore told His prophet (*Isaiah* 40:25), "To whom will you liken Me? To what am I equal?" If God were a physical being, then He would resemble other physical things.

1:9 Once we know this to be true, we might find it difficult to understand many passages in the Torah. We thus find such expressions as (*Exodus* 24:10), "beneath His feet," and (*ibid.* 31:18), "written with God's finger." In many places we likewise find expressions such as "the hand of God,"[4] "the eyes of God," [5] "the ears of God."[6]

All these expressions are actually adaptations to human intellect, which can only think in terms of the physical. The Torah thus speaks in the language of man.

They are all metaphors. For example, we find in the Torah

such expressions as (*Deuteronomy* 32:41), "I will sharpen My flashing sword." Can we then say that God has a sword, or that He needs a sword with which to kill? We understand, however, that the expression is used allegorically. The same is true of all similar expressions.

We can substantiate this view from the fact that different prophets describe God in utterly different ways. Thus, one prophet says that he perceived God (*Daniel* 7:9), "with a garment as white as snow." Another prophet describes Him (*Isaiah* 63:1), "with His garments stained red." Moses himself saw God at the Red Sea like a mighty man waging war, while at Sinai, he visualized Him as a prayer leader, wrapped [in his Tallis].[7]

From all this, we see that God has no form or figure. What is seen is merely a prophetic visualization.

God's true nature is beyond the reach of human intellect. Man is simply incapable of grasping or understanding God. We thus find (*Job* 11:7), "Can you by searching fathom God? Can you fathom the Almighty to perfection?"

1:10 We must then understand what Moses meant when he asked of God (*Exodus* 33:18), "Show me Your glory."[8]

What Moses desired was to know the true nature of God. He wanted to comprehend this as well as one knows a person when he sees his face. In such a case, the person's features are engraved in one's mind, and he is seen as an individual, distinct from all others.

This is what Moses desired. He wanted to comprehend God's nature to such a degree that it would be separated in his mind from everything else in existence.

God replied to Moses that this was impossible. The intellect of a living man, consisting of body and soul, could not possibly comprehend this. [He thus told Moses (*ibid.* 33:20), "You cannot see My face, for no man can see Me and live."]

But God did reveal things to Moses that had never before been revealed, and which never again will be revealed. In his mind, Moses was thus able to distinguish God from everything else that exists. But it was only like seeing a person's back, where all that can be seen is his body and clothing. One can still distinguish him as an individual [but it is not the same as when one sees his face]. The Torah alludes to this when it says [that God told Moses] (*ibid.* 33:23), "You will see My back, but My face shall not be seen."

1:11   Since God is not a body nor any other kind of physical entity, it is obvious that nothing associated with the physical can apply to Him.

We cannot apply to Him such concepts as combination and separation, position and size, up and down, right and left, back and front, sitting and standing.

He likewise does not exist in time. Such concepts as beginning, end and age therefore do not apply to Him.

God furthermore does not change, since there is nothing that can cause Him to change.

We therefore cannot apply to Him such concepts as life and death in a physical sense. We cannot use such terms as wisdom and foolishness in the same sense as we do when speaking of a human being. Such states as sleep and wakefulness, anger and laughter, joy and sadness, do not apply to Him at all. He does not keep quiet, nor does He speak as a person does.

Our sages thus teach us, "On high there is neither sitting nor standing, neither combination nor separation."

1:12   We must therefore realize that whenever the Torah or Prophets speak about God, they do so in a metaphorical and allegorical manner.

This is true of the expressions mentioned earlier. It is also true of such expressions as (*Psalms* 2:4), "He who sits in the heavens shall laugh"; (*Deuteronomy* 32:21) "They have provoked Me to anger with their vanity"; and (*ibid.* 28:63), "As God rejoices. . ." Regarding all such statements, our sages say that "the Torah speaks in the language of man." God Himself told His prophet (*Jeremiah* 7:19), "Do they indeed provoke Me to anger?"

God told the prophet (*Malachi* 3:6), "I am God, I do not change." But if God would be happy at some times and angry at others, he would indeed change. [It is therefore obvious that none of these states can apply to Him at all.]

All these states only exist in physical beings, living in this lowly dark world. We "dwell in houses of clay, whose foundations are in the dust." [9] God, however, is above all these things.

◆§ *Code, Repentance*
(*Yad, Tshuvah*)

3:7 Five are in the category of the nonbeliever (*Min*). . .One who admits that there is one Master, but claims that He is physical or has a form.

◆§ *Points for Discussion*

1. How are the second and third principles related?
2. What does the Torah mean when it says that man was created in the "image of God?"
3. Why does the Torah speak of God as if He were just like us?
4. Could Christianity accept this principle?
5. What nonphysical things affect our lives? Do these in any way resemble God?
6. Why is it impossible to comprehend God?
7. Why must the Torah speak in the language of man?
8. What do we mean when we say that God is holy? Relate this to the verse in *Yigdal*.
9. Why do we refer to God as "He," using the masculine gender?

אֲנִי מַאֲמִין

בָּאֱמוּנָה שְׁלֵמָה
שֶׁהַבּוֹרֵא, יִתְבָּרַךְ שְׁמוֹ,
הוּא רִאשׁוֹן
וְהוּא אַחֲרוֹן.

The Fourth Principle

אֲנִי מַאֲמִין בֶּאֱמוּנָה שְׁלֵמָה שֶׁהַבּוֹרֵא, יִתְבָּרַךְ שְׁמוֹ,
הוּא רִאשׁוֹן וְהוּא אַחֲרוֹן.

*I believe with perfect faith
that God is first and last.*

◈ Yigdal

He preceded all things that were created,
He is first, yet without beginning.

◈ Commentary on Mishnah

The fourth principle involves the absolute eternity of the One [whom we call God]. Nothing else shares His eternal quality. This is discussed many times in Scripture, and the Torah teaches it to us when it says of Him (*Deuteronomy 33:27*), "The eternal God is a refuge."

◈ Code, Repentance
(*Yad, Tshuvah*)

3:8 Five are in the category of the nonbeliever (*Min*): . . . One who says that God alone was not the first thing and Creator of all.

◈ Guide to the Perplexed
(*Moreh Nevuchim*)

2:13 Everything (other than God Himself) was created by God out of absolute nothingness. In the beginning, God alone existed. There was nothing else. He then created everything that exists from absolute nothingness. It all followed His will and desire.

Even time itself is among the things created by God. Time depends upon motion. In order for motion to exist, we must have things that move. And all things were created by God.

ৰ্জ Points for Discussion

1. How is this principle related to the previous one?

2. Discuss the following questions: What existed before the first thing? Who created the first thing?

3. Children often ask, "Who created God?" Discuss this question.

4. What do we mean when we say that God is last?

5. Why do we consider time as something that was created?

אֲנִי מַאֲמִין

בֶּאֱמוּנָה שְׁלֵמָה
שֶׁהַבּוֹרֵא, יִתְבָּרַךְ שְׁמוֹ,
לוֹ לְבַדּוֹ
רָאוּי לְהִתְפַּלֵּל,
וְאֵין רָאוּי לְהִתְפַּלֵּל
לְזוּלָתוֹ.

The Fifth Principle

אֲנִי מַאֲמִין בֶּאֱמוּנָה שְׁלֵמָה שֶׁהַבּוֹרֵא, יִתְבָּרַךְ שְׁמוֹ,
לוֹ לְבַדּוֹ רָאוּי לְהִתְפַּלֵּל, וְאֵין לְזוּלָתוֹ רָאוּי לְהִתְפַּלֵּל.

I believe with perfect faith
that it is only proper to pray to God.
One may not pray
to anyone or anything else.

◄§ Yigdal

He is the Lord of the world, and all things created,
Display His greatness and His majesty.

◄§ *Commentary on Mishnah*

The fifth principle teaches us that God is the only one whom we may serve and praise. We may sing only of His greatness and obey only His commandments.

We may not act in this way toward anything beneath Him, whether it be an angel, a star, one of the elements, or any combination of them. All these have a predetermined nature and, therefore, none can have authority or free will. Only God has these attributes.

It is therefore not proper to serve these things or make them intermediaries to bring us closer to God. All our thoughts should be directed only toward Him. Nothing else should even be considered.

This fifth principle forbids all forms of idolatry, and it constitutes a major portion of the Torah.

∽§ Code, Idolatry
(Yad, Avodas Kochavim)

1:1 In the days of Enosh, mankind succumbed to a grave error, demolishing the advice of the wise men living in that time. Enosh himself was among those who were caught up in this mistaken idea.[10]

This was their error:

They argued that God created stars and spheres with which to control the world, placing them on high and giving them honor. These creations are then the servants who minister to Him and it is therefore fitting to praise, glorify and honor them. Certainly God would want us to honor and praise those whom He Himself elevates and honors. They compared God to an earthly king, who wishes his subjects to honor those who stand before him, since this in itself demonstrates their respect for the king.

Following this false line of reasoning, they began to build temples to the stars and offer them sacrifices. They praised and glorified them with words, and bowed down before them. They [Enosh and his contemporaries] had become so confused and mistaken that they felt they were actually fulfilling God's will in this manner.

This is the foundation of idol worship.

Idolaters who really understand their belief also conceive it in this way. They never claim that there is no God other than the star that they worship.

The Prophet Jeremiah spoke of this when he said (*Jeremiah* 10:7,9), "Who would not fear You, O King of nations? It is Your due. For among all the wise ones of the nations of their kingdoms, there is none like You. For in one respect they are fools and simpletons: the vanities that they preach are nothing more than a block of wood."[11] They all know that God is unique. But their error is in thinking that their [idolatry, which is really] foolishness is God's will.

2:1 The main commandment regarding idolatry is not to worship anything that God created, whether it be an angel, a sphere, a star, one of the elements, or anything created from them.

Even though one knows that God is the true God, and only worships this thing in the manner that Enosh and his generation first did, he is still an idolater.

The Torah thus warns us (*Deuteronomy* 4:19), "Do not lift your eyes to the heavens, and see the sun, [moon and stars, and all the host of heaven, and be drawn to worship and serve them] which the Lord your God has allotted to all peoples." You shall not let your mind's eye rove and think that these control the world. You might see that they continue to exist and do not deteriorate, and then mistakenly think that one must bow down to them and serve them.

The Torah likewise says (*Deuteronomy* 11:16), "Watch yourselves, lest your hearts be deceived [and you turn aside and serve other gods and worship them]." You should not be deceived by the thoughts of your hearts to serve these and make them intermediaries between you and God.

❧ Code, Repentance
(*Yad, Tshuvah*)

3:7 Five are in the category of the nonbeliever (*Min*): . . . One who serves a star or constellation in order that it be an advocate between him and the Master of all worlds.

❧ Points for Discussion
1. Why is idolatry forbidden?
2. Why is it forbidden to worship an angel if one still believes in God? Why is this an error?
3. Christianity teaches that one can only approach God through Jesus. How would this principle apply to that belief?
4. How does belief in idolatry diminish our concept of God?
5. How does the verse in *Yigdal* relate to this principle?
6. An earthly king depends upon his subordinates to help him rule. Is this true of God? How does this relate to this principle?

אֲנִי מַאֲמִין

בֶּאֱמוּנָה שְׁלֵמָה
שֶׁכָּל־דִּבְרֵי נְבִיאִים
אֱמֶת.

The Sixth Principle

אֲנִי מַאֲמִין בֶּאֱמוּנָה שְׁלֵמָה שֶׁכָּל־דִּבְרֵי נְבִיאִים אֱמֶת.

*I believe with perfect faith
that all the words of the prophets are true.*

◆§ Yigdal

He has granted the bounty of His prophecy
To the men of His choice and glory.

◆§ Commentary on Mishnah

The sixth principle concerns prophecy.

We must realize that there exist human beings who have such lofty qualities and achieve such great perfection that their souls become prepared to receive pure spiritual wisdom.

Their human intellect can then become bound up with the Creative Mind (*Sechel HaPo'el*), and receive an inspired emanation from it. This is prophecy, and those people who achieve it are the prophets.

This is the concept of prophecy. A full explanation would require a lengthy discussion, but we do not intend here to cite proof-texts for every principle or explain how prophecy is attained. In passing, however, I will remind you that many verses in the Torah testify to the prophecy of many different prophets.

◆§ Code, Foundations of the Torah

(*Yad, Yesodey HaTorah*)

7:1 It is a foundation of our faith to know that God grants prophecy to man.

Such prophecy can only be attained by a person who has very great intelligence. He must have strong character, and not be overcome by his impulses in any way. He must also have constant control over his emotions and have an outlook that is both very broad and very firm.[12]

A person having all these qualities can then delve into the spiritual.[13] He can advance in these deep, subtle concepts, gaining a firm understanding and perception of them.

At the same time, he must also sanctify himself and separate himself from the ways of the common people who grope in the darkness of the times. He must achieve a constant diligence in not even thinking of nonessentials or considering the vanities and intrigues of the times.

He must work upon himself until his mind is constantly clear and directed on high. He must bind his intellect to the Throne of Glory, striving to comprehend the purity and holiness of the spiritual beings. He must furthermore contemplate the wisdom of God in everything and understand its significance, whether it be the highest spiritual entity or the lowliest thing on earth.

One who does this immediately becomes worthy of Divine Inspiration (*Ruach HaKodesh*).[14]

When one attains this spirit [of inspiration], his soul becomes bound up in the level of the angels. . .and he becomes a different individual completely. He can now understand things with a knowledge completely different than anything he ever had previously. The level that he has attained is far above that of other men who can merely use their intellect.

This is the meaning of what [the prophet Samuel told] King Saul (*I Samuel* 10:6): "[The spirit of God will descend upon you,] and you shall prophesy with them, and you shall be transformed into a different man."

7:2   There are many levels of prophecy. Just as one person may have greater intelligence than another, so one prophet can be greater in prophecy than another.

All prophets, however, have one thing in common. They all see their prophecy only in a dream or vision at night, or else during the day while in a trance. This is what the Torah means when it says (*Numbers* 12:6), "[If there be a prophet among

you, then I, God,] will make Myself known to him in a vision —
I will speak to him in a dream."

Prophecy is also a very traumatic experience. The prophet's
limbs tremble, his body becomes faint, and he loses control of
his thoughts. All that remains in his consciousness is a clear
understanding of what he is experiencing.

We thus find in the case of Abraham (*Genesis* 15:12),
"[Abraham fell into a trance,] and a great dark dread fell upon
him." Similarly, Daniel describes his vision, saying (*Daniel*
10:8), "[I saw this great vision, and I became powerless.] My
appearance was destroyed, and my strength deserted me. [I
heard the sound of his words, and I fell on the ground in a
trance.]"

7:3 When a prophet is given a message, it is given in the
form of an allegory. The interpretation of the allegory,
however, is immediately implanted in his mind, and he knows
its meaning.

Thus, for example, Jacob saw a ladder with angels going up
and down on it. This was an allegory for the empires that would
subjugate his children.[15]

The same was true of other prophets. Ezekiel saw a vision of
living creatures.[16] Jeremiah saw a boiling pot[17] and an
almond tree rod.[18] Ezekiel also saw a scroll,[19] and Zechariah,
a measure.[20]

In these instances, the prophet divulged both the allegory
and its interpretation. In some cases, only the interpretation
was revealed. Other times, only the allegory was recorded, and
this is true of some of the prophecies of Ezekiel and Zechariah.
All the prophets, however, only prophesied by means of
allegories and metaphors.[21]

7:4 A prophet cannot prophesy at will. He must concentrate
and seclude himself in a good, joyous mood. For one cannot
attain prophecy when he is depressed or languid, but only
when he is joyous.[22]

The prophets would therefore have people play music for
them when they were seeking prophecy.[23] We find (*I Samuel*
10:5), "[A band of prophets, coming from a high place, led by
harp, drum, flute and lyre,] and they were seeking prophecy."

That is, they were seeking to be worthy of a prophetic vision.

7:5 Those seeking prophecy were known as the "sons of the prophets."[24] Even though they did everything properly, it was possible that the Divine Presence would descend upon them, but it was also possible that it would not.

7:7 Sometimes a prophet experiences prophecy only for his sake alone. It then comes to broaden his outlook, increase his knowledge, and help him to learn more about these lofty concepts.

At other times, a prophet may be sent to a group of people, a city, or a national government. He then comes to prepare and instruct them, or to keep them from evil that they are doing.

When such a prophet is sent, he is given a sign or miracle in order to show the people that he was actually sent by God.

However, we do not accept everyone who performs a sign or miracle as a prophet. First, he must demonstrate that he is fit for prophecy. He must be outstanding in his generation, both in wisdom and in piety, and must follow the holy paths of prophecy, separating himself from all worldly things. Only then do we accept him when he performs a sign or miracle and says that God sent him.

When this happens we are commanded to obey such a prophet. The Torah thus says (*Deuteronomy* 18:15), "[God will raise up a prophet from among you. . .] and you shall hearken to him."

It is, of course, always possible that one may perform a sign or miracle and still not be a prophet. The miracle can always have something else behind it. Still we are commanded to obey such a prophet. We see that he is a great sage, fit for prophecy, and we therefore accept him as such.

We find a very similar case in the Torah. We are commanded to judge all legal cases on the basis of the testimony of two witnesses.[2][5] It is always possible that these witnesses may be lying, but we must still accept them, since they fulfill all our requirements.

The Torah therefore says (*Deuteronomy* 29:28), "Secret things are for the Lord our God, but what we can see is for us and for our children." It is likewise written (*I Samuel* 16:7),

"Man sees with his eyes, but [only] God sees into the heart."

10:1   When a prophet comes and claims to be sent by God, it is not necessary that he perform miracles like those of Moses, Elijah and Elisha, which actually violated the laws of nature. All that he must do is accurately predict the future. The Torah thus says (*Deuteronomy* 18:21, 22), "If you say in your heart, 'How can we know that the word was not spoken by God?' If the prophet speaks in God's name, and the word does not come true, then that word was not spoken by God, and the prophet has spoken deceitfully." From this, we also see the converse.

All that is therefore required is that the individual be fit for prophecy in his relationship to God. He must furthermore not teach that we add to or subtract from [the Torah], but only that we serve God according to its commandments. We merely says, "If you are a true prophet, then predict the future." He must then do so, and we wait to see whether or not his prediction comes true.

If even a single detail of his prediction does not come true, then we can be certain that this individual is a false prophet. If his prediction is completely accurate, we accept him.

10:2   We must then test this prophet a number of times. If his predictions all come true, then he is a true prophet. We thus find in the case of Samuel (*I Samuel* 3:18, 19), "[Samuel grew, and God was with him, and not one of his words did not come true.] And all Israel, from Dan to Beersheba, knew that Samuel had become established as a prophet of God."

10:3   We might find that horoscopists and fortunetellers also predict the future, but there is a vast difference between them and a true prophet. Even though a fortuneteller might predict the future, he cannot do so with unerring accuracy. Some predictions may come true, but many other do not. We thus find (*Isaiah* 47:13), "Let now the astrologers, stargazers and fortunetellers stand up, and tell you *something* of what will come upon you." They can only tell you *something*, but not everything. [26]

It is also possible that none of their predictions will come true at all. It is thus written (*Isaiah* 44:25), "He frustrates the signs of impostors, and makes fortunetellers look foolish."

The predictions of a [true] prophet, however, must all come true. We find (*I Kings* 10:10), "No word of God shall fall to the ground." God likewise told His prophet (*Jeremiah* 23:28), "Let the prophet who has a dream tell that dream, and let he who has My word speak the truth, for how does straw compare to wheat?" The prediction of fortunetellers and mediums are like straw, which may have a little wheat mixed with it. But God's word is like pure wheat, containing no straw at all.

The Torah teaches us that even when these astrologers and fortunetellers do predict the future, they are still charlatans. We learn truth from the prophets, and have no need for such things as mediums and horoscopists. The Torah tells us (*Deuteronomy* 18:10-15), "There shall not be anyone among you [. . .who uses fortunetelling, augury or divination. . .] For the other nations [. . .hearken to fortunetellers. But God does not permit you to do such things]. God will raise up a prophet from among you. . ."

We see from this that one of the main tasks of the prophet is to tell us the future and predict such things as bounty and famine, war and peace. Even the needs of an individual may be revealed to a prophet. Thus, when Saul lost something, he went to a prophet, who then told him where it was.[27]

This is the main task of the prophet. He does not come to start a new religion, or to add to or subtract from the commandments of the Torah.

10:4 A prophet may sometimes predict troubles, saying that an individual will die, that a famine will occur, or the like. In such cases, the fact that his predictions do not come true does not invalidate his status as a prophet.[28]

In such cases, we do not say that he failed in his prediction. We know that God is "slow to anger, rich in kindness and regretting evil."[29] It is therefore always possible that the people have repented and been forgiven by God. This indeed happened in such cases as when [Jonah warned] Nineveh.[30] It is also possible that God may have suspended their judgment, as in the case of Hezekiah.[31]

If a prophet predicts good, however, and it does not come

true, then we can be certain he is a false prophet. Anything good that God decrees is not retracted, even if it is only stated conditionally.[32]

There was actually only one case where God reversed a good prediction. Before the destruction of the First Temple (*Bais HaMikdash*), God promised that the righteous would not be killed together with the wicked. In this one case, God retracted His word [and the righteous were also destroyed]. This is explained in detail [in the Talmud] in the tract of *Shabbos*.[33]

A prophet is therefore only tested through a good prediction. We see this in Jeremiah's answer to Hananiah son of Azzur. Jeremiah was prophesying that evil would come, while Hananiah was predicting good. Jeremiah then told Hananiah, "If my prediction does not come true, it does not prove me to be a false prophet [since I am predicting evil]. But if yours does not come true, it shall be known that you are false [since you are predicting good]." We also find (*Jeremiah* 28:7,9), "Now listen to this. . . When a prophet predicts peace, and his words come true, then it shall be known that he is the prophet who is truly sent by God."[34]

10:5 If an established prophet testifies that another is a true prophet, we accept the latter without any further test. Thus, we see that after Moses testified regarding him, Joshua was accepted by all Israel, even before he provided any sign.[35] The same was true for all future generations.

Once a prophet is established and his predictions come true time after time, it is forbidden to suspect him or think that his prophecy is not true. As long as he follows the ways of prophecy, it is forbidden to test him unduly.

We therefore do not continually test a prophet. The Torah says (*Deuteronomy* 6:16), "You shall not test the Lord your God as you did at Massah." [It was at Massah that the people doubted the prophecy of Moses and asked for a further test,] saying (*Exodus* 17:7), "Is God among us or not?"

Once it is determined that an individual is a prophet, we must know and believe that God is among us and not disparage this prophet. We thus find [that God told Ezekiel] (*Ezekiel* 33:33), "[When it comes true — and it *will* come true—] then they will know that a prophet has been among them."[36]

⊸§ Code, Repentance

(Yad, Tshuvah)

Three are in the category of the heretic (*Apikores*): One who says that prophecy does not exist, and that there is no way in which God communicates information to man...

⊸§ Points for Discussion

1. How do we know what is good and what is evil? How are these things defined?

2. What do we mean when we say that Judaism is a revealed religion?

3. How does a revealed religion differ from other philosophies? What makes it superior?

4. Why is prophecy one of the fundamental principles of Judaism?

5. What is a prophet? How does one become a prophet?

6. Do prophets exist today? Why?

7. What conditions must be fulfilled before we accept someone as a prophet?

8. What is the relationship between music and prophecy? How does this relate to your own experience?

9. Why is predicting the future a hallmark of prophecy?

10. What does this principle teach us about the Bible?

אֲנִי מַאֲמִין

בֶּאֱמוּנָה שְׁלֵמָה
שֶׁנְּבוּאַת מֹשֶׁה רַבֵּנוּ,
עָלָיו הַשָּׁלוֹם,
הָיְתָה אֲמִתִּית,
וְשֶׁהוּא הָיָה
אָב לַנְּבִיאִים,
לַקּוֹדְמִים לְפָנָיו
וְלַבָּאִים אַחֲרָיו.

The Seventh Principle

אֲנִי מַאֲמִין בֶּאֱמוּנָה שְׁלֵמָה
שֶׁנְּבוּאַת מֹשֶׁה רַבֵּנוּ, עָלָיו הַשָּׁלוֹם, הָיְתָה אֲמִתִּית,
וְשֶׁהוּא הָיָה אָב לַנְּבִיאִים,
לַקוֹדְמִים לְפָנָיו וְלַבָּאִים אַחֲרָיו.

I believe with perfect faith
that the prophecy of Moses
is absolutely true.
He was the chief of all prophets,
both before and after him.

◆§ *Yigdal*

There has not arisen another like Moses,
A prophet who looked upon His image.

◆§ *Commentary on Mishnah*

The seventh principle involves Moses.

We believe that Moses was the chief of all prophets.[37] He was superior to all other prophets, whether they preceded him or arose afterwards.

Moses attained the highest possible human level. He perceived the Godly to a degree surpassing every human being that ever existed. He literally elevated himself from the level of the mere human to that of an angel.

Moses himself thus became like an angel. There was no barrier that he did not split and penetrate. Nothing physical held him back. He was not tainted by any deficiency, great or small. His thoughts, senses and feelings ceased to exist entirely. His conscious mind was completely separated and became a pure spiritual being. It is for this reason that we say that he spoke to God without needing an angel as a mediator.

I would very much like to explain this mystery and unlock its secrets in the Torah. [In the Torah, God says of Moses] (*Numbers* 12:8), "Mouth to mouth, I will speak to him," and this entire passage requires considerable explanation.

Before I could delve into this, however, I would first have to cite many proofs, propositions, introductions, and examples. First, I would have to explain the nature of angels, and how they differ from God Himself. The soul and all its powers would also have to be explained. The discussion would then have to be expanded to include an exposition of all the images that the prophet used to describe God and the angels. This, in turn, would involve a discussion of the Divine Stature (*Shiur Komah*)[38] and all that it involves.

Even this would not suffice, and no matter how concise such a discussion would be, it would involve an essay of at least a hundred pages. I will therefore leave these matters for a book of discourses that I plan to write. Otherwise, I will include this discussion in a work on the prophets that I am currently writing, or in a special volume explaining these [thirteen] principles.

Returning to this seventh principle, let us distinguish Moses' prophecy from that of all other prophets in four ways:

1. God spoke to all other prophets through an intermediary. Moses alone did not need any intermediary. This is what the Torah means when it says [in God's name] (*Numbers* 12:8), "Mouth to mouth, I will speak to him."

2. Every other prophet could only receive prophecy while sleeping. We therefore find in numerous places that prophecy is described as (*Genesis* 20:3), "a dream at night," and (*Job* 33:15), "a vision of night." If prophecy does occur during the day, it only comes when the prophet falls into a trance, where all his senses are obliterated and his mind becomes as passive as in a dream. This state is called a "vision" or an "insight."[39] To Moses, however, the word came by day, when he stood [fully awake] before the two cherubim. God Himself thus testified (*Exodus* 25:22), "I will meet with you there [and I will speak with you, from above the ark-cover, from between the

two cherubim that are on the ark of testimony]." God likewise said (*Numbers* 12:6-8), "If there be a prophet among you, [then I, God, will make Myself known to him in a vision, I will speak to him in a dream]. This is not true of My prophet Moses. . . Mouth to mouth, I will speak to him."

3. Even though other prophets only experienced a vision in a trance, and then, only through an angel, it was still a very traumatic experience for them. Their strength would fail, their stature would become disarrayed, and they would experience such dread that they would come close to death. After the angel Gabriel spoke to Daniel in a vision, Daniel said (*Daniel* 10:8), "I became powerless, my appearance was disarrayed, and my strength deserted me. . .and I fell on the ground in a trance." He later said (*ibid.* 10:16), "The vision caused me to become dislocated [and I had no strength left]." This, however, was not true of Moses. The word came to him without his experiencing any trembling or terror whatsoever. The Torah thus says (*Exodus* 33:11), "God spoke to Moses face to face, as a man speaks to his friend." Moses' prophecy was just like a friendly conversation, involving no agitation whatsoever. Moses did not tremble at the word, even though it was "face to face." This was because he was so completely attached to the spiritual, as discussed earlier.

4. Other prophets could not receive prophecy whenever they desired. It all depended on God's will. A prophet might wait days and years and still not achieve prophecy. All that he could do was plead to God to reveal a vision and then wait until it came. This might take days and months, and sometimes it might not ever come. There were numerous groups who purified their minds and constantly kept themselves in preparation for prophecy. We are told that when he sought prophecy, Elisha said (*II Kings* 3:15), "Now bring me a musician." Still even with this preparation, it was not certain that he would attain prophecy. Moses, on the other hand, could achieve prophecy whenever he desired.[40] The Torah quotes him as saying (*Numbers* 9:8), "Now wait, and I will hear what God commands in your case." God likewise told Moses (*Leviticus* 16:2), "Speak to Aaron your brother that he not

come at all times into the holy place." Our sages teach us that this means Aaron could not approach God whenever he pleased, but Moses could.[41]

❧ Code, Foundations of the Torah
(Yad, Yesodey HaTorah)

7:6 Moses was the master of all prophets. There are therefore numerous differences between Moses and all others.

All other prophets could only achieve prophecy in a dream or vision, while Moses could prophesy while standing fully awake. The Torah thus says (*Numbers* 7:89), "When Moses came into the Tent of Meeting (*Ohel Moed*) to speak to God, he heard the Voice speaking to him."

All other prophets only received prophecy through an angel.[42] All that they could see was an allegory or metaphor. Moses, however, did not receive his prophecy through an angel. God tells us (*Numbers* 12:8), "Mouth to mouth, I will speak to him." In another place the Torah says (*Exodus* 33:11), "God spoke to Moses face to face." We also find (*Numbers* 12:8), "He (Moses) gazes upon a vision of God." This teaches us that Moses did not see a mere allegory. He saw the thing as it was, without having to resort to any metaphor. The Torah thus says (*ibid.*), "[I speak to him...] manifestly, and not in allegory." Moses did not see an allegorical vision, but was able to see things as they truly are.

All other prophets were terrorized, confused and torn apart by their experience. This was not true of Moses, as the Torah says (*Exodus* 33:11), "[God spoke to Moses...] as a man speaks to his friend." A man is not terrorized by his friend's conversation. Moses likewise had enough mental strength to understand words of prophecy with his composure totally unaffected. All other prophets could not achieve prophecy whenever they desired. This was not true of Moses. When he wished, he could be enveloped by Divine Inspiration (*Ruach HaKodesh*), and prophecy would descend upon him. He would not have to concentrate and prepare himself for it, for he was in a constant state of concentration and preparation, just like a ministering angel. He could therefore prophesy at all times, and the Torah quotes him as saying (*Numbers* 9:8), "Now wait, and I will hear what God commands in your case."

God promised this to Moses when he said (*Deuteronomy* 5:27,28), "Go say to them, 'Return now to your tents.' But you stand here with Me [and I will speak to you]." We see from this that all other prophets had to return "to their tents" — to their worldly needs — after they were finished with their prophecy. They were once again like all other people, and therefore did not have to separate from their wives. Moses, on the other hand, never returned to his "first tent," and never again touched a woman.[43] His mind was continually bound to the Creator of all worlds, and the glory never left him. He became as holy as an angel. The Torah thus says that (*Exodus* 34:29), "the skin of his face sent forth beams of light."

8:1 The Jewish people did not believe in Moses because of any miracles that he might have performed. For when one believes in something because of miracles, he still may have doubts and suspect that they might have been performed by means of magic or trickery. All the miracles that Moses performed in the desert, however, were only done because they were necessary, and not to bring proof of his prophecy.

Thus, when it was necessary to defeat the Egyptians, he split the sea and saved us in its midst.[44] When we needed food, he provided us with the Manna.[45] When we were thirsty, he split the rock [to provide water].[46] When Korach and his band revolted, he caused the earth to swallow them up.[47] The same is true of all his other miracles.

But the main reason why we believe in Moses, is because of what happened at Mount Sinai. "Our eyes saw, and not a stranger's."[48] Our ears heard, and not another's. There was the fire, the thunder and lightning,[49] when Moses entered in the deep clouds.[50] The Voice spoke to him, and we ourselves heard it say, "Moses, Moses, speak to the people." Moses thus told the people (*Deuteronomy* 5:4), "Face to face, God spoke to you." The Torah likewise says (*ibid.* 5:3), "God did not make this covenant with our fathers [but with us, who are all here alive today]."

The revelation at Sinai is the only real proof that Moses'

prophecy was true and contained no trickery. God told Moses (*Exodus* 19:9), "Behold, I come to you in a thick cloud, so that the people may hear when I speak with you, so that they may believe in you forever." Before Sinai, the people did not believe with a faith strong enough to last forever. They might have believed, but they could have later had doubts and suspicions.

Those who received Moses' message were therefore themselves witnesses that his prophecy was true, and no further sign was needed.

Moses and the Jewish people were like two witnesses who have seen the same thing. Each witness in the pair knows that the other is speaking truthfully, and neither one needs any proof regarding the other. The same is true of Moses. The entire Jewish people were his witnesses after the revelation at Sinai, and no further signs were needed.

At the beginning of Moses' career, he was given miracles to perform in Egypt, and God told him (*Exodus* 3:18), "They shall hearken to your voice." But Moses knew that one who only believes because of miracles still has doubts, suspicions and similar thoughts. He therefore did not want to go, and told God (*ibid.* 4:1), "They will not believe me." God then told him that the miracles were only to establish the faith[51] until after the Exodus. After that, they would stand at Mount Sinai, and all suspicions would be removed. They would then know for certain that it was God who gave him the initial signs and sent him from the beginning, and they would no longer have any doubts. God therefore told Moses (*ibid.* 3:12), "This shall be your [true] sign that I have sent you. When you bring the people out of Egypt, you shall serve God on this mountain."

Therefore, when any other prophet comes, we do not believe him merely because he performs miracles. Just because he produces a miracle, it does not mean that we must accept everything he says. The only reason we accept a prophet is because the Torah says that if he produces a sign (*Deuteronomy* 18:15), "you shall hearken unto him."

This again is similar to the laws regarding evidence. Testimony offered by two witnesses is accepted as legal evidence, even though we can never know for certain that they are telling the truth. In the same way, we are commanded to hearken to such a prophet, even though we do not know for certain that his sign is true and not a result of magic and trickery.

8:3 Therefore, if a prophet comes and attempts to refute Moses' prophecy, we do not accept him, no matter what great miracles he performs.[52] Moses' prophecy did not depend on any miracles, and therefore cannot be disputed by miracles. We saw and heard with our own eyes and ears, exactly as Moses himself did.

Here again we can use the example of witnesses. If witnesses testify to something, and a person has seen with his own eyes that it is not true, then he is not bound to accept their testimony. He knows for certain that they are false witnesses.

The Torah therefore says (*Deuteronomy* 13:3,4), "[Even] if the sign or wonder comes to pass. . .you shall not hearken to the words of that [false] prophet." He might produce signs and miracles, but he is coming to contradict what we have seen with our own eyes. We only believe the evidence of miracles because of a commandment given to us by Moses. We therefore cannot possible accept any sign that comes to contradict Moses. We ourselves heard and saw his revelation.

⤳ Code, Repentance
(*Yad, Tshuvah*)

Three are in the category of the heretic (*Apikores*):. . .One who denies the prophecy of Moses. . .[53]

⊷§ *Points for Discussion*

1. Why is Moses so central to Judaism?

2. Why is it so important that he be the greatest of all prophets?

3. We speak here about the prophecy of Moses. Exactly what is this prophecy?

4. What is the most important single book in Judaism?

5. Compare the verse in *Yigdal* with *Deuteronomy* 34:10 and *Numbers* 12:8.

6. How would this principle apply to Christianity and Islam?

7. To what extent do miracles verify a prophet's authenticity?

8. How did Moses differ from all other prophets?

9. Will the Messiah be greater than Moses?

10. Why did Moses have to reach such a high degree of prophecy?

11. What sort of person was Moses?

אֲנִי מַאֲמִין

בֶּאֱמוּנָה שְׁלֵמָה
שֶׁכָּל־הַתּוֹרָה
הַמְצוּיָה עַתָּה בְּיָדֵינוּ,
הִיא הַנְּתוּנָה
לְמשֶׁה רַבֵּנוּ,
עָלָיו הַשָּׁלוֹם.

The Eighth Principle

אֲנִי מַאֲמִין בֶּאֱמוּנָה שְׁלֵמָה
שֶׁכָּל־הַתּוֹרָה הַמְּצוּיָה עַתָּה בְּיָדֵינוּ,
הִיא הַנְּתוּנָה לְמשֶׁה רַבֵּנוּ, עָלָיו הַשָּׁלוֹם.

I believe with perfect faith
that the entire Torah that we now have
is that which was given to Moses.

⋖ Yigdal

God gave a true Torah to His people,
Through His prophet, trusted in all His house.

⋖ *Commentary on Mishnah*

The eighth principle is that the Torah given to us by Moses originated from God. It is therefore called "God's word."

We do not know exactly how the Torah was transmitted to Moses. But when it was transmitted, Moses merely wrote it down like a secretary taking dictation. In this way, he wrote the events of his time and the other stories in the Torah, as well as the commandments.[54] Moses was therefore called a "secretary."

Every verse in the Torah is equally holy. The Torah might contain verses such as (*Genesis* 10:6), "the sons of Ham were Cush and Mizraim"; (*ibid.* 36:39), "his wife's name was Mehitabel"; and (*ibid.* 36:12), "Timneh was his concubine," [55] alongside of (*Exodus* 20:2), "I am the Lord your God. . ." and (*Deuteronomy* 6:4), "Hear O Israel, [the Lord is our God, the Lord is One]." All these verses are perfectly equal. They all originate from God, and are all part of God's Torah, which is perfect, pure, holy, and true.[56]

The person who says that some passages were written by Moses of his own accord is considered by our prophets and sages to be the worst sort of nonbeliever, and a perverter of the Torah.[57] Such a person claims that the Torah must be divided into a core and a shell, and that the stories and history contained in it were written by Moses and are of no true benefit.

Such a person is in the category of those who say, "the Torah is not from heaven."[58] Our sages teach that this category includes even one who says the entire Torah was given by God with the exception of a single word, which was composed by Moses and not spoken by God.[59] Regarding such a person, the Torah says (*Numbers* 15:31), "He has despised the word of God [. . .his soul shall be utterly cut off]."

If one really understands the Torah, then he finds every word filled with wondrous wisdom. It contains a depth that can never be plumbed completely — "it is broader than the earth and wider than the sea."[60] One need only follow the example of King David, the anointed of God and Jacob, who prayed (*Psalms* 119:18), "Uncover my eyes, that I may behold the wonders of Your Torah.' "

The same is true of the accepted explanation of the Torah, which was also given by God. [Following this oral tradition,] we make such things as the Succah, Lulav, Shofar, Tzitzis and Tefillin in exactly the manner that God dictated to Moses. Moses transmitted this to us as a trustworthy messenger.

The Torah teaches us this principle when it says (*Numbers* 16:28), "Moses said, 'Through this you shall know that God sent me to do all these things, and I did not do it on my own accord."

◂§ Introduction to Yad

Every commandment given to Moses on Mount Sinai was given together with an explanation. God thus told Moses (*Exodus* 24:12), "[Come up to Me to the mountain. . .] and I will give you the tablets of stone, the Torah and instruction." "Torah" refers to the written Torah, while "instruction" is its interpretation. We are thus commanded to keep the Torah according to its interpretation. This interpretation is what we call the Oral Torah (*Torah SheBaal Peh*).[61]

Moses wrote the entire Torah with his own hand shortly before he passed away. He gave a copy to each tribe, and another Torah was placed in the Ark as a testimony.[62] [Moses thus told the Levites] (*Deuteronomy* 31:26), "Take this scroll of the Torah and place it [by the side of the ark of the covenant. . .]."

The interpretation, however, was not written down but was orally taught to the elders, Joshua, and the rest of the Jews. Moses therefore said (*Deuteronomy* 13:1), "All this word that I instruct you, you shall keep and obey." It is for this reason that it is called the Oral Torah.

Although the Oral Torah was not written down, it was taught by Moses to his council, which was made up of seventy elders.[63] Elazar, Pinchas and Joshua thus all received the tradition from Moses. Joshua, however, was Moses' main disciple, and he was given [responsibility for] the Oral Torah, and received special instruction in it.[64]

Joshua likewise taught this tradition orally as long as he lived. There were then many elders who received the tradition from Joshua. . .

Rabbi Judah, the son of Rabbi Simeon, was known as Our Holy Rabbi[65]. . .And it was Our Holy Rabbi who wrote the Mishnah.[66]

From the time of Moses until Our Holy Rabbi, there was no book from which the Oral Torah could be taught publicly. In each generation, however, a prophet or the head of the Sanhedrin would write down his own notes in order that he might remember what he learned from his teachers. He would then use these notes in his oral teachings. Everyone listening would also take notes according to his ability.[67]

Similar notes were taken on laws that were not transmitted from generation to generation, but were derived through the Thirteen Principles [where they were used to expound the Torah][68] and agreed upon by the Sanhedrin.

This continued until the time of Our Holy Rabbi. He then gathered all the traditions, laws, explanations, and commentaries on the entire Torah, which had been handed down from

Moses and expounded by the Sanhedrin in each generation. This was then all compiled into the book known as the Mishnah.[69]

The Mishnah was then publicly taught to the sages and revealed to all the Jews. Everyone wrote it down, and it was spread to every community. The Oral Torah was thus preserved and not forgotten.

The reason why Our Holy Rabbi broke the tradition [of leaving the Oral Torah unwritten] was because he saw that the number of students was declining, new troubles continually arising, and the Roman Empire spreading throughout the world and constantly becoming stronger. The Jews were also being separated, travelling to the four corners of the globe. He therefore wrote a single volume that everyone could have. It was something that could be learned rapidly and not forgotten.

Our Holy Rabbi spent all his life together with his council, publicly teaching the Mishnah.

Among the sages who were part of Our Holy Rabbi's council were. . .Rabbi Chiya, Rav, Bar Kapara. . .Rabbi Yochanan and Rabbi Hoshia. . .Besides these, there were tens of thousands of other sages who received the tradition [from Our Holy Rabbi].

Rav then wrote the *Sifra* and *Sifri* (commentaries on *Leviticus*, *Numbers* and *Deuteronomy*) to explain and expound upon the main points of the Mishnah. Rabbi Chiya wrote the *Tosefta* to elucidate other concepts in the Mishnah. Rabbi Hoshia and Bar Kapara likewise wrote *Beraisos* to explain the words of the Mishnah. Finally, Rabbi Yochanan wrote the Jerusalem Talmud, in the land of Israel, some 300 years after the destruction of the Holy Temple. . .

Ravina and Rav Ashi were the last of the sages of the Talmud. It was Rav Ashi who wrote the Babylonian Talmud in Babylon, approximately a hundred years after Rabbi Yochanan had written the Jerusalem Talmud.[70] Both Talmuds (or Gemorahs) were commentaries on the Mishnah, explaining its depth and expounding all the new concepts that had been resolved in the courts since the time of Our Holy Rabbi.

The two Talmuds, the *Tosefta*, the *Sifra* and the *Sifri* all explain what is permitted and forbidden, clean and unclean, liable and innocent, fit and unfit. It was all as it had been handed down from generation to generation, and ultimately from Moses himself. . .

Ravina and Rav Ashi were therefore the last great Jewish sages to transcribe the Oral Torah. . .Every Jew therefore follows the Babylonian Talmud. . .This is because every single Jew had agreed to accept the teachings of the Talmud. . .for it included the teachings of all our sages, or at least the majority of them. They, in turn, had received the tradition regarding the foundations of the Torah from generation to generation, and ultimately from Moses himself. . .

⋅§ Code, Repentance

(Yad, Tshuvah)

3:8 Three are in the category of those who deny the Torah: A person who says that the Torah does not come from God, even if he only says this with respect to one verse, or even one word. If a person says that Moses wrote it on his own, then he denies the Torah. The same is true of one who denies its interpretation as included in the Oral Torah. Such a person is then like Tzaduk and Baithus [who denied the Oral Torah].[71]

⋅§ Code, Rebellion

(Yad, Mamrim)

1:1 [The Sanhedrin,] the great court in Jerusalem, is the basis of the Oral Torah. It stood as the pillar of Law, and from it laws and judgments emanated to all Israel. The Torah assures us [of this court's authority] when it says (*Deuteronomy* 17:11), "[You shall abide] by the Torah according to how they teach it to you." This in itself is a commandment of the Torah.

Everyone who believes in the Torah must therefore accept this court's authority and depend on it regarding all matters concerning our religion.

3:1 One who does not believe in the Oral Torah. . .is counted as a heretic (*Apikores*).

3:2 If one openly denies the authenticity of the Oral Torah, he is in the same category as all other heretics, people who deny that the Torah came from heaven, informers and renegades. All of these are not counted as Jews.

3:3   This is only true when one denies the Oral Torah on the basis of his own thoughts and opinions. This is the person who follows his own limited intellect and stubbornly denies the Oral Torah on his own. He thus follows the footsteps of Tzaduk, Baithus and their followers.

But this does not include the children of those who go astray or their descendants. These are raised among the Karaites[72] and are convinced by their parents. Such people are therefore in the same category as a person kidnapped by gentiles as an infant[73] and raised by them. He may not eagerly abide by the commandments, but he is like one under constraint.[74]

Even though such a child may later find out that he is a Jew and see Jews practicing their religion, he is still considered to be under constraint, since he was raised in such a misguided manner.

The same is true of those who follow the ways of their fathers who are Karaites who have strayed.

It is therefore fitting to bring them back and draw them with words of peace, until they return to the strength of the Torah.

ᐵ Points for Discussion

1. How was the Book of Genesis written?

2. What was the role of Moses in writing the Torah?

3. Compare this principle with the previous one.

4. What part of the Torah is uniquely Jewish?

5. What is the Oral Torah? Where do we now find it?

6. Who were responsible for insuring that the oral tradition remained accurate?

7. How was the Oral Torah put into writing? When?

8. Why was this not done until after the rise of Christianity?

9. How do we know how to read and translate the Torah? To what degree is this related to the oral tradition?

10. Where do we find the laws of Tehillim? Why?

11. Why was the Torah given in two parts, one written and the other oral?

12. Who were the Sadducees, Tzadukim, Baithusians and Karaites? What happened to them? What groups correspond to them today?

13. What is the status of one who grows up without knowledge of Judaism? How is this related to the concept of the Oral tradition?

בֶּאֱמוּנָה שְׁלֵמָה
שֶׁזֹּאת הַתּוֹרָה
לֹא תְהִי מֻחְלֶפֶת,
וְלֹא תְהִי תּוֹרָה אַחֶרֶת
מֵאֵת הַבּוֹרֵא,
יִתְבָּרַךְ שְׁמוֹ.

The Ninth Principle

אֲנִי מַאֲמִין בֶּאֱמוּנָה שְׁלֵמָה
שֶׁזֹּאת הַתּוֹרָה לֹא תְהֵא מֻחְלֶפֶת,
וְלֹא תְהֵא תּוֹרָה אַחֶרֶת מֵאֵת הַבּוֹרֵא יִתְבָּרַךְ שְׁמוֹ.

*I believe with perfect faith
that this Torah will not be changed,
and that there will never be another
Torah given by God.*

◆§ Yigdal

God will not replace nor change His Law
For all time, for anything else.

◆§ Commentary on Mishnah

The ninth principle involves permanence. The Torah is God's permanent word, and no one else can change it.

Nothing can be added to or subtracted from either the written Torah or the Oral Torah. It is thus written (*Deuteronomy* 13:1), "You shall not add to it, nor subtract from it." This has already been discussed in detail in our introduction to this *Commentary on the Mishnah.*

◆§ Code, Foundations of the Torah
(*Yad, Yesodey HaTorah*)

9:1 The Torah clearly states that its commandments will remain binding forever, with neither change, addition nor subtraction. The Torah thus states (*Deuteronomy* 13:1), "All this word that I command you, you shall keep and do. You shall not add to it, nor subtract from it." The Torah likewise says (*ibid.* 29:28), "things that are revealed belong to us and our children *forever*, to keep all the words of *this Torah.*" We thus see that we are commanded to keep the words of the Torah forever. Similarly, with regard to many laws, the Torah clearly states, "It shall be an everlasting statute, for all your generations."[75]

The Torah furthermore says (*ibid.* 30:11, 12), "[This commandment which I give you today. . .] is not in heaven." From this we learn that a prophet can no longer add anything to the Torah.[76]

Therefore, if any prophet comes to alter [the Torah, which is] the prophecy of Moses, we immediately know that he is a false prophet. It does not matter whether he is Jewish or non-Jewish, or how many signs or miracles he performs. If he says that God sent him to add or subtract a commandment of the Torah or explain it differently than our tradition from Moses, he is a false prophet. The same is true if he teaches that the commandments given to Israel were only given for a limited time and not forever. . .

In all such cases, we know that such a prophet is speaking presumptuously in God's name, making up something not told to him by God. For God Himself told Moses that this commandment (the Jewish religion) is "for us and for our children [forever]."

[And as the Torah says (*Numbers* 23:19),] "God is not man that he should speak falsely."

9:2   One may then wonder what God meant when He told Moses (*Deuteronomy* 18:18), "I will raise up a prophet like you from among your brothers."

But the truth is that such a prophet will not be sent to start any new religion. A prophet only comes to command us to keep the Torah and warn people who violate it. We thus find that the very last words of prophecy ever spoken were (*Malachi* 3:22), "Remember the Torah of Moses, My servant."

A prophet may likewise come to tell us things that have nothing at all to do with the commandments. Thus, for example, he might instruct us whether or not to go on a journey, wage a war, or build a wall. In such cases, we are commanded to obey his instructions. . . .

◄§ Code, Repentance
(Yad, Tshuvah)

Three are in the category of those who deny the Torah:. . . One who says that God has exchanged His religion for another, or that the Torah no longer applies, even though it was originally from God.

◄§ Points for Discussion

1. Why do we believe that the Torah will never be changed or substituted?

2. Christianity claims that the Torah was the "old testament," which has now been replaced by a "new testament." How would this principle apply to their belief?

3. How does this principle apply to Islam?

4. Many Jews feel that the commandments of the Torah are no longer valid since "times have changed." Discuss this belief.

5. Does God know the future? When He gave the Torah, could He anticipate what the present world would be like?

6. The Torah contains commandments regarding many things, such as sacrifices and the laws of purity, which no longer apply. Why does this not contradict this principle?

7. Will we still keep the Torah in the Messianic Age?

8. Can anything in the Torah ever become "old fashioned?"

9. Did God give the world any religion other than Judaism?

בֶּאֱמוּנָה שְׁלֵמָה
שֶׁהַבּוֹרֵא, יִתְבָּרַךְ שְׁמוֹ,
יוֹדֵעַ כָּל־מַעֲשֵׂה
בְּנֵי אָדָם
וְכָל־מַחְשְׁבוֹתָם,
שֶׁנֶּאֱמַר:
הַיֹּצֵר יַחַד לִבָּם,
הַמֵּבִין אֶל כָּל־מַעֲשֵׂיהֶם.

The Tenth Principle

אֲנִי מַאֲמִין בֶּאֱמוּנָה שְׁלֵמָה שֶׁהַבּוֹרֵא, יִתְבָּרַךְ שְׁמוֹ,
יוֹדֵעַ כָּל־מַעֲשֵׂה בְּנֵי אָדָם וְכָל־מַחְשְׁבוֹתָם,
שֶׁנֶּאֱמַר: הַיֹּצֵר יַחַד לִבָּם, הַמֵּבִין אֶל כָּל־מַעֲשֵׂיהֶם.

*I believe with perfect faith that God
knows all of man's deeds and thoughts.
It is thus written (Psalm 33:15),
"He has molded every heart together,
He understands what each one does."*

◄§ Yigdal

He sees, He knows our secrets,
He sees each thing's end at its very beginning.

◄§ Commentary on Mishnah

The tenth principle is that God knows all that men do, and never turns His eyes away from them. It denies the opinion of those who say (*Ezekiel* 9:9), "God has abandoned His world. [God does not see.]"[77]

This principle is taught by the Prophet when he says that God is (*Jeremiah* 32:19), "great in counsel, mighty in insight, whose eyes are open to all the ways of man." We also find it assumed in the Torah in such places as (*Genesis* 6:5), "God saw that the evil of man on earth was very great," and (*ibid.* 18:20), "The cry of Sodom and Gomorrah is great." These and similar passages all reflect this tenth principle.

◄§ Code, Foundations of the Torah
(Yad, Yesodey HaTorah)

2:9 Everything that exists (with the exception of God Himself) only exists because God gives it power to exist. This is true of everything, from the highest angelic form to the smallest insect in the interior of the earth.[78]

2:10 God knows Himself, and is aware of His own greatness, glory and reality, and He therefore must also know everything else. There is nothing that can be hidden from Him.[79]

God recognizes His true nature and knows it exactly as it is.

This knowledge is not something that can be separated from His essence. In this way, it is very different from ours. For our knowledge is not the same as our identity. But in the case of God, both He, His knowledge and His life are One. They are all One in every possible way and in the fullest definition of unity.

For if God lives with a "life" or knew with a "knowledge" that was not equivalent to His essence, then we would have to say that there was more than one God. For [neither His life nor His knowledge could be inferior to His essence, and therefore] we would have to say that there were many Gods. His essence, His life, and His knowledge [all being equal] would have to be considered [equally] as Gods.

This, of course, is not true. God is One in every possible way, in the fullest sense of unity.

We must therefore say that He Himself is the Knower, the thing that is known, and the knowledge itself.[80] It is all one.

This concept is beyond the power of speech to express, and beyond the power of the ear to hear. There is no way that the human mind can fully comprehend it.

We also know that this is true, however, from the very language of the scripture. When speaking of things other than God, it uses such expressions as "by the life of Pharaoh,"[81] and "by the life of your soul."[82] In the case of God, however, the scripture never uses the expression, "by the life of God." Rather, it always uses the expression, "by the Life — God."[83] This is because God and His life [are identical, and] not two separate entities, as in the case of physical beings and angels.

God therefore does not recognize and know creatures

because of themselves, as we do. Rather, He knows them because of Himself. Everything depends upon Him for existence, and since He knows Himself, He therefore knows everything.

◆§ Code, Repentance
(Yad, Tshuvah)

5:5 We may then ask a very legitimate question. [For we find a paradox between God's knowledge of the future and man's freedom of will.] We must either say that God knows the future and therefore knows whether one will be good or wicked, or else we must say that He does not know. If we say that God knows a person will be good, then it is impossible for him to be otherwise. If, on the other hand, we say that God knows that he will be good, and it is still possible for him to be evil, then we must say that God's knowledge is not complete.[84]

Before going further, you must realize that the answer to this question is "wider than the earth, and broader than the sea."[85] It involves a great number of important basic principles and lofty concepts. However, you must pay very close attention to what I am saying.

In the second chapter of the Code, on the Foundation of the Torah (*Yesodey HaTorah*), we discussed the fact that God does not "know" with a knowledge that is separate from His essence. In the case of man, we can speak of the individual and his knowledge as two separate things. In the case of God however, both He and His knowledge are one.

This, however, is beyond our power of understanding, just as man cannot understand God's true nature. This is what God meant [when He told Moses] (*Exodus* 33:20), "Man cannot see Me and live."

For the very same reason, man cannot understand God's knowledge. [God told us this through His] prophet, when He said (*Isaiah* 55:8), "My thoughts are not your thoughts, My ways are not your ways." We therefore do not have the ability to understand how God knows all things and deeds.

We know, however, without any doubt, that man has absolute free will, and that God does not force him nor decree upon him what to do. This is not only known from the traditions of our faith, but can also be proven philosophically. For this reason all prophecy teaches that man is judged for his deeds, and according to his deeds, whether they be good or evil. This is the foundation, and all prophecy depends upon it.

3:8 Three are in the category of the heretic (*Apiko-res*):...One who says that God does not know the deeds of man.

◄§ *Points for Discussion*

1. Why is this a fundamental principle? How is it related to the first principle?

2. If God does not change, how can He acquire knowledge?

3. Why do we say that God and his knowledge are one? Why are they not the same in the case of man?

4. Discuss the paradox of God's knowledge and free will. How does the Rambam treat this paradox?

5. Why is this paradox necessary? How can it strengthen our faith?

6. How does God know the future?

7. Why does the Rambam call free will the foundation of all prophecy?

8. How does God know our thoughts?

אֲנִי מַאֲמִין

בֶּאֱמוּנָה שְׁלֵמָה
שֶׁהַבּוֹרֵא, יִתְבָּרַךְ שְׁמוֹ,
גּוֹמֵל טוֹב
לְשׁוֹמְרֵי מִצְוֹתָיו,
וּמַעֲנִישׁ לְעוֹבְרֵי מִצְוֹתָיו.

The Eleventh Principle

אֲנִי מַאֲמִין בֶּאֱמוּנָה שְׁלֵמָה שֶׁהַבּוֹרֵא, יִתְבָּרַךְ שְׁמוֹ,
גּוֹמֵל טוֹב לְשׁוֹמְרֵי מִצְוֹתָיו, וּמַעֲנִישׁ לְעוֹבְרֵי מִצְוֹתָיו.

*I believe with perfect faith that God rewards
those who keep His commandments,
and punishes those who
transgress His commandments.*

◆§ Yigdal

He rewards man with love, as his deeds deserve,
He gives the wicked evil, according to their wrong.

◆§ Commentary on Mishnah

The eleventh principle is that God rewards those who obey
the commandments of the Torah, and punishes those who
violate its prohibitions.

The greatest possible reward is the World to Come,
while the greatest possible punishment is being cut off from
it. . .

The Torah teaches us this principle in the following
account. Moses said to God (*Exodus* 32:32), "If You will, then
forgive their sin, but if not, then extinguish me." God
answered (*ibid.* 32:33), "The one who has sinned against Me,
him will I erase from My book."

This shows that God knows both the obedient and the
sinner, rewarding one and punishing the other.

ᴥ§ Code, Repentance
(Yad, Tshuvah)

6:1 When either an individual or a nation sins. . .they deserve punishment, and God knows what punishment is fitting. In some cases one is punished through his body. . ., while in others he is punished through [the loss of] his possessions.

In other cases, his punishment might involve his minor children.[86] For young children, who are not yet obligated to keep the commandments, are considered like one's possessions.[87] The Torah says (*Deuteronomy* 24:16). "[Children shall not die because of their fathers,] every man shall die for his own sin." This, however, [does not refer to small children, but] only to an adult, who has full responsibility for his deeds.[88]

There are some cases in which a person is punished in the World to Come, and absolutely no harm comes to him in this world at all. In other cases, one may be punished both in this world and in the next.

6:2 This is only true when one does not repent. When a person repents, his repentance is like a shield protecting him from troubles.[89] And just as a person can sin through his own free will, so can he repent through his own free will.

8:1 The main reward of the righteous is in the World to Come. This is a life that is not terminated by death, and a good that is not mixed with any evil.

The Torah thus says (*Deuteronomy* 22:7), "You will have good, and your days will be long." Our traditions interpret this to say: "You will have good" — in a world where all is good — "and your days will be long" — in a world that goes on and on.[90] This is the World to Come.

◄§ Points for Discussion

1. What is the main good and evil involved in reward and punishment? Where is it defined?

2. Where is the main place of reward and punishment?

3. Why do we sometimes see good people suffering and evil people prospering?

4. Why does God reward good? Why does He punish evil?

5. What is the World to Come?

6. How is the principle related to that of the immortality of the soul?

אֲנִי מַאֲמִין

בֶּאֱמוּנָה שְׁלֵמָה
בְּבִיאַת הַמָּשִׁיחַ;
וְאַף עַל פִּי שֶׁיִּתְמַהְמֵהַּ,
עִם כָּל־זֶה אֲחַכֶּה־לּוֹ
בְּכָל־יוֹם שֶׁיָּבוֹא.

The Twelfth Principle

אֲנִי מַאֲמִין בֶּאֱמוּנָה שְׁלֵמָה בְּבִיאַת הַמָּשִׁיחַ;
וְאַף עַל פִּי שֶׁיִּתְמַהְמֵהַּ,
עִם כָּל־זֶה אֲחַכֶּה־לּוֹ בְּכָל־יוֹם שֶׁיָּבוֹא.

*I believe with perfect faith
in the coming of the Messiah.
No matter how long it takes,
I will await his coming every day.*

◦§ Yigdal

He will send our Messiah at the End of Days,
To redeem those who await His final salvation.

◦§ Commentary on Mishnah

The twelfth principle involves the Messianic Age.

We believe and are certain that the Messiah will come. We do not consider him late, and "although he tarry, we await him."[91]

We should not set a time for his coming, nor try to calculate when he will come from scriptural passages. Our sages thus teach us, "May the spirit of those who try to calculate the time of the end rot."[92]

We believe that the Messiah will be greater than any other king or ruler who has ever lived. This has been predicted by every prophet from Moses to Malachi.

One who doubts or minimizes this denies the Torah itself. For the Messiah is mentioned both in the account of Balaam[93] and at the end of Deuteronomy.[94]

Included in this principle is the belief that a Jewish king can only come from the family of David through his son Solomon. One who rejects this family denies God and His prophets.

◆§ *Commentary on Sanhedrin 10:1*

The Messianic age is when the Jews will regain their independence and all return to the land of Israel.

The Messiah will be a very great king, whose government will be in Zion. He will achieve great fame, and his reputation among the nations will be even greater than that of King Solomon. His great righteousness and the wonders that he will bring about will cause all peoples to make peace with him and all lands to serve him. Whoever rises up against him will be destroyed by God and given over into his hand.

All the Biblical passages that speak of the Messiah thus testify to his success, and to our prosperity that will accompany it.

Nothing will change in the Messianic age, however, except that the Jews will regain their independence. Our sages thus teach us, "There is no difference between this world and the Messianic Age, except with regard to our subjugation by other governments."[95]

Rich and poor, strong and weak, will still exist in the Messianic Age. It will be very easy for people to make a living, however, and with very little effort they will be able to accomplish very much. This is what our sages mean when they teach us, "In the Future, the land of Israel will bring forth white bread and cloaks of fine wool."[96] This saying is very much like the common expression that people use when someone finds something all prepared and they say, "he has found baked bread and cooked food." Agriculture and harvest will still exist, however, even in the Messianic Age, as the scripture clearly says (*Isaiah* 61:5), "Aliens shall be your plowmen and your vinedressers."

It is for this reason that the sage [who said that Israel will bring forth white bread] became angry at one of his disciples, who took this statement literally. [He answered that we indeed find similar things, even now in this world.] But even this answer, however, was given in the context of the disciple's misunderstanding, and was not the actual truth. We see that this is so, since the Talmud uses this as an example of the teaching (*Proverbs* 26:4), "Do not answer a fool according to his folly."

The main benefit of the Messianic Age will be that we will no longer be under the subjugation of foreign governments who prevent us from keeping all the commandments. It will be a time when the number of wise men will increase, as we find (*Isaiah* 11:9), "All the world will be filled with knowledge." War will no longer exist, as the prophet said (*ibid.* 2:4), "nation shall no longer lift up sword against nation." It will be an age of great perfection, through which we will become worthy to enter into the World to Come.

The Messiah will then die, and his son will rule in his place.[97] He, in turn, will be followed by *his* son. The Prophet speaks of the Messiah's death when he says (*Isaiah* 42:4), "He shall not fail nor be crushed until he has set right in the world."

His kingdom, however, will last for a very long time. This is because man's lifetime will be vastly extended. Worries and troubles will no longer exist, and therefore people will live much longer. We should therefore not be surprised that the Messiah's kingdom will last for thousands of years.[98] Our sages thus teach us that when this good is brought together, it will not be quickly dispersed.

We do not hope and long for the Messianic Age in order that we might have much grain and wealth. We do not want it so that we should be able to ride horses and indulge in wine and song, as those with confused ideas believe.

The main reason why our prophets and saints have desired the Messianic Age with such a great longing is because it will be highlighted by a community of the righteous and domi-nated by goodness and wisdom. It will be ruled by [the Messiah, who will be] a righteous and honest king, outstanding in wisdom, and close to God. The Scripture therefore says of him (*Psalms* 2:7), "God has said to him, you are My son, I have given birth to you today."

The people in that Age will obey all the commandments of the Torah without neglect or laziness, and nothing will hold them back. This is what the prophet predicted (*Jeremiah* 31:33), "Man will no longer teach his friend and his brother saying, 'know God.' For all of them will know Me, great and small alike." The scripture [speaking of the knowledge of God that comes through the Torah, as the previous verse] says (*ibid.* 31:32), "I will place My Torah in their hearts."[99] The Prophet likewise said in God's name (*Ezekiel* 36:26), "I will remove the heart of stone from your flesh..." There are many other similar passages that speak along these lines.

It is through this that we will be worthy of the World to Come, which is the final goal...

⋖§ Code, Repentance

(Yad, Tshuvah)

9:2 All Jews, including their prophets and sages, [have always] longed for the Messianic Age because they wanted relief from the oppressive governments which would not let them observe the Torah and its commandments properly. They wanted to find the tranquility to grow in wisdom, and thus become worthy of life in the World to Come.

The Messianic Age, on the other hand, will be part of our present world. The world will follow its present course with the one exception that the Jews will regain their total independence. Our sages thus teach us, "There is no difference between this world and the Messianic Age, except with regard to our subjugation by other governments."[100]

⋖§ Code, Governments

(Yad, Melachim)

11:1 The Messiah will be a king who will restore the kingdom of David to its original state. He will rebuild the Temple (*Beis HaMikdash*), and gather together all Jews, no matter where they are scattered.

All the laws of the Torah will be fulfilled as they were originally. The sacrificial system as well as the practices of the Sabbatical Year (*Shemitah*) and the Jubilee (*Yovel*) will all be restored.[101] We will then be able to once again observe all the commandments of the Torah.

A person who does not believe in the Messiah, or does not await his coming, denies the most essential teachings of the prophets. Beyond that, he also denies the teachings of both

Moses and the Torah.

The Torah itself testifies to the Messianic promise when it says (*Deuteronomy* 30:3-5), "God will restore your fortunes, have mercy on you, and gather you [again from all the countries where He has scattered you]. If He were to banish you to the ends of the heavens [the Lord your God will gather you, and bring you from there]. The Lord your God will bring you [to the land that your fathers occupied. You will occupy it again, and He will make you even more prosperous and numerous than your fathers]." This passage in the Torah includes everything that was predicted by all the prophets [regarding the Messiah].

In the account of Baalam, we likewise find a prophecy regarding the two Messiahs (or anointed ones). The first one was King David, who liberated the Jews from all their initial oppressors. The second is his descendant, the Messiah, who will liberate all Jews in the end.

This is his prophecy (*Numbers* 24:17):

"I see him, but not now" — King David.

"I behold him, but not near" — the Messiah.

"A star shall come forth from Jacob" — King David.

"A scepter shall arise from Israel" — the Messiah.

"He shall smite the squadrons of Moab" — King David.

We thus find that he (*II Samuel* 8:2) "smote Moab and measured them with a rope."

"He shall break down the sons of Seth" — the Messiah. We thus find that (*Zechariah* 9:10), "his rule shall be from sea to sea."

"Edom shall be his conquest" — King David. It is thus written (*II Samuel* 8:14), "all Edom became servants to David."

"And Seir, his enemy, shall be his tribute" — the Messiah. It is thus foretold (*Obadiah* 1:21), "Saviors shall come up on Mount Zion [and judge the mount of Esau, and the kingdom shall become that of God]."

11:2 We find further evidence [in the Torah] from the commandment concerning the Cities of Refuge (*Arey Miklat*).[102] The Torah thus says (*Deuteronomy* 19:8,9), "When God enlarges your borders . . . and you shall add three cities." This never took place, but it is certain that God would not give a commandment in vain.[103] [We therefore see that this will have to take place in the Messianic Age.]

We do not have to bring any proof, however, that the prophets speak of the Messiah, since all their writings are full of this concept.

11:3 Do not think that the Messiah will have to perform signs and miracles. He will not necessarily change the course of nature, bring the dead back to life, or anything else like that.[104]

We thus find that Rabbi Akiba, the greatest sage of the Mishnah, was willing to accept Ben Kosiba as the Messiah, at least until he was killed because of his sins.[105] It was only when he was killed that they realized that they had been wrong and he was not the true Messiah.

We see, however, that the sages did not ask him for any sign or miracle.

The main thing, however, [is that the Messiah will not change our religion in any way]. The Torah that we now have, with its laws and commandments, will remain the same forever. Nothing will be added to it nor subtracted from it.

11:4 We may assume that an individual is the Messiah if he fulfills the following conditions:

He must be a ruler, from the house of David, immersed in the Torah and its commandments like David his ancestor. He must also follow both the written and the Oral Torah, lead all Jews back to the Torah, strengthen the observance of its laws, and fight God's battles. If one fulfills these conditions, then we may assume that he is the Messiah.

If he does this successfully, and then rebuilds the Temple (*Beis HaMikdash*) on its original site and gathers all the dispersed Jews, then we may be certain that he is the Messiah.

He will then perfect the entire world and bring all men to serve God in unity. It has thus been predicted (*Zephaniah* 3:9), "I will then give all peoples a pure tongue, that they may call in the name of God, and all serve Him in one manner."

12:1 Do not think that the ways of the world or the laws of nature will change in the Messianic Age. This is not true. The world will continue as it is.

It is true that the prophet Isaiah predicted (*Isaiah* 11:6), "The wolf shall live with the sheep, the leopard shall lie down with the kid." This, however, is merely an allegory, meaning that the Jews will live safely, even with the wicked nations, who are likened to wolves and leopards. We thus find [that the Prophet says of the nations who will punish Israel] (*Jeremiah* 5:6), "A wolf from the plains shall ravish them, a leopard shall prowl in their cities."

All nations will return to the true religion and will no longer steal or oppress. They will eat that which they have honestly attained, together with Israel. This is what the Prophet means when he says (*Isaiah* 11:7), "The lion shall eat hay like the ox."

All prophecies such as these regarding the Messiah are allegorical. Only in the Messianic Age will we know the meaning of each allegory and what it comes to teach us.

12:2 Our sages [provided us with an important rule when they] said, "There is no difference between this world and the Messianic Age, except with regard to our subjection to other governments."[106]

From the simple meaning of a number of prophecies, we see that the Messianic Age will begin with the war of Gog and Magog.[107]

Before this war of Gog and Magog, a prophet will arise to rectify the Jews and prepare their hearts. The Prophet foresaw this when he said [in God's name] (*Malachi* 3:23), "Behold, I will send you Elijah the prophet [before the great and terrible day of God]."[108]

The prophet will not come to make the clean unclean or the unclean clean. He will not declare that certain individuals are illegitimate when they have been assumed to be legitimate. Neither will he legitimize those who are assumed to be illegitimate. His only task will be to bring peace to the world.[109] The prophecy thus concludes (*ibid.* 3:24), "He shall turn the hearts of the fathers to their children."

Others of our sages, however, say that Elijah will come immediately before the Messiah[110] [after the war of Gog and Magog].

In all cases such as these, no man knows what will happen until the time comes. These things were purposely left ambiguous by the prophets. Our [Talmudic] sages likewise did not have any clear tradition in this area, and could therefore only come to some conclusion by interpreting various Biblical passages. It is for this reason that we find so many opinions regarding these matters.

The main thing to remember, however, is that neither the order in which these things will occur, nor their details, are fundamentals of our faith. A person should therefore not involve himself in analyzing these traditions. He should not spend time on the Midrashim which were written about such topics, nor consider them overly important. For these things do not bring one to love or fear God.

One should likewise not attempt to calculate when the Messiah will come. Our sages thus said, "May the soul of those who calculate the end rot."[111] One must hope and believe in general, as we have explained.

12:4 Our sages and prophets did not long for the Messianic Age in order that they might rule the world and dominate the gentiles. They did not desire that the nations should honor them, or that they should be able to eat, drink and be merry.

They only wanted one thing, and that was to be free to involve themselves in the Torah and its wisdom. They wanted nothing to disturb or distract them, in order that they should be able to strive to become worthy of life in the World to Come. This has already been discussed in my code on Repentance.

12:5 In the Messianic Age, there will be neither war nor famine. Jealousy and competition will cease to exist, for all good things will be most plentiful, and all sorts of delicacies will be as common as dust.

The main occupation of humanity will only be to know God. The Jews will therefore become great sages, know many hidden things, and achieve the greatest understanding of God possible for a mortal human being. The Prophet thus predicted (*Isaiah* 11:9), "The earth shall be full of the knowledge of God, as the waters cover the sea."

◆§ Points for Discussion

1. Who will the Messiah be?
2. How will we know for sure that he is the Messiah?
3. Will he be a prophet? What consequences will this have?
4. Will he be a greater prophet than Moses? Why?
5. What is the reason for the Messianic Age?
6. Will the Messiah necessarily perform miracles? Why?
7. Will we still observe the Torah when the Messiah comes? Why?
8. Why don't we believe that Jesus was the Messiah?
9. What is the war of Gog and Magog?
10. Why will Elijah come before the Messiah?
11. Do you see any signs that the Messianic Age is approaching?
12. Can the Messiah come miraculously any day?
13. What is the "End of Days?"

אֲנִי מַאֲמִין

בֶּאֱמוּנָה שְׁלֵמָה
שֶׁתִּהְיֶה תְּחִיַּת הַמֵּתִים
בְּעֵת שֶׁיַּעֲלֶה רָצוֹן
מֵאֵת הַבּוֹרֵא,
יִתְבָּרַךְ שְׁמוֹ
וְיִתְעַלֶּה זִכְרוֹ
לָעַד וּלְנֵצַח נְצָחִים.

The Thirteenth Principle

אֲנִי מַאֲמִין בֶּאֱמוּנָה שְׁלֵמָה
שֶׁתִּהְיֶה תְּחִיַּת הַמֵּתִים בְּעֵת שֶׁיַּעֲלֶה רָצוֹן מֵאֵת הַבּוֹרֵא, יִתְבָּרַךְ שְׁמוֹ,
וְיִתְעַלֶּה זִכְרוֹ לָעַד וּלְנֵצַח נְצָחִים.

I believe with perfect faith
that the dead will be brought back to life
when God wills it to happen.

◆§ *Yigdal*

God will bring the dead to life with His great love;
May His glorious name be blessed for all time.

◆§ *Commentary on Mishnah*

The thirteenth principle involves the resurrection of the dead.

◆§ *Commentary on Sanhedrin 10:1*

The resurrection of the dead is one of the foundations handed down by Moses. One who does not believe in it cannot be associated with Judaism or its religion.

The resurrection, however, is just for the righteous. The Midrash thus says in *Bereshis Rabbah*, "Rain is for both the wicked and righteous, but the resurrection is only for the righteous."[112] It would be absurd for the wicked to be brought back to life, for even while they are alive, they are considered dead. Our sages teach us, "The wicked are considered dead, even during their lifetimes. But the righteous are considered alive, even after they die."[113]

⊷ Code, Repentance

(Yad, Tshuvah)

3:6   These have no portion in the World to Come. . .Those who deny the resurrection of the dead. . .[114]

⊷ Discourse on the Resurrection

(Maamar Techiyas HaMesim)

The concept of the resurrection is well known among all Jews, and there are none who dispute it. It is mentioned many times in our prayers and homilies, as well as in supplications written by the prophets and sages. Innumerable references to it may be found in the Talmud and Midrash.

This is its significance:

The body and soul will be reunited once again after they have been separated [by death]. There is no Jew who disputes this, and it cannot be interpreted other than literally. One may not accept the view of any Jew who believes otherwise. For we must understand that even though many other Biblical verses may be interpreted allegorically, this must be taken literally.

The concept of the resurrection, namely that body and soul will be reunited after death, is found in the book of Daniel in such a manner that it cannot be interpreted other than literally. We are told (*Daniel* 12:2), "Many who sleep in the dust shall awaken, some to everlasting life, and some to everlasting shame and reproach." Daniel was likewise told by the angel (*ibid.* 12:13), "Now go your way to the end and rest, and you shall arise to your destiny at the end of days". . .

We also see from many pertinent teachings that the men whose souls have been returned to their bodies will eat, drink, marry, have children, and finally die after living a very long time. . .[115]

1. Exactly what is the resurrection of the dead?

2. How is it related to the concept of the immortality of the soul?

3. Read the 37th chapter of Ezekiel. Did this really happen, or was it merely a vision? How is it related to the final resurrection?

4. What effect would a miracle like the resurrection have on the world? How would the world change? What would it be like afterward?

5. Rambam here writes that the resurrected dead will die once again. Many other sages, however, dispute this, and maintain that they will never die. Discuss the significance of these two opinions.

6. Those who hold that the resurrected dead will not die again maintain that the world of the resurrection will lead directly into the World to Come. The World to Come will then include both body and soul. Why do you think that man must also have a body in order to receive his final reward?

7. The Rambam disputes this view, and maintains that the World to Come is completely spiritual. Why does he reject the other opinion? Discuss both opinions.

8. How do you think the dead will be brought back to life? How about those whose bodies no longer exist? What about someone whose body was completely destroyed?

9. How would you react to coming face to face with someone close to you, whom you knew to have died?

NOTES

1. See *Moreh Nevuchim* 2:1. Also see introduction to Part 2, No. 16, *Cf. Or HaShem* 1:1:16, 1:2:23, *Amud HaAvodah, Hakdamah Gedolah* No. 15, 31.
2. Rashi *ad loc.*, however, explains this somewhat differently. Instead of "neither separation nor combination," he would read, "neither direction nor weariness."
3. Also see *Deuteronomy* 4:39.
4. *Exodus* 9:3, *Deuteronomy* 2:15, *Joshua* 4:24, *Judges* 2:15, *I Samuel* 5:6, 5:9, 7:13, 12:15, *II Kings* 3:15, *Isaiah* 19:16, 25:10, 41:20, 59:1, 66:14, *Ezekiel* 1:3, 3:22, 37:1, 40:1, *Job* 12:9, *Ruth* 1:13.
5. *Deuteronomy* 11:12, *Zechariah* 4:10, *Psalms* 34:16, *Proverbs* 5:21, 15:3, 22:12, *Cf. Genesis* 6:8, 38:7, 38:10, *Leviticus* 10:19, etc.
6. *Numbers* 11:1, 11:18, *I Samuel* 8:21.
7. *Cf. Mechilta*, Rashi, on *Exodus* 20:2; *Rosh HaShanah* 17b.
8. See *Moreh Nevuchim* 1:54, 64.
9. *Job* 4:19.
10. Enosh was the son of Seth, and the grandson of Adam. It was in his generation that idolatry began. See *Genesis 4:26, Targum J.*, Rashi *ad loc.*; *Shabbos* 118b, *Mechilta* on *Exodus* 20:3 (67b), *Sifri* (43) on *Deuteronomy* 11:16; 23:5, *Yerushalmi, Shekalim* 6:2 (26a). The question as to whether or not Enosh himself was involved in this idolatry is discussed in detail in the Radal on *Pirkey DeRabbi Eliezer* 18:52 and 22:4, note 2.
11. See *Metzudos*, Abarbanel *ad loc.*
12. *Shabbos* 92a, *Nedarim* 38a, *Avos* 4:1, *Shemonah Perakim* 7, *Moreh Nevuchim* 2:36.
13. That is, *Pardes* or Paradise. See *Yad Yesodey HaTorah* 4:13, *Chagigah* 14b.
14. *Cf. Avodah Zarah* 20b, *Yerushalmi Shabbos* 1:3 (8b), *Yerushalmi Shekalim* 3:3 (14b).
15. *Genesis* 28:12, *Bereshis Rabbah* 68:19.
16. *Ezekiel* 1:5 ff.
17. *Jeremiah* 1:13.
18. *Ibid.* 1:11.
19. *Ezekiel* 2:9.
20. *Zechariah* 5:6.
21. Others, however, disagree with the Rambam on this point, and hold that exact words were revealed to the prophet, especially where the prophecies were to be recorded in the Bible. See Rambam on *Numbers* 23:5, *Kuzari* 5:20 (50b), Sforno on *Numbers* 22:38 from *II Samuel* 23:2.
22. *Shabbos* 30b, *Pesachim* 117a.
23. *Ibid. Cf. II Kings* 3:15.
24. *I Kings* 20:35, *II Kings* 2:3, 2:5, 2:7, 2:15, 4:1, 4:38, 5:22, 6:1, 9:1. See *Targum ad loc.*
25. *Deuteronomy* 17:6, 19:15.
26. *Cf. Bereshis Rabbah* 85:3.
27. *I Samuel* 9:19 ff.
28. *Yerushalmi Sanhedrin* 11:5 (56b). *Cf. Tanchuma VaYera* 13.

29. *Job* 2:13, *Jonah* 4:2. *Cf. Exodus* 34:6, *Numbers* 14:18, *Psalms* 103:8, *Nehemiah* 9:17.
30. See *Jonah* 3:1.
31. *II Kings* 20:6, *Isaiah* 38:5, *II Chronicles* 32:26.
32. *Berachos* 7a.
33. *Shabbos* 55a. *Cf. Berachos* 4a.
34. See note 28.
35. *Cf. Yerushalmi Sanhedrin* 11:6 (57b).
36. See Rashi *ad loc.* Also see *Ezekiel* 2:5.
37. Literally, the "father" of all prophets. See *VaYikra Rabbah* 1:3.
38. The Kabbalistic interpretation of the anthropomorphic metaphor. See *Kuzari* 4:3 (24b), *Kol Yehudah ad loc.* , Ibn Ezra on *Exodus* 33:20.
39. That is *Mareh* and *Machazeh.* We find *Mareh* in *Numbers* 12:8, *Exodus* 3:3, *Ezekiel* 11:24, 43:3, *Daniel* 8:27, *Numbers* 8:4. *Machazeh* occurs in *Genesis* 15:1, *Numbers* 24:4, 24:16, *Ezekiel* 13:7.
40. *Cf. Sifri* (68), Rashi *ad loc.* Also see Rashi on *Exodus* 33:8, *Deuteronomy* 34:10.
41. *Sifra ad loc.*
42. See *Moreh Nevuchim* 2:34.
43. *Shabbos* 87a.
44. *Exodus* 14:15 ff.
45. *Exodus* 16.
46. *Numbers* 20:8.
47. *Numbers* 16:32.
48. *Cf. Job* 19:27.
49. *Exodus* 20:15.
50. *Ibid.* 20:18.
51. See *Exodus* 14:31.
52. *Sanhedrin* 90a.
53. *Sanhedrin* 10:1 (90a).
54 *Bereshis Rabbah* 8:7. *Cf. Baba Basra* 15a, *Menachos* 30a.
55. See *Sanhedrin* 99b.
56. *Psalms* 19:8.
57. *Sanhedrin* 99a. *Cf. Avos* 3:11.
58. See note 53.
59. *Sanhedrin* 99a, *Yerushalmi Sanhedrin* 10:1 (49b).
60. *Job* 11:9.
61. *Cf. Berachos* 5a.
62. *Devarim Rabbah* 9:4, *Midrash Tehillim* 90:3, *Pesikta* 31 (197a), *Yalkut* 1:550, *Tosefos Menachos* 30a "*MiKan,*" Rosh, *Pesachim* 10:13.
63. *Cf. Eruvin* 54b, *Sifra* (43c) on *Leviticus* 9:1, *Sifri* on *Deuteronomy* 15.
64. *Avos* 1:1.
65. *Cf. Shabbos* 118b.
66. This took place in the year 204 C.E. *Kitzur Kelaley HaTalmud* (on *Mavo HaTalmud*) "*K'sav.*"
67. *Cf. Shabbos* 6b, Rashi *ad loc.* "*Megillas.*"
68. That is, the Thirteen Principles of Rabbi Ishmael, brought in the prayer book at the beginning of the morning service. See introduction to *Sifra.*
69. The Rambam holds that it was actually put into writing by Rabbi. Rashi,

however, disagrees, and maintains that it was not actually written down until several generations later. See Rashi, *Shabbos* 13b *"Megillas," Eruvin* 62b *"KeGon," Baba Metzia* 33a *"VeAina," ibid.* 85b *"U'Misnisa," Succah* 28b *"Marki," Takois* 12b *"DeKeTkoi."* Also see *Tosefos Megillah* 32a *"VeHaShoneh," Sefer Mitzvos Gadol,* Introduction (3a), Negative Commandment 65 (16c), *Tshuvos Tashbatz* 1:73, 2:53, Maharatz Chayos, *Takois* 12b, *Succah* 50b, *Baba Metzia* 85b. For a detailed discussion, see *Iggeres Rav Sherira Gaon* and Maharatz Chayos, *Mavo HaTalmud* 33.

70. The Babylonian Talmud was finally redacted in the year 505 C.E. See note 66.

71. Their followers were knows as the Sadducees (*Tzadukim*) and Bathusians. See *Avos DeRabbi Nathan* 5:2, Rambam on *Avos* 1:3, *Chulin* 1:2, *Yadayim* 4:6, Rashbam, *Baba Basra* 115b, *Aruch "Basusin." Cf. Shabbos* 108a, *Menachos* (65a).

72. A sect that did not believe in the Oral Torah.

73. *Cf. Shabbos* 68 a,b.

74. One under constraint is exempt from punishment. See *Baba Kama* 28b, *Yad, Yesodey HaTorah* 5:4.

75. *Leviticus* 3:17, 10:9, 23:14, 23:31, 23:41, 24:3, *Numbers* 10:8, 15:5, 18:23.

76. *Baba Metzia* 59a, *Temurah* 16a; *Shabbos* 104a, *Yoma* 80a, *Megillah* 2b, *Yerushalmi Megillah* 1:5 (7a), *Targum J., Sifra* (115d) on *Leviticus* 27:34, *Devarim Rabbah* 8:6, *Ruth Rabbah* 4:7.

77. *Cf. Ezekiel* 8:12.

78. See *Moreh Nevuchim* 1:69.

79. *Ibid.* 3:20,21.

80. *Ibid.* 1:68. Also see *Likutey Amarim (Tanya)* 1:2 in *Hagah*, quoting *Pardes Rimonim* 8:13. *Cf. Shiur Komah* 13:12.

81. *Genesis* 42:15,16.

82. *I Samuel* 1:26, 17:55, 20:3, 25:26, *II Samuel* 11:11, 14:19, *II Kings* 2:2, 4:6, 4:30.

83. Or "as God lives." *Judges* 8:19, *I Samuel* 14:39, 14:45, 19:6, 20:3, 20:21, 25:26, 25:34, 26:10, 26:16, 28:10, 29:6, *II Samuel* 4:9, 12:5, 14:11, 15:21, 22:47, *I Kings* 1:29, 2:24, 17:1, 17:12, 18:10, 18:15, 22:14, *II Kings* 2:2, 2:4, 2:6, 3:14, 4:30, 5:16, 5:20, *Jeremiah* 4:2, 5:2, 12:16, 16:14,15, 23:7,8, 38:16, *Hosea* 4:15, *Psalms* 18:47, *Ruth* 3:13, *II Chronicles* 18:13.

84. See *Moreh Nevuchim* 3:20.

85. *Job* 11:9.

86. See *Shabbos* 32b, 105b, *Kesuvos* 8b, *Sotah* 49a, *Koheles Rabbah* 4:1. Also see *Sifra* (93a,b), *Targum J.,* Rashi on *Leviticus* 20:20, 20:21, *Yevamos* 55a, *Tosefos, Yevamos* 2a *"Eshes."*

87. This refers to boys under the age of 13, and girls under 12.

88. *Sifri* (280), Rashi *ad loc., BeMidbar Rabbah* 8:4.

89. *Avos* 4:11.

90. *Kiddushin* 39b, *Chulin* 142b.

91. *Habakkuk* 2:3.

92. *Sanhedrin* 97b.

93. *Numbers* 24:7.

94. *Deuteronomy* 30:3 ff.

95. *Berachos* 34b, *Shabbos* 63a, 151b, *Pesachim* 68a, *Sanhedrin* 91b, 99a.
96. *Shabbos* 30b.
97. See Bachya on *Genesis* 11:11, who holds that the Messiah will never die.
98. *Cf. Sanhedrin* 99a.
99. This is the "new covenant" mentioned in *Jeremiah* 31:31. Here we see that this merely refers to the renewed observance of the Torah.
100. See note 95.
101. See *Erchin* 32b, *Yad, Shemitah VeYovel* 12:16.
102. *Numbers* 35:9 ff.
103. See *Sifri* (185) *ad loc., Yerushalmi Makkos* 3:6 (7b), *Yad, Rotzeach* 8:4.
104. *Yerushalmi Takois* 4:5 (24a), *Eicha Rabbah* 2:4. *Cf. Sanhedrin* 97b.
105. In the above sources, we find that Bar Kosiba was killed by an act of God. For a different opinion, see *Sanhedrin* 93b. Ravad, Radbaz, *Kesef Mishneh*, here.
106. See note 95.
107. *Ezekiel* 38, 39. Also see *Berachos* 7b, *Shabbos* 118a, *Succah* 52b, *Megillah* 11a, *Sanhedrin* 17a, 97b, *Eduyos* 2:10, Targum J. on *Exodus* 40:10, *Numbers* 11:26, 24:17, *Deuteronomy* 32:29, Radak on *Zechariah* 14:1.
108. See *Tana Debei Eliahu Rabbah* 18 (86b), *Yeshuos Yaakov ad loc.* 51. Also see Radal on *Pirkey DeRabbi Eliezer* 43:85.
109. *Eduyos* 8:7.
110. *Eruvin Tosefos ad loc.* "*DeLo.*" Also see *Yad, Nezirus* 4:11.
111. See note 92.
112. This is actually found in *Takois* 7a. A somewhat similar saying occurs in *Bereshis Rabbah* 13:6 but it is not the saying brought here. This saying occurs nowhere in *Bereshis Rabbah*. It is most probable that the Rambam had a different reading in the Midrash.
113. *Berachos* 18b.
114. *Sanhedrin* 10:1 (90a).
115. See *Sanhedrin* 92a,b.

the infinite light

A book about God

Aryeh Kaplan

Introduction

"The Infinite Light", A Book about G-d

The first man was speechless when confronted by the divine question, Where are you? We, his descendants, are inarticulate in our response to man's question, Where is G-d?

Achieving an awareness of G-d is a difficult task. The pursuit of that awareness involves relentless study and questioning, as well as mitzvah observance and Torah living. As Jews, we do not rely on dreams and heavenly manifestations to actualize G-d's presence in our lives. The true appreciation of a purposeful, personal G-d can only derive from a purposeful life in accordance with a purposeful creation.

The first human being to recognize the existence of G-d through his own observation was Abraham. Some commentaries say that this spectacular feat was accomplished at the age of forty-six, when his mental powers had attained their greatest acuity. Others maintain that it was at the age of three that Abraham experienced the original, auto-induced personal revelation.

Rabbi Menachem Mendel of Kotzk explains that even according to the former opinion, Abraham's first 46 years were not wasted on the impotent emptiness of idolatry. They were years of searching, of questioning, of delving into the mysteries of human and universal existence. When at age 46, Abraham achieved the pinnacle of man's sensitivity to creation, it was not a thunderclap, not an apparition that preceded this discovery, but rather the calm, steady reflection of Abraham's magnificent mind and gigantic spirit.

It is instructive that it was Abraham, the paragon of righteousness in human affairs, who was privileged to be the first to recognize G-d, and to understand His concern for human behavior.

In contemporary society, particularly among young people we sense a not-quite conscious stirring, a movement within humanity, which searches and strives for meaning in life. Logotherapy, a school of psychodynamics, projects "meaning" as the central idea of human existence. There is a sense that man cannot achieve happiness purely through satisfaction of material goals. The high statistics of suicide in developed countries, as well as the almost universal statement that "life seemed meaningless" by attempted suicides, attest to this fact.

Ultimately, searching for meaning is striving for G-d. This book was conceived as an atlas to aid the searching Jew, in mapping his personal journey in the quest for the ultimate meaning of human existence, the knowledge of G-d, his Torah, and of Man's duty to observe the truths embodied in it.

Rabbi Judah Halevi once wrote, "If I were to see Him in a dream, I would continue to sleep forever." We present work in the hope that it will enable us to better see Him in our lives so that we may indeed seize our portion of eternity.

Kislev 6, 5740 November 26, 1979

Baruch Taub

Part One: Foundations

1.

In order to speak about Judaism, we must speak about man and about life in general. Judaism is, first of all, a way of life, and its depth touches upon the very foundations of human existence. If you truly understand Judaism, you know the ultimate secret of life's purpose.

One of the most important elements of life is purpose. There is an old song that asks, "Why was I born, why am I living? What do I get, what am I giving?" These are questions that man has been asking himself every since he first began using his mind.

Have you ever stopped and asked yourself such questions?
Why was I born?
What meaning does my life have?
Why am I myself?
How should I live this one life of mine?
What do I have to offer life?

When we are young, such questions often bother us. Among the problems of growing up, we try to find a philosophy of life to follow. But then, caught in the business world, the market place, and the toil of raising a family, we often forget these questions. And sometimes we are rudely awakened. When tragedy strikes, the questions are thrown at us like buckets of ice water. When we grow old — and we all do grow old— we may gaze back at a lifetime and wonder, "What did I live for?"

We have but one life and must make the most of it. We all want to do what is "right." We want somehow to justify our lives. Rare indeed is the person who can say, *This is wrong, but*

I will do it anyway."

We all have a feeling that some things are right and others are wrong. We have a feeling that there is meaning to life. But many of us go no further. Even when we ask the questions, we do not go very far in seeking answers.

A very wise man once said, "The unexamined life is not worth living."

People can spend their lives seeking pleasure, fame and riches, and never once stop to ask themselves if these things are really important. But unless one gives this serious thought, he will never know whether or not he is doing the right thing. He may spend his entire life pursuing useless and even dangerous goals.

The most fundamental principle of Judaism is the realization that the universe is purposeful, and that man has a purpose in life.[1]

Our sages thus teach us, "A person must have the wisdom . . . to know why he is and why he exists. He must look back at his life, and realize where he is going."[2]

Both man and nature have purpose because they were created by a purposeful Being. We call this Being God.[3]

It is impossible to imagine the world as having purpose without a Creator. Without God, the universe would be purposeless and human existence pointless. All life would be completely without meaning or hope.

For the sake of argument, let us look at the negative viewpoint more closely. Let us look at the world through the eyes of a man without belief and see it as the absolute atheist would. Since his world has no purposeful Creator, there is no purpose in existence. Mankind becomes nothing more than an accident, with no more consequence than a bacterium or a stone. Man can even be looked upon as a vile infection and a disease on the surface of this planet.

If there is no purpose to existence, all our hopes, desires and aspirations are nothing more than the mechanizations of the molecules and cells of our brain. We would have no alternative than to agree with a noted cynic who declared, "Man is a sick fly, taking a dizzy ride on a gigantic flywheel."

In a world without purpose there can be neither good nor

evil, since both of these concepts imply purpose. Without a belief in some ultimate purpose, all values become completely subjective, subject to the whim of the individual. Morality becomes a matter of convenience, to be thrown out when it does not serve one's immediate goal. One's philosophy of life can simply be, "If you can get away with it, do it."

If existence has neither purpose, meaning nor depth, our attitude toward the world, toward our fellow man, and toward society in general needs to be little more than "so what."

If there is no God, there is no purpose. And if there is no purpose, all man's endeavors are in vain. The Psalmist alludes to this, when he says, "If God does not build the house, in vain do the builders toil; if God does not watch the city, in vain do the sentries wake" (*Psalms* 127:1).

But we can also look at the other side of the question and gaze at the world through the eyes of true faith. If we believe in God as Creator of the universe, then creation has a mighty purpose and life has an infinitude of depth. If man is to find meaning in life, he must seek God's purpose in creation and spend his days trying to fulfill it. The existence of man, a creature who can search for purpose in life, is no longer a mere accident, but the most significant phenomenon in all creation. The concepts of good and evil take on awesome proportions. That which is in accordance with God's purpose is good, while that which goes against it is evil. We are nothing less than partners with God in fulfilling His purpose.

Deep down, no one really feels that everything is meaningless. But many of us lose sight of the true Root of all meaning, often hiding behind a facade of cliches and excuses. Deep down, however, all of us know that there is purpose in life, and ultimately, in all creation.

The old-fashioned materialist, who was convinced that human life was without goal or purpose and that man is an irresponsible particle of matter engulfed in a maelstrom of meaningless forces, was a man without wisdom. A great philosopher once summed up the folly of this way of thinking by saying, "People who spend their lives with the purpose of proving that it is purposeless, constitute an interesting subject of study."

The Bible flatly says that the nonbeliever is a fool. The Psalmist thus said, "The fool says in his heart, there is no God" (*Psalms* 14:1).[4]

What the Bible is saying is that one who does not believe is both stupid and blind. He does not see what there is to see. Not only is he blind, but he is also likely to act blindly. He does not recognize any purpose in existence, and is therefore likely to act without direction. He does not recognize Truth, and is apt to do everything wrong. He is so unperceptive that he cannot be trusted. He says that there is no God because he is a fool. He is too blind to see God all around him; or else he is too selfish to share his own world with its Creator.

In the entire Bible, you will not find a single philosophical argument for the existence of God. It is simply assumed. The Bible does not waste time trying to convince the atheist that he is wrong. He is considered a fool, too dull to understand, or too wicked to want to.

Belief, like beauty, is in the eye of the beholder. For over three thousand years, the existence of God was self-evident to the Jew. He needed no proof or demonstration.

The very existence of a universe implies a creator. The Psalmist thus said, "The heavens declare the glory of God, and the skies proclaim His handiwork" (*Psalms* 19:2). Their very existence is a hymn, declaring the glory of their Creator.[5]

The Prophet speaks of this most lucidly when he says (*Isaiah* 40:21,26):

> Do you not know?
> Have you not heard?
> Was it not told to you from the beginning?
> Do you not understand how the earth was founded?
> . . . Lift up your eyes to the stars
> And see Who has created them
> He numbers them all like an army,
> He calls them all by name . . .

2.

There is a legend that throws much light on this subject:[6]

A philosopher once came to Rabbi Meir and told him, "I don't believe in God. I feel that the universe came into being by itself, of its own accord, without any outside help."

Rabbi Meir did not reply. A few days later, he came to the philosopher, and showed him a beautiful piece of poetry, written in a fine hand on smooth white parchment.

The philosopher looked at the parchment and admired it. He asked, "Who is the great poet who wrote this lovely poem? Who was the talented scribe who copied it?"

Rabbi Meir shook his head and answered, "You are completely wrong. There was no poet. There was no scribe. This is what really happened. The parchment was lying on my desk next to a bottle of ink. A cat accidently knocked over the bottle, spilling ink all over the parchment. This poem was the result."

The philosopher looked at Rabbi Meir in amazement. He said, "But that is impossible! Such a lovely poem! Such perfect script! Such things do not come into being by themselves. There must be an author! There must be a scribe!"

Rabbi Meir smiled. He answered the philosopher, "You yourself have said it! How could the universe, which is much more beautiful than any poem, come into being by itself? There must be an Author. There must be a Creator."

What Rabbi Meir was dramatizing, of course, was the argument from design. We see a world that appears to be well planned and purposeful. Everything in nature fits into its place. Tremendously complex creatures, such as man himself, exist in this world. How can a sane man really believe that all of this came into being without a purposeful Creator?

There is a Midrash telling us that this is how Abraham first realized the existence of God. Abraham said, "Is it possible that a brightly illuminated castle can exist without an owner? Can one say that this world exists without a Creator?"[7]

Ultimately, there is a certain blindness involved in not seeing God. This is what the Prophet meant when he said (*Isaiah* 29:16):

How upside down are things!
Is the potter no better than the clay?
Can something say of its maker,
"He did not make me"?
Can a pot say of the potter,
"He has no skill"?

All that we must do is ask the right questions. The *Zohar*[8] quotes the verse, "Lift up your eyes to the stars, and see, *Who* has created *these*?" (*Isaiah* 40:26). The world that we see is *these* — *Eleh* in Hebrew. Look at *these*, and ask *Who* — *Mi* in Hebrew. Combine the two words, *Eleh* and *Mi* — these and Who — and you obtain *Elohim* — the Hebrew name for God. One must merely ask the right questions, and God appears in the answers.

A person need only look at himself, and he will see the handiwork of the Creator. The fact that you can think, or move your hand, is the greatest miracle possible. The Psalmist recognized this when he exclaimed, "I will thank God, for I am fearfully and wonderfully made" (*Psalms* 139:14).

All of this is summed up in one sentence in the Bible: "From my flesh, I will see God" (*Job* 19:26).[9] I can see God in the very fact that something as miraculous as my flesh can exist.

3.

It is told that King Frederic the Great once asked his Lutheran pastor to provide him with a visible proof of God's existence. The pastor answered with just two words: The Jews.

For the Jew, the question of God's existence is no mere philosophical exercise. It is linked to our very history. We have seen the rise of the Babylonians, the Persians, the Phoenicians, the Hittites, the Philistines, the Greeks and the Romans, all the great nations of the pagan era, and we have also witnessed their fall. All these great civilizations were born, reached maturity, and died. This is the pattern of history. All the great civilizations of antiquity have passed on. There is but one exception, and we are still reading and writing books.

We have a long history of miraculous survival and continous growth. Our people have lived through four thousand years of persecution, enslavement, slaughter, exile, torture, inquisition, pogrom and death camp. We were enslaved by the Egyptians, slaughtered by the Philistines, exiled by the Babylonians, dispersed by the Romans, and butchered and chased from land to land in Europe. But miracle of miracles, we are still here today.

There is absolutely no theory of history that can explain this in a natural manner. Social scientists may find many unusual records of survival among various peoples of the world, but nothing even comes remotely close to the story of the Jew.

The Midrash[10] tells us that the Roman emperor Hadrian once remarked to Rabbi Joshua, "Great indeed must be the lamb, Israel, that it can survive among seventy wolves." Rabbi Joshua replied, "Great is the Shepherd, Who rescues her and protects her."

We are familiar with the song in the Passover Hagaddah, where this theme is repeated:[11]

> This is what has stood up
> for our fathers and for us:
> Not one alone
> has stood up to finish us,
> But in every generation
> they rise to finish us;
> But God, blessed be He,
> saves us from their hand!

This great miracle of Jewish survival cannot be without meaning. It is something that is unique in the annals of history. If you want to see a real miracle, just look into a mirror. One of the greatest possible miracles is the fact that after four thousand years, there is still such a thing as a Jew.

God told us through His prophet, "You are My witnesses, says the Lord, and I am God" (*Isaiah* 43:12). The Midrash states that God is known as such in the world because we bear witness to Him.[12] In a sense, our very existence and survival bear witness to God.

4.

It is our history that defines our relationship with God and makes Judaism unique among world religions.

Once we see God as Creator, it is obvious that His creation

has purpose. It should also be obvious that He would eventually reveal this purpose to man. We believe that this took place at Mount Sinai.

To understand our reason for this belief, we must see how Judaism differs from all other religions.

Other religions begin with a single individual. He claims to have a special message, and gradually gathers a following. His followers spread the word and gather converts, and a new religion is born. Virtually every world religion follows this pattern.

The one exception is Judaism.

God gathered an entire people, three million strong,[13] to the foot of Mount Sinai, and proclaimed His message. Every man, woman and child heard God's voice, proclaiming the Ten Commandments. Thus was a bond forged between God and Israel.[14]

This was an event unique in the history of mankind. It remained imprinted deeply in the Jewish soul throughout all of our history. It was something that was not to be forgotten.

The Torah thus tells us, "Be most careful, and watch yourself, that you not forget the things that you saw with your own eyes. Do not let them pass from your minds as long as you live. Teach them to your children, and to your children's children: The day when you stood before God. . ." (*Deuteronomy* 4:9-10). This is stated in the most emphatic terms, and there are some who count it among the commandments of the Torah.[15]

The revelation at Sinai came just seven weeks after another unique event in Jewish history. This was the Exodus from Egypt. God revealed Himself to an entire people and literally changed the course of both nature and history. Here too was an event unique in the history of mankind.[16]

The Torah itself speaks of this when it says, "Did God ever venture to take a nation to Himself from another nation, with a challenge, with signs and wonders, as the Lord your God did in Egypt, before your very eyes? You have had sure proof that the Lord is God, there is no other" (*Deuteronomy* 4:34).

There may be other religions in the world, but none had the powerful beginning of Judaism. It is the Exodus that makes us unique.

The Exodus not only made us uniquely aware of God, but it also showed Him to be profoundly involved in the affairs of man.

The Torah warns us never to forget the Exodus. We thus find, "Beware, that you not forget God, Who brought you out of the land of Egypt, from the house of slavery" (*Deuteronomy* 6:12). There are some who count this among the commandments of the Torah.[17]

The impact of the Exodus remained imprinted on the Jewish mind throughout our history. We saw every persecutor as Pharaoh, with God standing on the sidelines, ready to repeat the miracle of the Exodus. This, in part, accounts for the miracle of our survival.

5.

In giving the Ten Commandments, God opened with the words "I am the Lord your God, Who took you out of the land of Egypt, from the house of slavery" (*Exodus* 20:2) [18]

There are some commentators who ask why God mentioned the Exodus, rather than the more universal fact that He is Creator of the universe.[19] In other words, why did He not say, "I am the Lord your God, Creator of heaven and earth"?

They answer that this is because the latter statement would allow us to make a serious mistake. We could erroneously think of God as Creator, and yet believe that He has no interest in the affairs of man.[20]

In the opening words of the Ten Commandments, God was telling us that He *is* involved in the affairs of man, and has a profound interest in everything we do. God gave the Exodus as an example, for it was here that the entire Jewish people experienced Him. To them, God was no mere philosophical abstraction. They actually saw His deeds, and were aware of Him to such an extent that they were able to point and say, "This is my God."[21]

One who does not accept the fact that God is involved and interested in our affairs and actions cannot be said to believe. He may claim to believe in God, but it is not the God of Israel. As such, he is considered a nonbeliever.[22]

We believe in God, both as the God of creation and as the

God of history. Judaism totally rejects the deistic concept of a God who created the world and then abandoned it with neither ruler, guide nor judge. Our sages teach us that one who says, "There is neither Judge nor judgment," is considered a nonbeliever.[23] It is of such people that the Prophet was speaking when he exclaimed, "They say: God does not see, God has forsaken the earth" (*Ezekiel* 8:12).

The entire history of Judaism bears witness to God's active involvement in the affairs of man. Indeed, this is born out by the history of mankind in general. The experience of men and nations clearly indicates that only good is stable. Evil, on the other hand, always tends to destroy itself.[24] This is what the Bible means when it says, "There are many thoughts in man's heart, but the counsel of God is what stands"(*Proverbs* 19:21).

The first Commandment, "I am the Lord your God," is interpreted by most authorities as an actual commandment to believe in God.[25] As such, it is the first and foremost commandment. Any moment that a person so much as thinks that he believes in God's existence, he is fulfilling this commandment.[26]

There are other authorities, however, who go a step further. They write that belief in God is much too basic a part of Judaism to be a mere commandment.[27] Rather, they see this as an introduction to the commandments, and a statement that forms the very basis of Judaism.

The second of the Ten Commandments tells us, "You shall have no other gods before Me" (*Exodus* 20:3). Essentially, this is a commandment not to believe in any deity other than the One True God, Creator of all things.[28]

Like the first Commandment, this can be fulfilled by mere thought. Thus, a person can fulfill this commandment at any time merely by thinking that he does not believe in any other God.[29] Conversely, one who even thinks and believes any idolatrous idea is guilty of violating this commandment and may be punished accordingly. The Prophet thus said, "These men have set up idols in their hearts"(*Ezekiel* 14:3).[30]

The Commandment states, "You shall not have any other gods *before Me*." When God said, "before Me," He was stressing that one may not believe in any other deity, even if he also believes in God.[31] One who sets up any mediator between God and man is similarly guilty of violating this commandment.[32]

Let us look into this a bit more closely. If a person believes in God, then what need does he have for any other deity? The answer that some non-Jewish thinkers give is that God is so high that He is unapproachable without a mediator. The second commandment teaches us that this, too, is idolatry.

God is infinite. To say that He needs a mediator to hear our prayers is to deny His infinite wisdom.

It is therefore a foundation of our faith to believe that all prayer must be addressed directly to God.[33]

One who calls any other being a god is guilty of idolatry.[34]

Our sages thus teach us, "One who takes God's name in partnership with something else is torn out of this world. It is written, 'only to God alone' (*Exodus* 22:19)."[35]

The prohibition against idolatry applies both to Jew and non-Jew alike.[36] Some authorities, however, say that this is only true where an actual act of idolatry is involved.[37] The prohibition against believing in a "partner" or mediator, in this opinion, applies only to the Jew. These codifiers maintain that as long as a non-Jew believes in God, he may also accept another being as a deity or mediator.[38] They cite as evidence for this the passage, "That you not . . . be drawn away, and worship these things, which the Lord your God has allotted to all the other peoples . . ." (*Deuteronomy* 4:19).[39] According to this interpretation, the Torah is saying that belief in other deities is permissible to non-Jews, and may indeed be a partial fulfillment of God's ultimate purpose.[40] For a Jew, of course, belief in Christianity is not only forbidden, but is in direct conflict with the second of the Ten Commandments. Furthermore, many authorities extend the prohibition against idolatry to forbid even a non-Jew to believe in a mediator between God and man.[41]

God Himself proclaimed the first two of the Ten Commandments to the entire Jewish nation. The first two therefore are given in the first person: "*I* am the Lord" and "You shall have no other gods before *Me*." In these two cases, God Himself is speaking. The following Commandments, on the other hand, speak of God in the third person. Thus, the third Commandment says, "You shall not take the name of the Lord your God in vain" (*Exodus* 20:7). Here God is not saying "do not take *My* name in vain." Rather, someone else is speaking of God. Our traditions thus teach us that only the first two of the Ten Commandments were given to the Jewish people directly by God Himself.[42] All the others, however were transmitted through Moses. Our sages interpret the following passage as speaking of the first two Commandments: "God has spoken once, two [Commandments] which I heard" (*Psalm* 62:12).[43]

These first two Commandments constitute the very essence of Judaism. If a person denies the existence of God or accepts any other being as a deity, he is denying this essence. Our sages call him a *Kofer Belkkar*, literally, one who "denies the essence."[44] They further teach us that no man is more refuted by God than the one who rejects Him.[45]

The first five of the Ten Commandments all involve essentials of Judaism. The Commandment not to take God's name in vain relates to God's involvement with the world. If one truly believes that God is interested in man's deeds, he cannot openly show Him disrespect. One who grossly disrespects God's name is really demonstrating his lack of belief.[46]

The fourth Commandment, regarding the Sabbath, is also related to our basic beliefs. Keeping the Sabbath is the one act by which we demonstrate our belief in God as Creator of the universe. One who does not keep the Sabbath denies this belief by his actions, and therefore thrusts himself out of the fold of believers in Judaism.[47]

The fifth Commandment tells us to honor our parents, which again touches upon our faith. The sum total of our traditions has been handed down from generation to generation. Unless a bond of trust and respect exists between generations, these traditions cannot endure.[48] Through the traditions handed down from our ancestors, we know about God and His teachings, as the Torah itself says, "Ask your father and he will inform you, your elders, and they will tell you" (*Deuteronomy* 32:7).

6.

Belief in God is the very foundation of Judaism. However, faith is not just the utterance of words. It is firm belief and conviction with mind and heart, to be acted upon through a course prescribed by God.[49] Faith which does not predicate obedience to God is an absurdity.[50]

Speaking about God is very much like speaking about love. One can spend a lifetime speaking and reading about love, and never have the slightest idea of what it is all about. When one actually experiences it, however, lengthy discussions are no longer needed. The same is true of God. One cannot understand Him unless one experiences Him.

The only way to experience God is through the observance and study of our religious teachings. One who does not do this ultimately denies God.[51] On the other hand, if one studies God's teachings and keeps His commandments, he will ultimately find God.[52] Our sages thus teach us that God says, "If they would only abandon Me but keep My Torah, its light would bring them back."[53]

If one ignores God's commandments, he will ultimately also forget God. The Torah therefore warns us, "Beware that you do not forget the Lord your God by not keeping His commandments, His ordinances and His statutes" (Deuteronomy 8:11). Some authorities count this warning among the commandments of the Torah.[54]

It is not enough merely to believe. One must actually live in God's presence. This is what the Psalmist meant when he exclaimed, "I have set God before me at all times" (Psalms 16:8).[55]

I can gaze at a beautiful sunset and try to describe it. But unless you open your eyes and see it for yourself, my words are in vain. You must see it to understand and appreciate it.

I can describe the most delicious fruit. But you must taste it to understand what I am saying.

The same is true of God. The Psalmist thus says, "Taste and see that God is good, happy is the man who embraces Him" (Psalms 34:9).

Part Two: God

1.

What do we know about God?

Mostly, we know about God from our own experiences, both as individuals and as a people. We know Him from such great events as the Exodus and the Revelation at Sinai. We know Him from the many times that He intervened to guide the history and destiny of our people. We know Him from the careers of people who have been touched by Him.

But most of all, most of us know God through our own experiences. There have been times in all our lives when we have felt close to God, or experienced His hand guiding our lives. It is very easy to forget these times, but if we look back and think, we can remember.

We seek God in many ways. We approach Him in prayer. We keep His commandments. We look at the world and stand in awe at His Handiwork.

Who at some time has not contemplated nature and stood awestruck, realizing that he is gazing at the handiwork of God? Who at some time has not shared Job's experience, when he exclaims (*Job* 12:7-9):

> Now ask the beasts, they will teach you,
>   The birds of the sky, they will tell you;
> Or speak to the earth, it will teach you,
>   The fish of the sea, they will tell you;
> Who cannot learn from all these
>   That God's hand has done this?
> In His hand is every living soul,
>   The breath of all human flesh.

We experience God in our own lives and also know of Him from the history of our ancestors. We therefore call Him, "our

God and God of our fathers." He is our God because we ourselves have experienced Him, but He is also God of our fathers, because we know even more about Him from our traditions and history. This is what our people said at the Red Sea, "This is my God, I will glorify Him; my father's God, I will praise Him" (*Exodus* 15:2).

We know God for His mighty deeds, but also from his small miracles. God fashioned the stars, but He also listens to the cry of the small child. The Psalmist expresses this most beautifully when he says, "He rides upon the skies, His name is God . . . the Father of orphans, the Judge of widows, He is God in His holy place. God gives the friendless a home, and frees the captive, bringing him to safety" (*Psalms* 68:5-6). Our sages thus teach us, "Wherever you find God's greatness, you also find His humility."[1]

We know God as the Highest, and yet, we seek Him with humility. As long as one is filled with his own egotism, he has no room for God. Our sages teach us that God says that He cannot abide in the same world with the haughty man.[2] A man must surrender his own ego before he can truly find God. This is God's message, "I dwell in a high and holy place, but I am with the brokenhearted and humble. I revive the humble spirit and give new life to the broken heart" (*Isaiah* 57:15).

We know God through love. It is He who bids us, "You shall love your neighbor as yourself" (*Leviticus*). We know of this love as a reflection of our love for God, as the Torah says, "You shall love the Lord your God, with all your heart, with all your soul, and with all your might" (*Deuteronomy* 6:5). We know of His infinite love for us, as He announced through His prophet, "I love you with an infinite world of love, and so, have drawn you to Me with affection" (*Jeremiah* 31:3). And there are times when we can say along with the Psalmist, "O God, my God, I seek You, my soul thirsts, my flesh longs for You, like a dry and thirsty land that has no water" (*Psalms* 63:2).

We know God through our hope in the future. We know Him through our prayers for life, health and prosperity. We know Him through our hopes for Israel, for all mankind, for peace and brotherhood among men. We know Him through our optimism that the world will be good in the end.

One of the most profound prayers ever written is the *Amidah* (or *Shemoneh Esreh*), the silent, standing prayer, that every Jew has repeated three times each day for the past 2500 years. In the opening lines of this prayer we express our most basic feelings toward God:

> Blessed are You O Lord,
> Our God and God of our fathers,
> God of Abraham, God of Isaac,
> And God of Jacob;
> Great, mighty and revered God,
> Highest One,
> Giver of love and goodness,
> Master of all,
> Who remembers the love of the fathers
> And brings help to their children's children
> For His name's sake, with love.
> King, Helper, Savior and Shield.

2.

What can we say about God?

We know about God mostly from traditions found in the Bible. God Himself revealed these things when He spoke to His prophets. Looking in the Bible, we can obtain a very profound concept of God.

Many great thinkers among our sages have written about God. They have delved into all our traditions, analyzing and clarifying them. It is no exaggeration to say that some of the best minds that have ever lived have dealt with the question of God. But for most of them, this was more than a mere intellectual exercise. Their writings were guided by a most deep inspiration and feeling for God. As they thought about God and delved into His mystery, they were also experiencing Him. Thus, our traditions combine both the intellectual and the mystical.

But above all, our traditions go back to the Bible. Almost everything written about God can be found in this Book, if one knows where to look. Searching it carefully, we can build up a picture.

3.

It is clear from all our traditions that we define God primarily as the Creator of all things. We find this in the very opening verse of the Torah, which says, "In the beginning, God created the heaven and the earth." This is a statement about creation, but it also tells us that God is the Creator.[3]

When we speak of God as Creator of "heaven and earth," we are not just speaking of the visible world. God's creation includes every possible thing that exists. The Bible clearly tells us that there is absolutely nothing that is outside the domain of God's creation, as He told His prophet, "I am God, I make all things" (*Isaiah* 44:24).

We may be able to conceive of other universes. There may be worlds beyond our imagination. All of them, however, ultimately emanate from God. This is what the Psalmist meant when he said, "Your dominion is a kingdom of all worlds" (*Psalms* 145:13).[4]

There are many things that are difficult to imagine as emanating from God. For example, there is much evil in the world, and one may be tempted to think of it as coming from a separate power, independent of God. Nothing could be further from the truth; everything ultimately comes from God. If we understand God's purpose in creation, we understand why evil must exist. But it is most important to realize that there is no power independent of God's creation. He therefore told His prophet, "I form light and create darkness, I make peace and create evil, I am God, I do all these things" (*Isaiah* 45:7).

The very word "create" — *Bara* in Hebrew — implies creating something out of nothing. Otherwise, we use the word "make" or "form." When we say that God created the universe, we mean that He created it absolutely *ex nihilo* — out of nothing. This is alluded to in the verse, "He hangs the world upon nothingness" (*Job* 26:7).[5]

The Midrash[6] tells us that a philosopher once remarked to Rabban Gamaleil, "Your God is a wonderful artist, but He had fine materials to work with. When He made the world, He fashioned it out of waste and desolation, darkness, wind, water and depths."[7] Rabban Gamaliel replied, "Your words are mere wind! All of these things were also created by God."

The act of creation involved absolutely no effort on the part of God. When the Torah says that He "rested" on the seventh day, it does not mean that He rested because He was weary or tired after six days of hard work. Rather, it means that God stopped creating after six days, since the world was completed with the creation of man. The act of creation, however, involved absolutely no effort on the part of God, as the prophet Isaiah taught, "Do you not know? Have you not heard? The Lord, the everlasting God, Creator of the wide world, grows neither weary nor faint" (*Isaiah* 40:28).

This is because God is absolutely infinite. To an infinite Being, the entire universe is like nothing, and therefore, its creation involves no effort. The Bible thus says, "Everything on earth is like nothing to Him, He does as He wills with the host of heaven and the hordes of the earth" (*Daniel* 4:32). Every possible thing, even the creation of a universe, is infinitely easy for an infinite God.

In order to emphasize the fact that God's creation involved no effort, the Torah speaks of it as being done with words. Each act of creation begins with the expression "And God said."[8] The Psalmist explicitly states, "With the word of God were the heavens made, with the breath of His mouth, all their host ... For He spoke and it was, He commanded, and it stood" (*Psalms* 33:6,9). The Midrash comments of this: "Not with work nor effort did God create the universe, but with a mere word."[9]

In expressing the absence of effort in the act of creation, our sages teach us that it did not even involve a word, but a mere letter of the alphabet. This furthermore was not just any letter, but the one letter that is most easily pronounced. They teach us that the world was created with the letter *Heh*, the Hebrew equivalent of "H".[10] Pronouncing this letter involves no more effort than the slightest breath. With such a small effort God created the universe.

When we say that the world was created with God's word, we are, of course, using a metaphor. God did not actually speak in a physical sense.[11] He merely willed the existence of all things. His very wisdom and knowledge implied creation. When the

Torah says that He spoke, it merely does so to tell us that creation was a willful act. In actuality, however, God's creation came about as a direct result of His wisdom and knowledge.[12] The Prophet said, "He made the earth with His power, founded the world with His wisdom, and unfurled the skies with His understanding" (*Jeremiah* 10:12)[13].

Of course, this also means that creation was an intelligent and purposeful act. God does not act blindly, but with infinite wisdom. We find this concept echoed in the verse, "God founded the earth with wisdom, and fixed the heavens with understanding"(*Proverbs* 3:19).

We therefore see God's work as ultimately perfect. The Torah tells us, "The Creator's work is perfect, for all His ways are just" (*Deuteronomy* 32:4). The Psalmist, too, sings, "God's way is perfect, His word is tried" (*Psalms* 18:31). We may not be able to see the ultimate perfection in creation, but, in truth, everything has its own perfect time and place. This is the meaning of the verse, "He has made everything perfect in its time" (*Ecclesiastes* 3:11).

Once we say that God is Creator of *everything*, it becomes obvious that there can be no other creator. If there were a second creator, God would have created everything but *it*. The fact that God is Creator of everything therefore implies that He is One and Unique. We hear this in His word to His prophet, "Thus speaks God, Who created the heavens, God, Who formed and made the earth . . . I am God, there is none else" (*Isaiah* 45:18). We shall speak at length of God's unity in a later section.

As Creator of all things, God takes a keen interest in His world, down to the smallest details. The same God Who spins the galaxies also takes care of the hungry child. Nothing in all creation is too trivial for His attention. The Psalmist tells of this in his song, "He made heaven, earth and sea, and all that is in them, He is a true Watcher forever. He provides justice to the oppressed, He gives bread to the hungry" (*Psalms* 146:6-7).

The belief that God is creator of the universe is a foundation of our faith.[14] As discussed earlier, belief in a purposeful Creator is what gives both man and the universe a sense of purpose in existence. The fact that everything was created by one God also provides us with a concept of unity in all creation. It makes every human being a brother under the fatherhood of God. If we are all God's creatures, placed on earth to fulfill His purpose, what possible reason can we have for hatred and warfare? The prophet Malachi expresses this most clearly when he says, "Have we not all one Father? Has not one God created us? Why then do we deal treacherously with one another?" (*Malachi* 2:10).

4.

We can really say very little about God other than that He is the Creator of all things. About God Himself, we can say nothing. We know that He exists, but beyond that, no mind can penetrate.

This is essentially what God told Moses when he asked His name. God replied that His name is, "I Am what I Am" (*Exodus* 3:4). God was saying, "I am. I exist. There is nothing more you can understand about Me."

The only positive thing we can say about God is that He exists. We may experience God, but we cannot understand Him.

Although we cannot comprehend God, we do know Him as Creator, and as such, we understand that certain things must be true about Him. For example, we cannot say that He is any less than any of His creatures. Thus, the very fact that we can see and hear implies that God can do no less. We see this in the words of the Psalmist, "He made the ear, shall He not hear? He formed the eye, shall He not see?" (*Psalms* 94:9).

We therefore say that God at least has every kind of perfection found in the world. Here again, we do not know exactly what this means when speaking of God Himself, but we see His power manifest in creation. All these qualities ultimately come from God, therefore, we cannot say that He Himself does not have them. King David expresses this thought in his prayer, "Yours O God is the greatness, the power, the glory, the victory, the majesty, and everything in heaven and earth . . . For it is in Your hand to give strength and power to all" (*I Chronicles* 29:11-12). From the fact that God can grant all these powers, we know that He can also use them.

We must constantly remember that God is the sole Creator of all things. He was the very first, and everything else emanated from Him. It is therefore obvious that God has power over all things. Everything came from Him; therefore, nothing can stop Him or prevent Him from doing as He wishes. God thus told His prophet, "I am God from the beginning of time,[15] none can deliver from my hand. When I act, who can reverse it?" (*Isaiah* 43:13). God is saying that He is the very first and therefore is Creator and Master of all. His power is unlimited, nothing can hold Him back.

We therefore say that God is omnipotent — all powerful. He is the One Creator and Master of all things and there is no power in existence that can turn Him back or frustrate His ultimate purpose. We hear this in the words of Job when he says, "He is in Unity, who can hold Him back? He does what His own will desires" (*Job* 23:13).[16] The same concept is also expressed in Jehoshephat's prayer, "God of our fathers, You alone are God in heaven. You rule over all kingdoms. In Your hand is mighty power, and none can withstand You" (*II Chronicles* 20:5).

This is one of the important things that we believe about God. He is all powerful and nothing can stand in His way. He rules the world according to His desire. This was one of the very first things that God revealed about Himself when He asked of Abraham, "Is anything too difficult for God?" (*Genesis* 18:4).

God repeats the question to Job, saying, "I am the Lord, God of all flesh. Is anything too difficult for Me?" (*Job* 32:27). He expresses the same thought in the song of *Deuteronomy* when He says, "I bring both death and life, I wound and I heal. None can deliver from My hand" (*Deuteronomy* 32:39). The same concept is stated in the Prophet's words, "When God decides, who shall cancel it? When He stretches forth His hand, who shall turn it back?" (*Isaiah* 14:27). The Psalmist sums up the idea of God's omnipotence when he sings, "Our God is in heaven, He does whatever He pleases" (*Psalms* 115:3).

God has only to send forth His word and His will is done. As we discussed earlier, this word is not actual speech, but a command that is even more tenuous than thought. When God wills something, it is as good as done. This is what He meant when He told His prophet, "The word that leaves My mouth shall not return to Me unfulfilled. It shall accomplish what I planned, and succeed in what it was sent to do" (*Isaiah* 55:10).

As Creator of the world, God not only is just, but He also defines justice. We cannot think of such concepts as justice and good as independent of God. Even these are His creations, and are therefore defined by Him. To set up an independent standard of justice and good by which to judge God is to place something on the same level as God, and this, of course, we cannot do. God expressed this idea to His prophet when He said, "I have made the world, and man and beast on the face of the earth . . . and I give it to whom I see fit" (*Jeremiah* 27:5). Eliyahu told Job essentially the same thing, saying, "Who can tell Him what course to take? Who can say, 'You have done wrong'?" (*Job* 36:23).

Since there is no force that can turn God back, there is nothing that can make Him change His mind. Everything in creation fulfills His purpose, and everything that He does leads toward it. No power exists that can change this purpose. This is what God meant when He told His prophet, "I have spoken, I have decided, and I do not repent nor turn back from it" (*Jeremiah* 4:28). It is also what the Torah says, "God is not man that He should lie, nor is He mortal that He should change His mind. Shall He say and not do, or speak and not fulfill it?" (*Numbers* 23:19).

It is for this reason that God is called True. The prophet teaches us, "The Lord, God, is Truth. He is the Living God, King of the world" (*Jeremiah* 10:10). Our sages explain this verse by stating: "Why is He true? Because He is the Living God, King of the world. A mortal king may make a promise and not be able to keep it. But God is always able to make His word come true."[17] Our sages similarly teach us that God's seal is Truth.[18]

As Creator, God is Master of all creation. Everything that exists is His and is here to fulfill His purpose. The Torah tells us this, saying, "It all belongs to God: the heaven, the heaven of heaven, the earth, and everything in it" (*Deuteronomy* 10:14). It is also what the prophet means when he says, "This is the plan prepared for the world: It is the Hand stretched over all nations" (*Isaiah* 14:26).

God is the ultimate Ruler over all mankind. Man is given freedom, but ultimately the world's destiny is in God's hands. We are utterly and totally dependent on God, as He Himself told His prophet, "As clay in the potter's hand, so are you in Mine. At one instant, I may decree upon a nation to pluck up, break down and destroy . . . At another instant, I may decree upon a nation to build up and plant" (*Jeremiah* 18:6-9).

We therefore call God the "King of the universe." This was one of the first things that the Jews realized when they left Egypt, and they exclaimed in the song of the Red Sea, "God is King forever and ever" (*Exodus* 15:18).[19]

We call God a King, but He is like no earthly king. A human monarch may rule, but there are limits to his power. Only God is a King with unlimited ability. The Psalmist thus sings, "God is most high and awesome, a great King over all the world" (*Psalms* 47:3). The prophet Jeremiah sums it all up when he prays, "There is nothing like You, O God, You are great, and Your name is Mighty" (*Jeremiah* 10:6).

5.

As mentioned, there is very little we can say about God Himself. However, we can, to some extent, understand His relationship to His creation.[20]

One of the best analogies of the relationship between God and the world is that of the soul to the body. In a sense, we can call God the "soul" of the universe. Of course, the analogy is far from exact, since God cannot be compared to anything else in creation. But it does serve the useful purpose of clarifying His relationship with the world.

Our sages use the analogy of the soul to the body to explain God's relationship to the world in six basic ways:[21]

> Just as the soul is one in the body,
>> so is God one in the universe.
> Just as the soul is pure and above the body,
>> so is God pure and above the world.

Just as the soul does not eat or drink,
so God does not eat or drink.
Just as the soul fills the body,
so God fills the world.
Just as the soul sustains the body,
so God sustains the world.
Just as the soul sees and is unseen,
so God sees and is unseen.

These are very basic statements about God. All of them are mentioned many times in our traditions and will be discussed at length. Here we will merely outline them:

1. God is one in the world. He is an absolute unity.

2. God is pure and above the world. He does not partake of any worldly quality. He has neither body, shape nor form. Nothing in all creation can be compared to Him. He is even above such basic worldly concepts as space and time.

3. God does not eat or drink. He is in no way dependent on His creation. Absolutely nothing can be given to God, for ultimately, everything is His.

4. God fills the world. There is no place empty of His presence.

5. God sustains the world. His life-force permeates all creation and gives it existence. If this were removed even for an instant, all creation would instantly cease to exist.

6. God sees and is not seen. He is aware of every single thing in the world, but no creature can see or comprehend God. There is nothing in all creation that can grasp His majesty.

These six concepts provide us with our basic knowledge regarding God's relationship to the world, and we will discuss each one at length. There are a few additional ways in which our sages use this analogy, and we will explore these briefly.

Our sages teach us:

Just as the soul dwells in the innermost chamber,
so God dwells in the innermost chamber.

Here, our sages are teaching us that even though God fills all creation, He does so in a hidden manner. God is everywhere, and yet, no matter how deeply we probe, we cannot detect His presence.[22]

Just as the soul survives the body,
so God survives the world.

This is closely related to the statement that God does not in any way need creation. If the world were to cease to exist, God would still remain the same.

Just as the soul does not sleep,
so God does not sleep.

This alludes to God's constant providence, whereby He is continuously aware of everything in the world and in direct control of all things. There is absolutely no time that His attention is in any way diverted from His creation. This is what the Psalmist meant when he sang, "The Guardian of Israel does not doze nor sleep" (*Psalms* 121:4). God's providence is constant and continuous.

6.

One of the most important foundations of our faith is the belief that God is one.[23]

The Torah says, "Here O Israel, the Lord is our God, the Lord is One" (*Deuteronomy* 6:4).

This is the *Sh'ma*, our declaration of faith. Twice each day, the believing Jew cries out these words. They are among the first things a Jew learns as a child, and the last words that he utters before he dies. On every Jewish doorpost, there is a Mezuzah proclaiming these very same words. They are found again in the Tefillin, bound daily next to the heart and mind. All these proclaim this most basic principle of Judaism.

What this tells us is that all things come from One ultimate Source. All creation is bound together by God. There is One unifying Force in the universe, God alone, unique and incomparable. The Torah thus tells us, "Know it this day, and set it in your heart, that the Lord is God, in heaven above, and on the earth below, there is no other" (*Deuteronomy* 4:39).

As Creator of all things, God stands alone. There can be only one Creator of all things. The Psalmist thus sings, "Who besides the Lord is God? Who besides our God is Creator?" (*Psalms* 18:32).

There can only be one First Thing. Anything else is no

longer first. God alone is the First Thing, as He told His prophet, "I am first and I am last, and beside Me there is no God . . . There is no other God besides Me, no other Creator. This I know" (*Isaiah* 44:6,8).

Man must ultimately depend on God. All of our prayers are directed toward Him. God is the One who has all power, and all our hopes and aspirations depend on Him. God thus told us through His prophet, "Before Me, there was no God, and none shall be after Me. I Myself am God, and none but I can save you" (*Isaiah* 43:10,11).

For over a thousand years the Jews alone proclaimed that God was One. For the first thousand years of our existence, the rest of the world believed in a host of pagan gods, each with a different power. Even those who believed in God felt that He was too high to be concerned with man, and therefore acted only through mediators. These mediators then became their gods.[24] Others believed that there were two primary forces, one for good and the other for evil.[25] Alone of all peoples, the Jews believed that everything ultimately and directly emanated from one Source, namely, God. Our experience at the Exodus, reinforced throughout our history, also taught us that God Himself is concerned with man, and to Him alone we must pray. God spoke of this when He told us through His prophet, "I am the Lord your God since your days in Egypt. You know that there is no God but Me, and no one else can save you" (*Hosea* 13:4).

We see the processes of history gradually bringing the entire world to belief in one God. The pagan world gradually gave way to religions professing belief in the one God of Israel. More and more, people are becoming convinced of this truth and in the end, the entire world will believe. The Prophet thus proclaimed, "God shall be King over all the world, and on that day, God will be One, and His name One" (*Zechariah* 14:9).

7.

Just as God is One, so is He unique. There is absolutely no power that can compare to Him. He is the One from whom all power emanates. This was one of the first things the Jewish people understood about God after the Exodus, and they sang by the Red Sea, "Who is like You, O God, among the mighty? Who is like You, majestic in holiness, awesome in praise, working wonders?" (*Exodus* 15:11).

Nothing else can possibly resemble God. He is the Creator of all things, and as such, is unique. Hannah thus said in her prayer, "There is none holy like God, for there is none besides Him. There is no Creator like our God" (*I Samuel* 2:2). God Himself told His prophet, "To whom will you liken Me, or make Me equal, or compare Me that we may be alike? . . . I am God, and there is none else. I am God, and there is none like Me" (*Isaiah* 46:5,9).

As Creator, God stands unique. Other beings may be great and powerful, but they can never be the one Creator of all. No matter what, this difference must exist.[26] God may have created many lofty beings, but none can even come close to resembling Him. The Psalmist thus sang (*Psalms* 89:7):

Who in the skies can compare to God?
Who is like Him of the sons of might?
A God too dreadful for the holy ones,
Too great and awesome for all around Him.
O Lord of Host, who is like You?
Mighty God, girded with faith.

8.

One of the foundations of our faith is the belief that God does not have any body, shape or form. After the revelation at Sinai, God specifically warned us, "Consider this carefully: You saw no manner of form on the day that God spoke to you at Horeb (Sinai)" (*Deuteronomy* 4:15).[27]

The fact that God has no body or form should be perfectly obvious. If God had any shape, it would provide us with a means of comparison. Since we have already determined that He cannot be compared to anything, it is clear that He has no body or form.

This also follows from the fact that God is infinite. God cannot have a body, because anything with a body must be bounded and finite. The Prophet sums up this line of reasoning when he says, "All the nations are like nothing before Him.

They are like zero and nothingness to Him. To whom then will you liken God? What likeness will you compare to Him?" (*Isaiah* 40:17, 18).[28]

The very fact that there is nothing in our experience that compares to God makes it utterly impossible really to speak of Him. Our vocabulary, and indeed, our very thought processes, can only deal with things we know. Since God can in no way be compared to anything in our experience, we do not even have the vocabulary with which to speak about Him.[29]

Our sages teach us that God borrows terms from His creatures to express His relationship with the world.[30] God can only speak to us in language that we understand. We therefore have a rule: "The Torah speaks in the language of man."[31]

We normally address God as we would address another person. It is therefore natural for the Torah to do so. Thus, when the Torah describes God's action, it may speak of God's hand. When it says that He sees us, it may speak of His eye. In saying that we are lower than He, it may say that we are under His feet.[32] None of these expressions, however, is meant to imply that God has any body or form. They are merely spoken in allegory, relating to His power and action in the world.[33]

Although these anthropomorphisms are spoken in allegory, they do have a precise meaning. They speak of the various qualities that God uses in running His universe, and as such, are the basic ingredients of His providence. We find a hint of their meaning in Elijah's introduction in the *Tikuney Zohar*, where he says:[34]

> Love is the right hand,
>> Power is the left;
> Glory is the body,
>> Victory and Splendor are the two feet . . .
> Wisdom is the brain,
>> Understanding is the heart . . .
> Majesty is the mouth . . .

All these spiritual qualities also exist in man. The Torah therefore says, "God created man in His image" (*Genesis* 1:27). We are not speaking of physical form, but of spiritual quality. As we mentioned earlier, God can to some extent be thought of as the soul of the world. As such, His spiritual qualities may parallel those of the human soul. In a spiritual sense, then, man is created in the "image of God".[35] Furthermore, since man's body parallels his soul, it too partakes of the divine.[36]

Every time God uses an anthropomorphism to describe Himself, He does so to teach us a lesson. There is a Midrash that expresses this most lucidly:[37]

> When our fathers stood at Mount Sinai to receive the Torah, they did not see any form. They did not see the form of any man, any creature, or even of any soul that God created in His world. It is thus written, "Consider this carefully: You saw no manner of form on the day that God spoke to you at Horeb."
>
> You want to argue that God is fire .. You ask, is it not written, "God is a consuming fire" (*Deuteronomy* 4:24)?
>
> Let me give you an example:
>
> A king once had a family and servants who did not act correctly. He said to them, "I am a bear upon you! I am a lion upon you! I am the angel of death upon you! All because of your deeds!"
>
> When the Torah says, "God is a consuming fire," we must interpret it the same way ... Thus, it is also written, "God will judge with fire ..." (*Isaiah* 66:16).

9.

When we say that God is pure and holy, we mean that He is totally separated from anything worldly. In general, the word "holy" means different, separated, special and set aside.[38] When we apply it to God, it means that He does not partake of any worldly quality. There is nothing in the world that can give us even the slightest clue of God's true essence. We find an allusion to this in the verse, " 'To whom will you liken Me that I be an equal?' says the Holy One" (*Isaiah* 40:25). In this verse we see that God is called the "Holy One" precisely because He cannot be likened to anything in His creation.

What do we mean when we say that God is totally divorced from all worldly things?

First of all, we mean that He is not physical in any sense, and therefore, not made of matter. This should be obvious, since God is the Creator of all matter. We mean that God has no body, shape or form, as we have already discussed. If we look into this a bit more deeply, however, we understand that as soon as we say that God has no body or form, we are also saying that it is utterly impossible to imagine Him. We have absolutely no way of picturing something without form, and therefore, have no way of imagining God. When we say that God does not partake of anything worldly, we are also saying that He is utterly beyond our imagination.

There are other worldly things that are even more basic than matter and form. There are things like space and time, which are the most elementary ingredients of the physical world. It is utterly impossible even to begin to imagine a world without space. It is like trying to look through the back of your head. And to imagine a universe without time is even more hopeless. We cannot even see two times at once. The absence of time is utterly beyond our ability to comprehend.

One of the ways in which God is holy is in the fact that He exists in a realm where neither space nor time exist. The Prophecy says of God, "He dwells in eternity on high, His name is holy" (*Isaiah* 57:15). Eternity is where neither space nor time exist. God is in this unimaginable domain, and is therefore called "holy."

To try to speak or philosophize about the realm of God is utterly impossible. Our minds cannot even begin to operate in a realm where neither space or time exist. We do not have the vocabulary to express the elements of such a domain. This is but one reason why God is absolutely beyond our understanding.[39]

All this is well expressed by an anecdote recorded in the Midrash:[40]

A philosopher once asked Rabban Gamaliel, "Where is God?"

The Rabbi answered, "I do not know."

The philosopher retorted, "He is your praise and wisdom. You pray to Him every day. How can you say that you do not know where He is?"

Rabban Gamaliel looked at the philosopher and said, "You

are asking me about something that is very far off, way beyond our world. I will ask you about something that is very close to you. Where is your soul?"

The philosopher was puzzled. He replied, "I really do not know."

Rabbi Gamaliel said, "Then your words are mere wind. You do not even know the place of something that is actually a part of you. How can you question me about something that is beyond understanding?"

What Rabban Gamaliel was telling the philosopher is that there are some things that the mind cannot even begin to grasp. To ask questions about these things is not wisdom, but foolishness. To ask where God is, is like asking where is thought or love or goodness. There are things outside the physical domain, and to apply physical terms to them is to lose sight of their true meaning.

The Midrash also tells us that even the highest angels cannot comprehend God's place. They therefore merely praise God by singing, "Blessed is God's glory from His place" (Ezekiel 3:12).[41] Even these celestial creatures, who themselves live in a realm beyond physical space, still cannot comprehend the domain of God. It is holy — utterly unique and different than anything in all creation.

When we say that God is the Creator of all things, we must say that He is the Creator of space and time as well.[42] Before He created the world, He created a realm of space and time in which to place it.[43] Thus, it is God Who defines space and time, and we cannot say that He is defined by them.

There is another Midrash that throws light on this most obscure subject.[44] The Midrash notes that in many places, God is called Makom, which literally means "place." The Midrash asks, "Why is God called 'Place'?" It answers, "Because He is the Place of the world. The world is not His place."

The Midrash is not merely telling us that God is bigger than the universe and therefore contains it inside of Himself. It is speaking in a much deeper sense. It is God Who defines the very concept of "place." He is Creator of space and time, and as such, is what makes them exist. As Creator of the concept of "place," God is the Place of all creation.

The Midrash finds an allusion to this in a verse in the Torah that literally reads, "Behold, 'place' is with Me" (Exodus 33:21).[45] "Place" is something that is with God, defined by Him. An even more remarkable allusion is found by the Midrash[46] in the Psalm (Psalms 90:1,2):

God, You have been our abode for all generations,
Before the mountains were born,
Before the world was formed,
From eternity to eternity, You are God.

What the Psalm is saying is that God Himself dwells in Eternity, and as such, is the "abode" of all creation. God is "from eternity to eternity," beyond the realm of space and time. It is therefore He who creates space and time as an "abode" for His creation.

According to many thinkers, space and time are properties of matter.[47] Therefore, when God created a universe of matter, He also created space and time.

Although the Bible does not discuss it in philosophical terms, there are numerous allusions to the fact that God is Creator and Master of time and space. Thus, for example, the Psalmist sings, "Yours is the day, Yours is also the night . . . You have set the borders of the world, You have made summer and winter" (Psalms 74:16, 17). The Psalmist alludes again to the creation of space when he says to God, "You created north and south" (I.e., Ibid. 89:13). Direction is the most elementary ingredient of space, and here we see that it, too, is created by God. In utter nothingness there is neither space nor direction. The first act of creation is therefore the creation of space out of nothingness. Job alludes to this most remarkably when he says, "He stretches the north over nothingness" (Job 26:7).[48] Another allusion is found in God's word to His prophet, which states, "I am He, I am the first, I am also the last. My hand laid the foundation of the world, My right hand spread out the heavens. When I call to them, they stand together" (Isaiah 48:12).

Since God encompasses all space and time, we see Him as infinite in them. Just as God's kingdom extends to all worlds, so is it infinite in time. The Psalmist thus says, "Your kingdom is a kingdom spanning all eternities, and Your dominion is throughout every generation" (Psalms 145:13).

The concept of God's eternity is repeated over and over in the Bible. In the Song of the Red Sea, our fathers sang, "God shall be King forever and ever" (Exodus 15:18). The Psalmist echoes these words when he says, "God is King forever" (Psalms 9:8).[49] Even in our darkest hour, we did not forget this lesson, as we chant in our dirge, "You, O God, sit forever, Your throne endures from generation to generation" (Lamentations 5:19).

God exists outside of time, and therefore, we cannot apply any concepts involving time to Him. Thus, we cannot say that God has a beginning or end, or that the concept of age applies to Him in any way. In one place, the Talmud flatly asked, "How can we possibly say that God grows old?"[50]

All change takes place in time. When something changes, it is in one state at one moment, and in another at the next. Since God exists outside of time, it is impossible for Him to change. God thus told His prophet, "I am God. I do not change" (Malachi 3:6). The Psalmist, also, sang, "You are the same, Your years never end" (Psalms 102:28).

God is therefore the unmoved Mover. He can bring about change in His world without changing Himself. He is the creator of time, and as such, can do whatever He desires with it. Thus, it is not incomprehensible that He can cause change without being changed Himself.[51]

Even the creation of the universe did not change God in any way. He did not suddenly make up His mind to create a world. The plan of creation existed in timeless eternity, and was only brought into time when time itself was created.[52] God, however, remains exactly the same after as before creation.[53]

This is expressed most clearly in our prayer Adon Olam:

> Lord of the world, Who was King
> Before all forms were created;
> When all things were made by His will,
> Only then was His name called King.

What this song is saying is that God was the same King

before creation as He was after it. The only difference is that now He is *called* King. Before creation, there was nothing to call Him King.

These concepts are most difficult to understand. As we have repeated several times, it is actually impossible to imagine a realm where neither change nor time exist. We are glancing through a crack in the door, but the human mind can never really enter into it, at least not in this life.

In many places in the Torah, we find accounts of God expressing such emotions as joy or anger. At first glance, these may seem to imply changes in God's emotions. But further thought should remind us of our previous discussion of human terms when used in relationship to God. Here again, we are merely perceiving God's acts, and ascribing the same emotions to Him as we ourselves would feel if we were doing the same thing. Thus, for example, when God does something to punish, we say that He is angry. When He bountifully rewards, we say that He is happy. In all these cases, however, we are merely expressing how we would feel if we were doing these things. It is most important to realize that they do not imply any change in God Himself.[54]

God literally never changes His mind, and therefore, His truth is absolute. A human being can say something in all sincerity one day, but feel quite differently the next. This is not true of God. He never changes; and that which is true in His realm today is also true tomorrow. God is therefore the only absolute truth.

The Prophet thus says, "The Lord, God, is Truth" (*Jeremiah* 10:10). The Midrash gives the following explanation:[55]

> What is God's seal? Our Rabbi said in the name of Rabbi Reuven, "God's seal is Truth."[56]
>
> Resh Lakish asked, "Why is *Emeth* the Hebrew word for truth?"
>
> He replied, "Because it is spelled *Aleph Mem Tav*. *Aleph* is the first letter of the Hebrew alphabet, *Mem* is the middle letter, and *Tav* is the last letter of the alphabet. God thus says, 'I am first and I am last.' "

The Midrash is making precisely this point. In saying that

God is Truth, we are also saying that He is eternal. Truth is something that is absolute and does not change. When we say that God is Truth, we are saying that He is outside the realm of change.[57]

The final consequence of God's eternity is the fact that He knows the future. Since He is outside of time, future and past are exactly the same to Him, and His knowledge of the future is therefore exactly the same as His knowledge of the past. This will be discussed at length in the section on God's omniscience, but it also concerns our present discussion. God knows the future because He exists outside of time, as He Himself told His prophet, "I call the generations from the beginning, I, God, am First, and with the last, I am the same" (*Isaiah* 41:4). The prophet is alluding to the reason why God can know the future and "call the generations from the beginning." This is because He is outside of time, abiding in unchanging Eternity from the beginning to the end.[58]

As Creator of both, God sees space and time alike. He can look at time just like we look at space. We are constantly moving though time, and can therefore only see the present. We are like a person driving down a road, who only sees a small part of the road at any given time. A person in an airplane, however, can see the entire road at once. In a similar way, God sees all time, from the beginning to the end, all at once. This is what the Talmud means when it says, "He sees it all with a single glance."[59]

10.

When our sages teach us that God does not eat or drink, they are telling us that He derives nothing at all from the world. God is the Creator and Giver, and there is no one who can give Him anything. God thus speaks through the Psalmist and says, "Even if I were hungry, I would not tell you, for the earth and everything in it are Mine" (*Psalms* 50:12). The Midrash tells us that God is saying, "Can you give oil to the olive or wine to the grape? If not, how can you give anything to Me?"[60]

God is saying that the olive and the grape are the givers of oil and wine; therefore, one cannot give these products to them. Furthermore, even these are creations of God. God is the Giver of everything; and therefore, one certainly cannot give anything to Him.

There is a story in the Talmud (*Chulin* 61a) that illustrates this point quite clearly:

A king once said to Rabbi Joshua, "I would like to prepare a meal for your God."

Rabbi Joshua told the king that this could not be done, assuring him that God has no need for this, having many servants to provide for Him. When the king insisted, the Rabbi advised him to prepare a meal on a large open space on the bank of the Ravisa River. The king assembled a large army, and they worked all summer, gathering grain for this "meal." Before they were able to finish their preparation, however, a strong wind came and blew it all into the river. They worked again all that autumn, amassing a huge mountain of grain for the "meal." But again a torrential rain came, washing it all into the river.

The king asked Rabbi Joshua, "Who is taking away your God's meal?"

The Rabbi replied, "These are merely His janitors, who sweep and mop before Him."

The king then agreed that nothing could be given to God.

What this story is telling us is that God's power is infinite. Even if He had any needs, He could supply them Himself. However, no such needs exist in the first place.

God has absolutely no need for the world. We cannot even say that creation filled some inner need for God.[61] Creation was an act of pure love and altruism, with God gaining absolutely nothing from it at all. Nothing can change God, and even though He is the Creator of the world, He can exist exactly the same without it.[62] The Psalmist speaks of this when he sings (*Psalms* 102:26-28):

> Long ago, You founded the earth,
> The heavens are the work of Your hands.
> They will perish, but You will remain . . .
> You are the same, Your years have no end.

One might be tempted to think that God may have created the world out of curiosity, to see how it would turn out. But even this is not true. We have already discussed how God knows the future exactly as He knows the past and present. He did not gain any new knowledge with the creation of the world or with anything else that happens in it. It is God who defines knowledge, and nothing can impart new knowledge to Him. This is what Job meant when he asked, "Can anyone grant God knowledge, when He judges even the highest?" (*Job* 21:22). The highest reaches of wisdom and knowledge are judged and defined by God. Who can add anything to His knowledge?

The Prophet echoes this question when he says (*Isaiah* 40:13-14):

> Who can affect God's spirit?
> What counselor can instruct Him?
> Whom has He consulted for understanding?
> Who taught Him the way of justice?
> Or gave Him lessons in wisdom?

Our good deeds do not affect God or benefit Him in any way. Our sins do not do anything to harm Him. All morality and good were created only for our own benefit.[63] Our sages thus taught us, "The commandments were only given to purify His creatures."[64] God Himself is not affected by any of them, as Elihu told Job (*Job* 35:6-8),

> If you sin, how does it touch Him?
> If you do much evil, how can you harm Him?
> If you do good, what do you give Him?
> What does He gain from your deeds?
> Your evil is only against man,
> And your good is only for mortals.

Our sages teach us that all the good that man does only benefits the man who does it, even in religious acts directed toward God.[65] Although God wants our service, He in no way needs it.

God Himself sums this up in His theophany to Job when He says, "Who has given Me anything beforehand that I should repay him? Everything under heaven is Mine" (*Job* 41:3). God does not reward good because it benefits Him, but because it is good. No one can give God anything at all, even good deeds. Our sages comment on this passage and tell us that God is saying, "Who can hang a Mezuzah if I do not give him a house? Who can build a Succah if I do not give him place?"[66] We cannot do anything unless God gives us the means. Therefore, everything that we do is ultimately done with things that belong to God. Indeed, our very existence belongs to God. This being the case, what can we give Him?[67]

God is the Giver of all things. As such, there is nothing that He can receive from His creation.

11.

From all this, we might begin to think of God as being very remote, beyond the realm of human experience. We might be led to believe that God is far away, disinterested in human suffering and indifferent to our prayers. But the exact opposite is true. God may transcend the very fabric of space and time. He might be absolutely unimaginable. But still, He is very close.

Our understanding of God is twofold. We see Him as both imminent and transcendental. He both encompasses and fills all creation.[68] This is what the Psalmist means when he sings, (*Psalms* 113:5,6)

> Who is like the Lord our God
> Who is enthroned on high,
> Yet looks down low
> Upon both heaven and earth.

Of course, this apparent duality exists only because of our imperfect understanding of God. He Himself is an absolute unity.[69]

We look at God in both of these ways. We see God as a King, sitting remotely on an exalted throne, far above the reaches of our imagination. But we also see Him as our heavenly Father, close at hand and ready to listen to our troubles and share our problems.

One of our well-known prayers addresses God as *Avinu Malkenu* — "our Father, our King." First we approach God as our Father, who is close and relates to our needs. Only then do we remind ourselves that He is also our King, remote, transcendental, heavenly and exalted.

We find this same idea in every blessing we make. We begin each blessing with the words, "Blessed are You, O Lord, our God, King of the universe." In every blessing we must recognize God's majesty,[70] calling Him King and Master of the world. But before we call God King of the world, we insert another idea. We call Him "our God." Before we proclaim that God is the transcendental King of the universe, we recall that He is also *our* God. He is ours to speak to, to pray to and to bare our hearts to.

Whenever we speak of God, we state that He is first and foremost *our* God. Only after we remind ourselves of this do we proclaim that He is King of the universe.

We find the same concept in the *Sh'ma*, our declaration of faith, where we declare "Hear O Israel, the Lord is our God, the Lord is One" (*Deuteronomy* 6:4).[71] When we say that God is One, we are proclaiming one of the deepest of all mysteries. We say that God is One — over all the stars and galaxies of the universe. God is One with an awesome unity that is beyond all human comprehension. Before we proclaim this great truth, we pause to reflect on another equally important truth: "The Lord is *our* God." He is ours, and listens to our prayers when we call upon Him. God may exist in majestic Unity, but He is also ours to call upon.

Our sages teach us that He is our God in this world, but One in the next. In the future world, God will open our minds so that we will be able to comprehend the mystery of His unity. But here in this world He is our God, and we know Him only by the way we ourselves can relate to Him.[72]

This concept is expressed most vividly in the *Kedushah*, the song of the angels. As we have seen, one part of their song is "Blessed is God's glory from His place" (*Ezekiel* 3:12). The angels are praising a transcendental God, far above the comprehension of even the highest beings. They are chanting of God's glory in a place beyond, far above all creation.

But there is another part of their song preceding this. The angels also sing, "Holy, holy, holy, is the Lord of Hosts, all the world is filled with His glory" (*Isaiah* 6:3). Here they are singing to an imminent God, who is near and fills all the world. God may be far above our minds, further than the stars and the infinite places beyond the stars. And yet, He is also very close to us. We therefore say in the Sabbath *Kedushah* prayer, "His glory fills the world, His servants ask one another, 'Where is the place of His glory?' "

Our sages teach us that "just as the soul fills the body, so God fills the world." There is absolutely no place empty of God.[73] God's essence permeates every atom of our being and every spark of our soul. His power extends to the very essence of every element of creation.

God's omnipresence is most beautifully expressed by the Psalmist, who sings (*Psalms* 139:7-12):

> Where can I go from Your spirit?
>> Where can I flee from Your presence?
> If I climb the heavens, You are there,
>> If I plumb the depths, You are there.
> If I flew to the point of sunrise,
>> Or dwelt at the limit of the sea,
> Your hand would still guide me,
>> Your right hand would hold me.
> If I asked darkness to cover me,
>> The black of the night to hide me,
> The darkness is not dark to You
>> The night is as bright as day,
>> Both light and darkness are the same.

There is no place in all creation where one can in any way escape God's presence. From the highest heaven to the lowest pit, He permeates all things. God Himself expressed this to His prophet when He said, "If they dig down to the bowels of the earth, My hand will haul them out. If they scale the heavens, My hands will drag them down" (*Amos* 9:2).

This concept is illuminated by a Midrashic anecdote.[74] A Roman once asked Rabban Gamaliel, "Why did God appear to Moses in a lowly bush?"

The Rabbi replied, "If God had appeared in a carob or fig tree, you would have asked the same question. God appeared in a lowly bush to teach us that He fills all creation. He could speak to Moses even from the most lowly thornbush."

Rabbi Pinchas sheds even more light on this concept in

another Midrash.[75] He says, "When a mortal king is in his bedroom, he is not in his throne room. When he is in his throne room, he is not in his bedroom. But the Holy One fills the highest and the lowest. It is thus written, 'His glory is in heaven and in earth'(*Psalms* 148:13)."

Since God fills all creation, He is close when we call Him. The Psalmist thus sings, "God is near to all who call Him, to all who call Him in truth" (*Psalms* 145:18). We do not have to seek in far places or indulge in deep philosophical speculation to find God. All we need do is call upon Him with sincerity and truth.

We also experience God's closeness when we do obey His commandments. Keeping the commandments is the main way in which we approach God.[76] This is what the Torah means when it says "Love the Lord your God, obey His word, so that you may hold fast to Him" (*Deuteronomy* 30:22). The Psalmist is also expressing this when he sings, "You are close, O God, for all Your commandments are truth" (*Psalms* 119:151).

Although God fills all creation, there are times when we see and feel His presence more than others. There are places where God tells us that His presence is to be found. For example, we are taught that the Divine Presence is in every congregation of worship, as it is written, "God stands in the Godly congregation" (*Psalms* 82:1).[77]

The idea is expanded in the following Talmudic anecdote:[78]

A nonbeliever once said to Rabban Gamaliel, "You say that God is in every congregation of ten. But there are many such congregations. How many can God be?"

Rabban Gamaliel asked him if the sun was shining where they were now standing. When the other replied that it was, the Rabbi asked him, "Then is the sun also shining over your house?"

The nonbeliever replied, "Of course it is. The sun shines over all the earth."

Rabban Gamaliel replied, "The sun is only one of God's multitude of servants. If it can shine over the entire world, God's glory certainly can."

God Himself told those who sought Him that He would always be close to them. Thus, He told Jacob, "I am with you, and will keep you wherever you go" (*Genesis* 28:15). This closeness to God is perhaps best expressed in the most famous of psalms, where the Psalmist sings out (*Psalms* 23):

> God is my Shepherd,
>   I have no wants;
> He lets me lie in green pastures,
>   He leads me to still waters,
>   He restores my soul.
> He guides me in straight paths
>   For the sake of His name.
> Though I pass through the valley
>   Of the shadow of death
> I will fear no evil
>   For You are with me.
> Your rod and Your staff,
>   They comfort me.

When the Torah says that God is in a place, it is not really saying anything about God. God is in every place, and cannot be restricted to any one locality. When we say that God is in a place, we are really saying something about that place. We are saying that it is a place where God's presence is felt, or where His miracles are seen.[79] The *Mekhilta*, the most ancient Midrash on the Book of *Exodus*, expresses this very clearly:[80]

> It is written, "And God went before them by day in a pillar of cloud . . . and by night in a pillar of fire" (*Exodus* 13:21). But how is it possible to say this? Is it not written, "The whole earth is filled with His glory"? (*Isaiah* 6:3).
>
> Rabbi Antoninos explained this with the following example:
>
> A king once sat in judgment and remained in court until after dark. His children remained in court so that they would be able to accompany him home.
>
> When the king left for his palace, he took a lantern and carried it, lighting the way for his children. His officers and nobles saw this and offered to carry the lantern for the king.
>
> The king then told them, "I do not carry the lamp

because I lack someone else to carry it. I carry it to show my love for my children."

Rabbi Antoninos explained that the same is true of God. He reveals His glory before His children as an expression of love for them.

The Talmud takes this idea one step further and teaches us a general lesson: "It is not the place that gives honor to the man. It is the man who gives honor to the place." It then derives this lesson from God Himself. As long as God's presence was on Mount Sinai, no one was allowed to climb it. As long as His glory was in the tabernacle, no unclean man could approach it. But when His glory left these places, any one could enter.[81]

What the Talmud is teaching us is that God may say that His glory is in a certain place, but that does not mean that it is not elsewhere. When God tells us that His glory is in a given location, He is saying that He is the One "who gives honor to the place." Hillel thus said in God's name, "When I am here, everything is here. When I am not here, nothing is here."[82]

God's glory fills all creation, but it can only be felt where man prepares the way. It is not enough to say that we believe that God fills all creation. We must do something about it. We must act as if we realize that He is everywhere. The Talmud teaches us that a person who sins in a hidden place is pushing away the feet of the Divine Presence.[83]

We cannot come close to God by building beautiful synagogues and temples. The only way is by being humble and obeying God's word. God Himself told us this through His prophet (*Isaiah* 66:1,2):

The heavens are My throne,
    The earth is My footstool,
Where will you build a house for Me?
    Where shall My resting place be?
Everything was made by My hand,
    And all this is Mine ...
But My eyes are drawn to the man
    Of humble and contrite spirit
    Who trembles at My word.

There is an anecdote that sums this up. It is told that the famed Chassidic leader, Rabbi Menachem Mendel of Kotzk, once asked his disciples, "Where does God live?" They quickly answered, "God lives everywhere." But the Rabbi would not accept their answer. He taught them, "God lives wherever man lets Him in."

One of the reasons why we cannot see God is because He is so very close to us. We cannot see Him for the very same reason that we cannot see the atmosphere. We live, breathe and move in an ocean of air, and yet it remains invisible to us. We understand that the atmosphere is invisible because of its very nature and closeness to us.

God is invisible for much the same reason. The reason we cannot see Him is not so much because He is so far away, as because He is so near to us. He fills all creation and there is no place empty of Him; therefore, we have no comparison with which to detect His presence. Of course there are deeper reasons, but they are beyond the scope of this work.

The only time we are aware of the air around us is when we feel it, such as when the wind blows. Similarly, the only time we are aware of God is when He acts to reveal His presence. This may be the reason why the Hebrew language has the same word, *Ruach*, for both wind and spirit.

We can feel God's presence if we only let Him in. It may be during the synagogue prayers, or while singing the Sabbath *zemiroth*. It may be while dancing on Simchath Torah, or while binding oneself with Tefillin. Or it might be when one just steals away to be alone with God, deep in the woods, on a lonely mountain peak, or standing in a field, gazing at the passing clouds and wondering at the meaning of it all. Who has not looked up at the heavens on a clear bright night and stared with fixed attention, as if he could penetrate the fathomless depths of space and probe the hearts of the stars and steal their secret?

This may indeed have been the experience of the Psalmist. It might have been a clear night, and as he gazed up at the heavens, he compared their glory to his own small self. Gazing at a myriad of stars, he burst into song (*Psalms* 8:4-6):

When I look at Your heavens,
The work of Your fingers,
The moon and the stars
That You have established:
What is man that You think of him?
Mere mortal that You remember him?
But You have made him a little less than God,
You crowned him with glory and honor.

There are times when we feel that God is there, right next to us. At times like these we can realize just how close God really is. Our whole being, body and soul, can be swallowed up in the Absolute Being that is God. We become steeped and saturated with God, and feel Him closer to us than existence itself.

12.

Our sages teach us, "Just as the soul sustains the body, so God sustains the world." As discussed earlier, this means that God's life-force permeates all creation and constantly gives it existence. Thus, existence itself is a direct result of God's constant power. This is the meaning of the song of the Levites, who chanted to God: "You made the heavens, the heavens of heaven . . . the earth and everything in it . . . and You give life to all" (Nechemiah 9:6). God constantly gives life and existence to all creation.

Our sages interpret this verse and teach us, "Do not read MeChayeh — gives life — but MeHaveh — gives existence."[84] The verse would then read, "You give existence to all." The power that God gives His creation is more than mere life. It is existence itself. Daniel therefore calls God "The Life of the world" (Daniel 12:7).[85]

A human craftsman can build a house and then forget it. But God's creation is more than that. Not only was God's will responsible for creation, it is also responsible for the continued existence of all things. Nothing can exist without God willing it to exist. If He did not constantly will the existence of everything in creation, it would utterly cease to exist.[86] Elihu thus told Job, "If He would gather to Himself His spirit and breath, then all flesh would perish together" (Job 34:14,15).[87] The Psalmist, too, sang, "You hide Your face, they vanish; You withdraw their spirit, they perish" (*Psalms* 104:29).

In our daily morning prayer, we say, "In His goodness, He constantly renews the act of creation." Thus it is written, "He *makes* great lights, for His love is infinite" (*Psalms* 136:7). The prayer quotes this verse, stressing that the word "makes" is used, in the present tense, rather than "made" in the past. God did not just make the world. He constantly "makes" it, continually renewing the act of creation.

The Midrash[88] teaches us that the very same word with which God created the universe constantly sustains its existence. This is base upon the following Psalm (*Psalms* 119:89-91):

> Eternal is Your word, O God,
>   Planted firm in the heavens,
> Your faithfulness lasts for all ages,
>   You founded the earth and it stands.
> Creation is maintained by Your ruling,
>   For all things are Your servants.

13.

The belief that God knows all the deeds of man is one of the foundations of our faith.[89]

As discussed earlier, God's being both fills and constantly sustains all creation. The very fact that God's presence is everywhere allows Him to be continuously aware of everything that takes place in His creation. God gives existence to everything, and there is no place to hide from Him. This is what He Himself told His prophet, "I am a God near at hand . . . not a God far off. Can a man hide himself in secret places that I not see him? . . . Do I not fill heaven and earth?" (*Jeremiah* 22:23,24).

As mentioned earlier, our sages teach us, "Just as the soul sees and is not seen, so God sees and is not seen." Our sages are telling us that the fact that God sees and the fact that He is not seen are related. Both stem from the fact that He is so near and permeates all creation. As discussed earlier, this is one of the main reasons why we cannot see Him. It is also the reason why He sees all.

There is no place in all creation that escapes God's scrutiny. He perceives everything that happens in the world, never lifting His gaze from it. The wise Solomon thus said, "God's eyes are in every place, keeping watch on the evil and the good" (*Proverbs* 15:3). Job was also expressing this when he said, "He looks to the ends of the earth, and sees under the whole heaven" (*Job* 28:24).

There is no place where one can hide from God. Light and darkness are absolutely the same to Him. Nothing in all creation can be hidden from Him. Here again we find the words of Job, "He uncovers deep things out of darkness, and brings the deep gloom to light" (*Job* 12:22). He repeats the same theme when he exclaims, "He brings hidden things forth to light" (ibid. 28:11).

God is constantly aware of every single human being, and indeed, of everything in all creation. This is what Solomon meant when he said, "The ways of man are before God's eyes" (*Proverbs* 5:21). Elihu also expressed this concept to Job, saying, "His eyes keep watch over all man's ways. He observes their every step. There is no darkness nor deep shadow where the sinner can hide" (*Job* 34:21). God Himself told this to His prophet, declaring, "My eyes are upon all their ways, they are not hidden from My face. Their sin is never concealed from My eyes" (*Jeremiah* 16:17).

The Psalmist was completely aware that God was always watching him. It was he who set God continuously before him. He cried out, "O God, You know my folly, my sins are not hidden from You" (*Psalms* 69:6). In a Psalm quoted earlier, he sings of this (*Psalms* 139:1-6):

O God, You examine me and know me:
You know when I sit and stand,
    You read my thoughts from far off.
When I walk or lie down, You are watching,
    You know well all of my ways.
The word is not yet on my tongue,
    Before You, O God, know about it . . .
Such knowledge is beyond my grasp,
    A height my mind cannot reach.

There is no secret before God and no hiding place in all creation where things can be concealed from Him. The deepest recesses of man's heart are wide open before Him. Daniel thus tells us, "He uncovers deep secrets. He knows what lies in darkness, the light dwells with Him" (*Daniel* 2:22).

The Midrash explains this with a parable.[90] A master architect was appointed as tax collector. Once, he was sent to a city that he himself had built. When he designed this city, he built into it many underground passages and secret chambers.

Upon hearing that a new tax collector was coming, the citizens hid their money in these secret chambers, thinking that he would not be able to find them. When the architect-tax collector got wind of this, he told the people, "I myself built these hiding places. Do you think you can hide things from me in them?"

The Midrash explains that God is like this architect. He tells us, "I created you and formed the innermost recesses of your hearts. What can you possibly hide from Me there?"

There are people who ask the question, "If God rules over the entire universe, how can He pay attention to me? How can He maintain His attention over every single individual in all creation?"

We must understand that just as God Himself is infinite, so is His intellect unbounded. A human mind may be able to concentrate on only one thing at a time. God, however, has no such restrictions. He can be aware of an infinite number of things, happening in an infinite number of places, all with one glance. God can maintain His gaze on the uncountable stars and galaxies of the universe, knowing exactly what is happening on each and every one of them at all times. There is not a single atom in all creation that escapes His constant scrutiny. This is what the Psalmist is teaching us when he sings, "He numbers the stars and calls them all by name ... His understanding is infinite" (*Psalms* 147:4,5). We may not be able to conceive of infinite understanding, but this is but another thing about God that is too deep for our grasp. The prophet thus tells us "no man can fathom His understanding" (*Isaiah* 40:28).

Beyond man's deeds, God scrutinizes the very convolutions

of our brains and gazes at the depths of our souls. He not only knows our deeds, but also our very thoughts. The human mind was also created by God, and it lies open and transparent before Him. The Psalmist tells us of this when he chants (*Psalms* 33:13-15):

God looks down from heaven,
He sees the whole human race;
From His place He watches,
Probing all who live on earth.
He has molded every heart together,
He knows what each one does.

Even the innermost secrets of our hearts are thus open before God. The Psalmist speaks of this when he says, "He knows the secrets of the heart" (ibid. 44:22). He repeats this again, exclaiming, "He knows the thoughts of man" (ibid. 94:11). For there are things in creation that are much more hidden than even man's thoughts, and these are nevertheless revealed before God. There are many secrets that only He knows, and in comparison, man's thoughts are a simple thing to probe. The wise Solomon thus declared, "The pit and destruction lie open before God, how much more so, the hearts of man" (*Proverbs* 15:11).

It is impossible to fool God. He not only knows our actions, but also our motives. God Himself told His prophet, "I, God, search the heart" (*Jeremiah* 17:10). The Prophet reiterates these words, saying, "God . . . probes the heart" (ibid. 20:12). These were also the words of the prophet Samuel, who said, "Man looks at appearances, but God looks at the heart" (*I Samuel* 16:7).

A man might even fool himself, but God cannot be tricked. He not only knows our conscious motives, but even the depths of our unconscious. The wise Solomon taught us, "A man's ways may strike him as pure, but God weighs the spirit" (*Proverbs* 16:2).

A person cannot think of anything or even begin to plan it, before God knows what is in his mind. One cannot hide even his most secret thoughts from God. This is what King David told his son Solomon: "God searches every heart and knows every plan that it devises" (*I Chronicles* 28:9). Our sages comment on this: "Before a man speaks, God knows what is in his heart."[92] Another Midrash explains this even further:[93]

Before a thought is formed in a man's heart, it is already revealed to God. Rabbi Yoden said in Rabbi Isaac's name, "Before it even begins to take form."

Just as God fills all space. He also fills all time. As we discussed earlier, God knows the future just as He knows the past and present.[94] We cannot comprehend time at all, and therefore, cannot fully understand how this is possible. Only God can see the future with absolute clarity, as He Himself told His prophet: "I am God: There is none like Me, Who can declare the end from the beginning. From ancient times, I reveal what is to be" (*Isaiah* 46:9,10).

God knew the destiny of the entire universe even before it was created. He knows every man's life even before he is born. He thus told His prophet: "Before I formed you in the womb, I knew you" (*Jeremiah* 1:5). Our sages therefore teach us, "God knows man's thoughts even before there is any thought of creating him."[95]

The Psalmist also sang of this in the 139th Psalm that we quoted earlier. Here he speaks of how God knew his entire destiny even before he was born (*Psalms* 139:15,16):

> My bones were not hidden from You
> When I was formed in secret,
> Woven in the depths of the womb.
> You saw my unformed substance,
> It was all written in Your book.
> My days were listed and determined,
> Before the first one was even formed.

In order to give us free will, God must, to some extent, restrict His knowledge of the future. As we shall see, there are many ways in which God restricts Himself, especially with regard to His knowledge. For example, in a sense, God restricts Himself from seeing evil, as the Prophet exclaims: "Your eyes are too pure to look upon evil, You cannot gaze upon wrongdoing . . ." (*Habakkuk* 1:13).[96]

It may be difficult to understand how God can know everything, yet at the same time restrict His gaze from seeing evil, but this is only one of the many ways where our limited intellect cannot comprehend the divine. One can also say that although God really knows the future, He restricts this knowledge when dealing with man. The Talmud thus teaches us, "God knows the future, but only judges man according to the present."[97]

This idea is expressed most clearly in a story brought in the Midrash:[98]

Just before the flood, the Torah tells us that, "God regretted that He had made man on the earth, and it grieved His heart" (Genesis 6:6). The Midrash discusses this paradox in terms of an anecdote.

A Roman was once conversing with Rabbi Joshua ben Korcha. He asked, "Do you not say that God knows the future?"

When the Rabbi replied in the affirmative, the Roman pressed the question further, "But it is written that God regretted that He made man and was grieved in His heart. Did He not know what man would end up doing?"

Rabbi Joshua responded by asking the Roman, "Do you have any children?"

When the Roman replied that he had several sons, Rabbi Joshua asked, "What did you do when they were born? Did you rejoice or did you mourn?"

"I rejoiced and made a great celebration," replied the Roman.

The sage pressed the point, "But why did you not mourn? Did you not know for sure that the child would eventually die? There is no man who can escape death."

The Roman answered, "Mourning is for the time of sadness. But in a time of joy we rejoice."

Rabbi Joshua replied, "That answers your question. The same is true of God."

Rabbi Joshua was really giving the Roman a very profound answer. He taught him that a person can know something beyond the shadow of a doubt, and yet ignore this knowledge completely. One knows for certain that a newborn child will eventually die, but still, he ignores this fact and rejoices in the child's birth. If man can ignore certain knowledge, how much more so is this possible for God. God's power is infinite, not only to do, but also to restrict Himself in order to make creation follow His plan.

14.

The final thing that we know about God is that He is absolutely hidden. Not only can we not see God with our eyes, but even our minds are inadequate to the task of perceiving Him.

The Torah speaks of this when Moses asked God to let him perceive His glory. He asked God, "I beseech You, let me behold Your glory" (*Exodus* 33:18). God answered him, "You cannot see My face, for no man can see Me and live" (ibid. 33:20). If a man were to see God, he would absolutely cease to exist. There might be a prophetic vision or symbol, but God Himself cannot be seen.[99]

This is well illustrated by the following Midrashic anecdote:[100]

King Adroninos once was having a conversation with Rabbi Joshua. He asked, "Is there a Master of the world?"

"Is the world then without meaning or purpose?" countered the Rabbi.

When the king asked Rabbi Joshua who was this Master and Creator, the Rabbi answered quite positively that it was God.

The king looked a bit puzzled. He said to the sage, "I am a king. It would be ridiculous for me never to show myself to my subjects. They would forget me completely. Why doesn't God reveal Himself once or twice a year, so that people would see and fear Him?"

The Rabbi answered, "God does not reveal Himself because no man could bear His glory. Is it not written, 'no man can see Me and live'?"

The king insisted and said, "If you do not show me your God, I will not believe that He exists."

Rabbi Joshua replied, "Very well. If you really want to see God, look up and gaze at the summer sun."

"But who can possibly gaze at the sun?" exclaimed the

monarch.

The Rabbi smiled and said, "Listen to your own words. The sun is only one of God's vast multitude of servants. Still, no man can gaze at it. But God's glory fills the universe. How could a mere mortal possibly gaze at it?"

Rabbi Joshua is teaching us an important lesson about why we cannot see God. This lesson is really deeper than it might appear at first glance. It is telling us that God cannot reveal Himself because man could no more exist in the presence of God's glory than in the center of the sun. Existence itself is merely a mirror of God's power. In God's presence, it would be like sunlight inside of the sun. The light would have absolutely no independent existence. In the same manner, if God were to reveal Himself, then there would not be able to be any independent existence in all creation.[101] Our sages teach us, "What good is a torch in broad daylight?"[102] Existence in God's presence would be less than the light of a candle in the center of the sun.

As we discussed in the previous section, one of God's great powers is that of restricting Himself. If a human being can restrict himself, we cannot say less about God. The prophet thus speaks to God and says, "You are a God who hides Himself" (*Isaiah* 45:15). The Psalmist sings, "He dwells in the highest mystery, He rests in the shadow of Shadai" (*Psalms* 91:1). The Midrash explains this verse by saying, "The Holy One dwells in the shadow of the world. He sees all and yet is unseen."[103]

Since it is God Who hides Himself, no one can in any way uncover Him. Elihu told this to Job when he said, "When He hides His face, who can behold Him?" (*Job* 34:29).

We cannot perceive or comprehend God both because He is too close and because He is too far. God has given man the ability to understand the world, but man's power does not extend beyond that. There is a limit beyond which man's intellect can no longer function, and God's realm lies far beyond that limit. The wise Solomon taught us this lesson when he said, "He has permitted man to consider the world, but man cannot comprehend the work of God from the beginning to the end" (*Ecclesiastes* 3:11).

Man's intellect can soar beyond the stars and to the far reaches past the stars. But his mind is still limited by his physical nature. This was the lesson that Eliphaz the Yemenite taught Job when he said, "God is in the zenith of the heavens. He looks down at the stars, high as they are" (*Job* 22:12).

To reach God would be like trying to remember before your existence. It would be like trying to recall your existence in your mother's womb, before your very mind came into being. No thought symbols exist in our minds to even begin to handle such things. Here again, we see Solomon's wisdom declaring, "As you remember not the way your spirit and bones grew in the womb, neither can you know the work of God, Who is behind it all" (*Ecclesiastes* 11:5).

One can keep on counting forever and not reach infinity. One can probe to the very limits of intellect and never reach the infinite God. Were man to fathom the deepest mysteries of all creation, he would not even reach the outskirts of God's true greatness.

Job speaks of this. He tells of all the unknowable mysteries of creation and despairs of ever even being able to peer deeper than through the shallowest surface of these mysteries. Then, after speaking of these mysteries, he says, "These are but the fringes of His power, a faint whisper that we hear of Him. But who can fathom the thunder of His might?" (*Job* 26:15).

What Job is saying is that all that we can comprehend is like the merest whisper, while in comparison, God's power is like the loudest thunder. Elihu echoes these same words to Job, "With His voice, God thunders wondrously, He does great things that we cannot understand" (ibid. 37:5). Again, he says, "God's greatness exceeds our knowledge, the number of His years is beyond computing" (ibid. 36:26). There is no way that we can grasp the infinite.

Another one of Job's friends expresses the utter hopelessness of ever attempting to probe the depths of the Divine. He speaks to Job and tells him (ibid. 11:7-9):

Can you probe the depths of God?
Can you fathom Almighty's mystery?
It is higher than heaven, what can you do?

> Deeper than deep, what can you know?
> Longer than the earth is its measure,
> And broader than the sea.

The idea of God's total transcendence and the impossibility of understanding Him is best expressed by Elijah, who says to God in his introduction to the *Tikuney Zohar*: "No thought can grasp You at all."[104] Rabbi Schneur Zalman of Liadi, the founder of Chabad, interprets this by saying, "Just as a physical hand cannot grasp a thought, so too, man's intellect cannot grasp God."[105] God is a dimension even beyond thought. Our minds may reach out to Him, but can no more grasp Him than our hands can grasp a thought.[106]

We come to God with faith and prayer rather than with true understanding. Ultimately, all we know about God is what He Himself revealed to us. Beyond that, God is totally beyond the reach of the human intellect. He is hidden, not only from our sight, but also from our minds. We might reach up to grasp a star, but our hands would never even come close to touching one. The same is true of God. He Himself tells us this, when He speaks to His prophet and says (*Isaiah* 55:8,9):

> My thoughts are not your thoughts,
> My ways are not your ways . . .
> As the heavens are higher than the earth
> So are My ways higher than yours
> And My thoughts above your thoughts.

NOTES

PART ONE: FOUNDATIONS

1. Cf. *Mesilath Yesharim* 1.
2. *Zohar Chadash* 70d. Cf. *Avoth* 3:1.
3. *Yad, Yesodey HaTorah* 1:1-5.
4. Also see *Psalms* 53:2.
5. *Moreh Nevuchim* 1:44.
6. *Chovoth HaLevavoth* 1:6 end.
7. *Bereshith Rabbah* 39:1.
8. *Zohar* 1:2a.
9. *Chovoth HaLevavoth* 2:5; *Pardes Rimonim* 8:1; *Shnei Luchoth HaB'rith* (*Shaar HaGadol*), Jerusalem 5720, 1:46b. Cf. *Bereshith Rabbah* 48:2.
10. *Tanchuma, Toldos* 5.
11. *VeHi SheAmdah,* in Passover Hagaddah.
12. *Sifri* (346) on *Deuteronomy* 33:5, *Midrash Tehillim* 123:2; *Pesikta* 12 (102b); *Yalkut* 1:275, 2:317; Abarbanel ad loc.
13. See *Targum J., Mechilta* on *Exodus* 12:37.
14. *Yad, Yesodey HaTorah* 8:1; *Kuzari* 1:87.
15. Ramban ad loc. and on Additions to *Sefer HaMitzvoth,* negative commandment #2; *Sefer Mitzvoth Gadol* (*Smag*), negative commandment #13.
16. *Moreh Nevuchim* 2:35.
17. Ramban loc. cit. #1, quoting *Halakhoth Gedoloth.* Cf. *Sefer Mitzvoth Gadol,* negative commandment #64.
18. This is repeated in Deuteronomy 5:6.
19. Ibn Ezra, Ramban, ad loc.; *Kuzari* 1:25; *Chinuch* 25.
20. Cf. *Kuzari* 1:1,2. See also *Ezekiel* 8:12, 9:9.
21. *Exodus* 15:2.
22. See *Likutey Halakhoth* (*Yoreh Deah*) *Shavuoth* 2:2.
23. Cf. *VaYikra Rabbah* 28:1; *Targum J.* on *Genesis* 4:8.
24. Cf. *Avoth* 4:11, 5:17.
25. *Yad, Yesodey HaTorah* 1:6; *Sefer HaMitzvoth,* positive commandment #1; *Sefer Mitzvoth Gadol,* positive #1, *Zohar* 21:25a, 3:256b. See also Josephus, *Antiquities* 3:5:5, who also appears to concur with this opinion. Cf. *Makkoth* 24a.
26. *Chinuch* 25. This may also answer the objection of the Ramban, quoted in the following note. However, the Ramban might counter by placing this in the category of remembering rather than believing. See note 17.
27. Ramban of *Sefer HaMitzvoth,* loc. cit. See also *Halachoth Gedoloth* and *Sefer HaMitzvoth* of Rabbi Saadia Gaon, who also omit it.
28. *Yad, Yesodey HaTorah* 1:6, *Sefer HaMitzvoth,* negative commandment #1; *Sefer Mitzvoth Gadol,* negative 1.
29. *Chinuch* 26.
30. *Kiddushin* 40a; *Yerushalmi Nazir* 4:3 (17a); *Tosefta Nazir* 3:6, from *Ezekiel* 14:5. Cf. Radak ad loc. *Zohar* 2:150b.
31. *Sefer Mitzvoth Gadol,* loc. cit. See *Mekhilta* and Ibn Ezra on *Exodus* 22:19. Cf. *2 Kings* 17:33, and Rashi and Radak on *Judges* 10:6, from *Pesikta Eicha Rabbah* 10, *Betza* 25b.

32. *Yad, Avodath Kochavim* 1:1; *Moreh Nevukhim* 1:36.
33. *Thirteen Principles of Faith* #5.
34. *Sanhedrin* 7:6 (60b); *Ramban* on *Exodus* 20:3.
35. *Sanhedrin* 63a: *Succah* 45b; *Yad, Shavuoth* 11:2.
36. *Yad, Melakhim* 9:3.
37. See *Yad,* loc. cit., which states that a non-Jew is only liable for those types of idolatry for which a Jew incurs a death penalty, cf. *Minchath Chinukh* 26:6. However, this only involves the *deed* of idolatry, cf. *Sanhedrin* 63a; *Yad, Avodath Kochavim* 3:4.
38. See *Tosafoth, Bekhoroth* 2b s.v. "Sh'ma"; *Sanhedrin* 63b s.v. "*Asur*"; *Orach Chaim* 156:1 in *Hagah; Rosh, Sanhedrin* 7:3, *Pilpula Charifta* ad loc.; *Darkey Moshe, Yoreh Deah* 151; *Shach* ibid. 151:7; *Mach'tzith HaShekel, Orach Chaim* 156:2; *Teshuvoth Tashbatz* 1:139; *Teshuvoth VeShev HaKohen* 38; *Mishnath Chakhamim* on *Yad, Yesodey HaTorah,* quoted in *Pithchey Teshuvah, Yoreh Deah* 147:2; *Maharatz Chayoth* on *Horioth* 8b. There is another opinion that this is only forbidden in the land of Israel, cf. *Maharatz Chayoth* on *Berakhoth* 57a; *Ramban* on *Leviticus* 18:25; Rabbi Yaakov Emden, *Mor U'Ketzia* 224.
39. Cf. *Rashbam* ad loc.; *Derech Mitzvothekha* (Chabad) p. 59b.
40. Cf. *Kuzari* 4:23; *Rambam,* end of *Halkhoth Melachim* (Amsterdam, 1702), quoted in *Ramban, Torath HaShem Temimah,* in *Kithvey Ramban,* Jerusalem, 5723, p. 1:144; *Teshuvoth Rambam* 58; *Teshuvoth Rivash* 119; *Akedath Yitzchok* 88.
41. *Teshuvoth Node BeYehudah, Yoreh Deah,* end of 2:148; *Teshuvoth Meil Tzadakah* 22; *Teshuvoth Shaar Ephraim* 24; all quoted in *Pithchey Teshuvah, Yoreh Deah* 147:2; *Pri Megadim, Eshel Avraham* 156:2, *Sifthey Daath (Yoreh Deah)* 65:11); *Chatham Sofer* on *Orach Chaim* 156:1; *Minchath Chinukh* 86.
42. *Makkoth* 24a. However, see *Shir HaShirim Rabbah* 1:13, where we find an opinion that disputes this and maintains that all Ten Commandments were given directly at Sinai. See *Ramban* on *Exodus* 20:7, and on *Sefer HaMitzvoth, Shoresh* #1. Also see *Pirkey DeRabbi Eliezer* 41, *Radal* ad loc. 41:77; *Sh'moth Rabbah* 42:7. In *Moreh Nevukhim* 2:33, we find that the very fact of revelation demonstrated these two commandments. See also *Kol Yehudah* on *Kuzari* 1:87 (52b) s.v. "VeEleh."
43. *Moreh Nevukhim* loc. cit.; *Rashi, Makkoth* 22a s.v. "*MiPi.*"
44. *Yad, Yesodey HaTorah* 1:6; *Avodath Kokhavim* 2:4; *Kiddushin* 40a.
45. *Tosefta Shavuoth* 3:5.
46. *Ramban* ad loc.; *Abarbanel* of *Moreh* 2:31.
47. *Moreh Nevukhim* 2:31, 3:32, 3:41; *Sefer HaChinukh* 32; Ibn Ezra, Bachya, on *Exodus* 20:8; *Ramban* on *Deuteronomy* 5:15; *Menorath HaMaor* 159; *Akedath Yitzchok* 4, 55; *Sh'nei Luchoth HaB'rith (Mesekhta Shabbath)* 2:10b. Cf. *Mekhilta* on *Exodus* 31:14.
48. *Moreh Nevukhim* 1:34; *Radak* on I *Chronicles* 28:29.
49. Cf. *Kuzari* 1:114, 4:13.
50. Cf. Ibn Ezra on *Proverbs* 30:19.
51. *Sifra* and *Rashi* on *Leviticus* 26:15; *Yalkut* 1:673.
52. Cf. *Pesachim* 59b; *Nazir* 23b; *Yoreh Deah* 146:20.

53. Reading of *Reshith Chakhmah, Shaar HaTeshuvah #7* (New York, 5728) 123c, of *Yerushalmi Chaggigah* 1:7 (6b). See *Pesikta Eicha Rabbah* 2; *Pesikta* 15 (121a); *Yalkut* 2:282
54. See note 17.
55. See Rashi, Radak ad loc.; *Moreh Nevukhim* 3:51, 52; *Orach Chaim* 1:1 in *Hagah.* cf. *Sanhedrin* 22a; *Reshith Chachmah, Shaar HaYira* 1 (8d).

PART TWO: GOD

1. *Megillah* 31a.
2. *Sotah* 5a.
3. See *Emunoth VeDeyoth* 1:1; *Yad, Yesodey HaTorah* 1:1, 1:5; *Mechilta* on *Exodus* 6:2 (120a); *Sifra* on *Leviticus* 18:2 (85c).
4. *Metzudoth, Targum* ad loc.; *Reshith Chakhmah* 1:1 (9c).
5. *Yad, Teshuvah* 3:7, Raavad ad loc.; *Ramban* on *Genesis* 1:1; *Emunoth VeDeyoth* 5:8 (74a); *Kuzari* 1:67 (41a).
6. *Bereshith Rabbah* 1:12. See Raavad loc. cit.
7. Alluding to the things mentioned in Genesis 1:2. According to the Ramban ad loc., the philosopher was referring to the primeval matter of the Hyle, the primitive Form, and the four elements of the ancient world, fire, air, water, and dust. See also *Torath HaShem Temimah* p. 156.
8. *Ramban* on *Genesis* 1:3. Also see *Kuzari* 4:25 (44a). Cf. *Midrash Tehillim* 107:3.
9. *Bereshith Rabbah* 12:10, 4:7.
10. *Minachoth* 29b; Rashi on *Genesis* 2:4. See also *Etz Yosef* on *Bereshith Rabbah* 12:10.
11. Ramban loc. cit., *Moreh Nevukhim* 1:66
12. *Magid Devarav LeYaakov* 102.
13. Cf. *Jeremiah* 51:15.
14. *Ramban* on *Genesis* 1:1, *Thirteen Principles of Faith #1, Yad, Teshuvah* 3:7.
15. See *Targum* ad loc.
16. See Malbim, *Metzudoth* ad loc.
17. *Yerushalmi Berakhoth* 1:5 (9b); *VaYikra Rabbah* 26:1. See Rashi, Radak ad loc.; *Yad, Yesodey HaTorah* 1:4.
18. *Shabbath* 55a.
19. See also Psalms 10:16, 29:10, 146:10.
20. *Chovoth HaLevavoth* 1:10 (Warsaw 5635) p. 40a: *Moreh Nevukhim* 1:58; *Kuzari* 2:2; *Ikkarim* 2:22.
21. *Midrash Tehillim* 103:4, according to reading and interpretation of *Shomer Emunim (HaKadmon)* 2:9-11. For other versions and readings, see *Berakhoth* 10a; *VaYikra Rabbah* 4:8; *Devarim Rabbah* 2:26; *Pirkey DeRabbi Eliezer* 34; *Tikuney Zohar* 13 (28a). See also *Derech HaShem #1*.
22. See *Iyun Yaakov* on *Berakhoth* 10a (in *Eyn Yaakov #50*).
23. *Thirteen Principles of Faith #2 Yad, Teshuvah* 3:7.
24. *Yad, Avodath Kochavim* 1; *Daath Tevunah* (Rabbi Moshe Chaim Luzzato, Tel Aviv, 5726) p. 13.
25. *Daath Tevunah* loc. cit. See also *Sifri HaAzinu #329*. Cf. *Berakhoth* 33b.

Notes □ 167

26. See *Pardes Rimonim* 2:7; *Shefa Tal* 1:3.
27. *Thirteen Principles of Faith* #3; *Yad, Teshuvah* 3:6, Raavad ad loc.; *Iggereth Techiyath HaMethim* p. 4; *Ikkarim* 1:2, 2:7; *Pardes Rimonim* 1:9.
28. See *Chovoth HaLevavoth* 1:10 (41b); *Yad, Yesodey HaTorah* 1:8, 1:11, from *Chagigah* 15a; *Moreh Nevukhim* 1:35, 2:1 end; *Kuzari* 5:18 #6.
29. *Chovoth HaLevavoth* 39b; *Moreh Nevukhim* 1:58; *Pardes Rimonim* 3:1, 4:8; *Ikkarim* 2:22. See also *Zohar* 2:42b; *Nefesh HaChaim* 2:2.
30. *Mekhilta* (65a), Rashi on *Exodus* 19:18; *Tanchuma Yithro* 13; *Bereshith Rabbah* 27:1; *Koheleth Rabbah* 2:24; *Pesikta* 4 (36b); *Moreh Nevuchim* 1:26, 1:47; *Emunoth VeDeyoth* 2:10; *Chovoth HaLevavoth* 1:10; *Kuzari* 4:3 (18a). See also Ramban on *Genesis* 46:1; *Tifereth Yisrael* (Maharal) 33.
31. *Berakhoth* 31b and parallels; *Sifra* on *Leviticus* 20:2; *Yad Yesodey HaTorah* 1:12; *Chovoth HaLevavoth* loc. cit.
32. Cf. *Exodus* 24:10.
33. *Yad,* loc. cit.
34. *Tikuney Zohar* 17a.
35. *Nefesh HaChaim* 1:1; *Pardes Rimonim* 31:8; *Etz Chaim, Drush Egolim VaYashar* 5; *Shomer Emunim (HaKadmon)* 1:25.
36. *Zohar* 1:90b, 2:96b, 3:71b; *Likutey Amarim (Tanya)* 1:4.
37. *Tana DeBei Eliahu Rabbah*, end of #1.
38. *Kuzari* 4:3, *Tosafoth, Kiddushin* 3b, s.v. *"DeAsar."* See also *Leviticus* 19:2, 21:8, *Isaiah* 6:3; *VaYikra Rabbah* 24:9.
39. *Emunoth VeDeyoth* 1:4.
40. *Midrash Tehillim* 103:5.
41. *Chagigah* 13b.
42. *Emunoth VeDeyoth* 2:11,12, *Sh'vil Emunah* ad loc. #10; *Moreh Nevukhim* 2:13, 2:30; *Ikkurim* 2:18; *Pardes Rimonim* 3:1, 4:7; *Torath HaOlah (Isserles)* 3:59; *Yaaroth Devash* on *Megillah* 9a; *Asarah Maamaros* 1:16; *Derech Mitzvothekha (Chabad)* 57a. Also see *Bereshith Rabbah* 3:8.
43. *Pardes Rimonim* 6:3.
44. *Bereshith Rabbah* 68:10; *Sh'moth Rabbah* 45:6; *Midrash Tehillim* 50; *Pesikta Rabathai* 21 (104b); *Yalkut* 2:841; *Radak* on *Psalm* 90:1; *Nefesh HaChaim* 3:1-3.
45. Cf. *Rashi, Baaley Tosafoth* ad loc.
46. Ibid. Cf. *Radak* ad loc.
47. See note 42. Also see Albert Einstein, *Relativity, the Special and General Theory* (Crown, New York, 1961), Appendix 5.
48. *Sanhedrin* 38a; *Yerushalmi Sanhedrin* 4:9 (23b); *Bereshith Rabbah* 8:5.
49. See also *Psalms* 22:10, 102:13.
50. *Yebomoth* 16b. See also *Yad, Yesodey HaTorah* 1:10; *Emunoth VeDeyoth* 2:10; *Kuzari* 5:18 #5; *Ikkarim* 2:19. Cf. *Bereshith Rabbah* 81:2; *Mekhilta* on *Exodus* 22:3 (67b); *VaYikra Rabbah* 19:2 end; Ibn Ezra on *Ecclesiastes* 3:15.
51. *Cheredim* #5 (Jerusalem, 5718) p. 42; *Elemah Rabathai* 1:1:15.
52. *Emunoth VeDeyoth*, end of #1; *Shomer Emunim (HaKadmon)* 2:17. Cf. *Etz Chaim, Drush Egolim VeYashar* #1.
53. *Shnei Luchoth HaB'rith, Beth HaShem* 1:6a, note; *Cheredim* #5 (p. 40).
54. *Yad, Yesodey HaTorah* 1:11; *Moreh Nevuchim* 1:54; *Emunoth VeDeyoth*

2:11; *Ikkarim* 2:14.

55. *Bereshith Rabbah* 81:2.
56. See above, note 18.
57. *Ikkurim* 2:27.
58. See Rabbi Moshe Almosnino, *Pirkey Moshe,* quoted in *Midrash Shmuel* and *Tosafoth Yom Tov* on *Avoth* 3:15; *Yesod Emunah* (Rabbi Baruch Kasover) 2; *Sh'vil Emunah* (on *Emunoth VeDevoth*) 4:4:11. Also see *Kol Yehudah* (on *Kuzari*) 5:20 (47b); *Otzar Nechemad* (on *Kuzari*) 1:1 (11b), s.v. *"Kol."*
59. *Rosh HaShanah* 18a. See Rambam, *Tosafoth Yom Tov* ibid. 1:2.
60. *Pesikta* 6 (57b).
61. *Yad, Yesodey HaTorah* 2:3; *Moreh Nevuchim* 3:13; *Emunoth VeDeyoth* 1:4, *Sh'vil Emunah* ad loc. 1:4:9; *Reshith Chachmah* 1:1 (8d).
62. See *VaYikra Rabbah* 4:8; *Midrash Sh'muel* 5.
63. See Ramban on *Deuteronomy* 22:6; *Sefer HaChinukh* 545; *Nefesh HaChaim* 2:4. Cf. Radak on *Psalms* 16:2.
64. *Bereshith Rabbah* 44:1; *VaYikra Rabbah* 13:3; *Tanchuma Shemini* 8; *Midrash Tehillim* 18:25; *Yalkut* 2:121; *Moreh Nevuchim* 3:26; *Avodath HaKodesh* 2:3; *Shnei Luchoth HaB'rith, Shaar HaGadol* (1:48b); *Tifereth Yisrael* (Maharal) 7.
65. *Yerushalmi Nedarim* 9:1 (29a).
66. *VaYikra Rabbah* 27:2; *BaMidbar Rabbah* 14:2; *Tanchuma Kedoshim* 16.
67. See *Zohar* 2:274a.
68. *Zohar* 3:225a; *Likutey Amarim* (Tanya) 2:7 (83b); *Nefesh HaChaim* 3:4; *Reshith Chachmah,* 1:1 (9a).
69. *Shnei Luchoth HaBrith* 1:44a, 1:64b; *Likutey Amarim* (Tanya) 84a.
70. *Berachoth* 12a; *Zohar* 3:272b.
71. Cf. *Sifri* ad loc. #31.
72. Ibid.
73. *Zohar Chadash, Yithro* 35c.
74. *Bamidbar Rabbah* 12:4; *Pesikta* 1 (2b).
75. *Midrash Tehillim* 24:5.
76. *Kuzari* 1:79 (47a), 1:98 (66b), 2:46 (54b), 3:23 (31b).
77. *Berachoth* 6a; *Avoth* 3:5.
78. *Sanhedrin* 39a.
79. *Ibn Ezra* on *Exodus* 13:21; *Emunoth VeDeyoth* 2:11; *Kuzari* 2:7,8; *Moreh Nevuchim* 1:27; Ramban on *Genesis* 47:1.
80. *Mechilta* on *Exodus* 13:21 (25a).
81. *Taanith* 21b.
82. *Succoth* 53a, according to Rashi.
83. *Kiddushin* 31a.
84. See *Pardes Rimonim* 6:8; *Likutey Amarim* (Tanya) 2:2 (77b).
85. See *Metzudoth* ad loc.; *Tosafoth Yom Tov* on *Tamid* 7:4 s.v. *"LeChayay."*
86. *Zohar* 2:42b; *Tikuney Zohar* 3a, 62a; *Reshith Chochmah* 7a, 8c,d; Radak on *Jeremiah* 23:24.
87. *Shomer Emunim* (HaKadmon) 2:11.
88. *Midrash Tehillim* 119:36.
89. *Thirteen Principles of Faith* #10.
90. *Tanchuma Nasa* 5; *Yalkut* 2:305.

91. See *Yerushalmi Rosh HaShanah* 1:3 (8a).
92. *Sh'moth Rabbah* 21:3.
93. *Bereshith Rabbah* 9:3.
94. *Sanhedrin* 90b.
95. *Tanna DeBei Eliahu Zuta* 23 (50b).
96. *Elemah Rabathai* 1:2:18; *Or HaChaim* on *Genesis* 6:6; *Meshekh Chakhmah* on *Genesis* 1:26.
97. *Yerushalmi Rosh HaShanah* 1:3 (7b).
98. *Bereshith Rabbah* 27:7.
99. *Sifri*, Rashi, on *Numbers* 12:8.
100. *Yalkut* 1:396. Cf. *Chulin* 60a.
101. *Shefa Tal*, Introduction (4d); *Likutey Amarim* (Tanya) 2:6 (81a).
102. *Chulin* 60b. Cf. *Zohar* 3:47b.
103. *Bamidbar Rabbah* 12:3.
104. *Tikuney Zohar* 17a.
105. *Likutey Amarim* (Yanya) 2:9 (86b).
106. Cf. *Chagigah* 13b; *Yad, Yesodey HaTorah* 2:8.

IF YOU WERE GOD

IMMORTALITY AND THE SOUL

A WORLD OF LOVE

IF YOU
WERE GOD

I form light and create darkness,
   I make peace and create evil,
   I am God, I do all these things . . .
Woe to the man who strives with his Maker . . .
   "What are you making?"
   or shall it say,
   "Your work has no place?"
Woe to the man who says to his Father,
   "Why have you conceived me?"
   or to his mother,
   "Why did you bear me?" . . .
Surely, You are a God Who hides,
   the God of Israel,
   the One Who saves.

Isaiah 45

I. The Problem

You are given an island where several tribes live.

By nature and culture, these tribes are exploitative and belligerent. This results in much suffering on the island, caused by war, poverty and prejudice.

They have been living this way for centuries without any sign of improvement.

❧ Your Assignment:

To try to improve this society.

To teach its members to live together in harmony and reduce suffering to a minimum or eliminate it entirely.

To create a healthy society.

❧ Your Resources:

You have all the resources that a highly advanced technology can offer.

You have the entire island under surveillance and can see what is happening in any place at any time.

You have such devices as cloud-seeding equipment and can plant underground explosives. Within reason, you can control weather, flooding, volcanoes and earthquakes, and produce any "natural" phenomenon on cue.

You also have devices that can be used to implant ideas through subliminal suggestion. You can implant ideas to entire populations or to certain select leaders.

However, you must take into account the severe limitations of subliminal suggestion. If you try to implant any ideas that go against the basic nature of the populace, they will be totally rejected and your efforts will be in vain.

One alternative would be to implant ideas that somehow

would make use of the acknowledged bad nature of these people.

ᴥᶳ Your Restrictions:

Under no circumstances are the natives of this island to be aware of your presence.

This supersedes all other considerations.

The cultural shock caused by your revealing yourself would disrupt the entire fabric of the island culture. It would cause much suffering and more than offset any good that you could possibly accomplish.

The natives would be reduced to a state of almost vegetable-like dependence from which they would be unlikely to recover. If they did recover, they might rebel so violently as to eliminate any positive values they might have originally had.

Therefore, the restriction that you not reveal yourself must be followed *without exception under any circumstances.*

But aside from this restriction, you have a free hand to proceed as humanely or as ruthlessly as you see fit.

In short, you have the opportunity to play God.

What would you do?

II. The Questions

Many people say that these days it is very difficult to believe. We live in a generation that has seen the brutal murder of the six million. We have seen children burned to death in Vietnam, babies starved in Biafra, and a nation systematically decimated in Bangladesh. We see starvation, poverty and inequality wherever we look. Good people suffer and the dishonest seem to thrive.

Many people ask what seems to be a legitimate question: Why does God allow these things? Why doesn't He do something about it?

To some extent, the answer should be obvious. It is man, not God, who brings most evil to the world.[1] God does not make wars — men do. God did not kill the six million — men did. God does not oppress the poor — men do. God does not drop napalm — men do.

But people come back and argue that this does not really answer the question. The basic dilemma still remains: Why did God create the possibility of evil? Why does He allow it to exist at all?

To even begin to understand this, we must delve into the very purpose of creation.

This purpose requires a creature responsible for its own actions. This in turn requires that men have free will.

If God would have wanted a race of puppets, then He would have created puppets. If He would have wanted robots, then He would have made robots. But this is not what God wanted. He wanted human beings, with free will, responsible for their actions.

But as soon as you have free will, you have the possibility of evil.

If You Were God □ 179

The deeper we probe, the clearer this becomes.

To the best of our understanding, God created the universe as an act of love.[2] It was an act of love so immense that the human mind cannot even begin to fathom it. God created the world basically as a vehicle upon which He could bestow His good.[3]

But God's love is so great that any good that He bestows must be the greatest good possible. Anything less would simply not be enough.

But what is the greatest good? What is the ultimate good that God can bestow on His creation?

If you think for a moment the answer should be obvious. The ultimate good is God Himself. The greatest good that He can bestow is Himself. There is no greater good than achieving a degree of unity with the Creator Himself. It is for this reason that God gave man the ability to resemble Himself.[4]

God therefore gave man free will.

Just as God acts as a free Being, so does man. Just as God operates without prior restraint, so does man. Just as God can do good as a matter of His own choice, so can man. According to many commentators, this is the meaning of man being created in the "image" of God.[5]

But if God's purpose does not permit man to be a robot, neither does it permit him to be a prisoner.

Just as man has free will, he must also have freedom of choice. A man locked up in prison may have the same free will as everybody else, but there is little that he can do with it. For man to resemble his Creator to the greatest possible extent, he must exist in an arena where he has a maximum freedom of choice. The more man resembles God in His omnipotence, the closer he can resemble Him in his free choice of the good.

To make this freedom of choice real, God also had to create the possibility of evil.[6] If nothing but good were possible, it would produce no benefit. To use the Talmudic metaphor, it would be like carrying a lamp in broad daylight.[7] The *Zohar* thus states, "The advantage of wisdom comes from darkness. If there were no darkness, then light would not be discernible, and would produce no benefit . . . Thus, it is written (*Ecclesiates* 7:14), 'God has made one thing opposite the other.' "[8]

Just as God's purpose does not allow man to be a physical prisoner, neither does it permit him to exist in an intellectual prison. How would man behave if God were to constantly reveal Himself? Would he really be free? If man were constantly made aware that he was standing in the King's presence, could he go against His will? If God's existence were constantly apparent, this awareness would make man a prisoner.

This is one reason why God created a world which follows natural laws, and in this way conceals Himself.[9] Thus, our sages teach us, "The world follows its natural pattern, and the fools who do evil will eventually be judged."[10]

This is the concept of the Sabbath. After the initial act of creation, God withdrew, as it were, and allowed the world to operate according to laws of nature which He had created.[11] The "clock" had been made and wound up, and now could run with a minimum of interference. When we observe the Sabbath, we similarly refrain from interfering or making any permanent changes in the order of nature.[12]

But the questioner can probe still deeper. He can ask: Why did God allow so much evil to exist in man's nature to begin with? Why does it seem so natural for man to oppress his neighbor and make him suffer?

But here also, we must realize that man's arena of action is here in the physical world, and therefore he must be part of a universe where God's presence is eclipsed. The spiritual in man may soar in the highest transcendental realms, but man's body is essentially that of an animal.[13] Our sages teach us that man partakes of the essence of both angel and beast.[14] The Zohar goes a step further and tells us that in addition to the divine soul which separates man from lower forms of life, man also has an animal soul.[15]

When man first came into existence, there was a basic harmony existing between these two parts of his nature. His intellect and animal nature were able to exist together without any intrinsic conflict. He had the opportunity to live in harmony with nature, devoting all his energies to the spiritual.[16]

However, there was an element of temptation in this Garden

of Eden. Man's destiny was to transcend his animal nature on a spiritual plane. But he also had the temptation to transcend it on a physical level, to partake of the Tree of Good and Evil.

Man succumbed to this temptation.

This Knowledge then came between the two basic elements in man, the animal and the human.[17] Man was no longer like the animal, bound to nature, in harmony with his basic nature. He still had all the desires, lusts and aggressive nature of the animal. But he also acquired the ability to use his intellect so that his animal nature would be directed against his fellow human beings. It is this conflict between his animal and human nature that thrusts man in the direction of evil. We are therefore taught that it is man's animal nature that is responsible for the *Yetzer HaRa, the evil in man.* [18]

But here again, God cannot be blamed.

The decision to partake of the Tree of Knowledge — to transcend his animal nature on a worldly plane — was a decision that man made as a matter of free choice.

As soon as man partook of the Tree of Knowledge, he *knew* good and evil. Morality became a matter of knowledge and conscious choice, rather than part of man's basic nature. He would now have to wrestle with a new nature, where the animal and angel in him are in conflict.

But we can probe still further. We can ask: Why could man not have been made better? Why did God not make him into something that was more angel and less animal?

Here too, the fault was man's. Our sages teach us that the prohibition against tasting the fruit of the Tree of Knowledge was only temporary. Man's spiritual nature was gradually developing in such a manner that he would have eventually been strong enough to master his animal instincts. When this time arrived, he could have partaken of the Tree of Knowledge without endangering his spiritual essence.[19]

Man was indeed destined to be more angel and less animal. However, this was now to be a gradual process. It was aborted by man's impatience, his partaking of Knowledge before its time. It was this Knowledge that brought him in conflict with his animal nature, and stunted his spiritual development, making the beast dominant.

This thread runs through the entire history of mankind. Man's knowledge gave him a technology that could create instruments of destruction, but his moral strength was not great enough to avoid misusing them. This has reached its peak in our generation, where man has the power to destroy his entire planet, either with nuclear weapons, or by poisoning his environment. Man's knowledge gives him tremendous power, but he still has not learned how to use this power for the good. This is the reason why the Messianic Age must soon arrive. Only then will man learn how to use his knowledge for the good.[20]

Until then, man is faced with this great dilemma. He has the knowledge to create great societies, but they always get out of control and degenerate. He can make great technological strides, but he does not have the moral strength to use them for good. One of the saddest comments on the human predicament is the fact that many of our greatest technological advancements have been made to further the cause of warfare.

Still, the basic question does not seem to go away. Admittedly, man has an evil nature and it is his own fault. But why doesn't God intervene? Why doesn't He open up the heavens and stop all this evil? Why didn't He send down a bolt of lightning and destroy the concentration camps? Why didn't He send down some kind of manna for the starving babies of Biafra and Bangladesh? Why didn't He stop the napalm bombs from burning innocent Vietnamese children? Why doesn't He pull off a miracle and make all the world's nuclear bombs disappear? After all, He is God. He certainly can do it. So why doesn't He?

We are taught, however, that an overabundance of light does not rectify the vessels, but shatters them.[21]

What would happen to our society if miracles suddenly started taking place? How would we react to it?

Could we go about our daily affairs as if nothing had happened? Could the vast, complex structures, upon which our civilization rests, continue to exist if this direct awareness of God were suddenly thrust upon us?

Take a city like New York. It takes the efforts of tens of thousands to provide food and other necessities to such a huge city, and further thousands just to transport these needs. It takes another army to provide the city with water, electricity, heat, and the removal of waste. Could this structure survive the awareness of miracles? And if it did not, would not the suffering be all the greater? If God began a miraculous intervention, would He not have to do it all the way? Indeed, this might take place in the Messianic Age, but then, the time must be ripe.

How would we react to miracles? Probably very much in the same way primitive societies react to the "miracles" of those that are more advanced. The first reaction is one of shock, or what sociologists call cultural shock. The natives first lose interest in everything and become completely dependent on the more advanced culture. They cease to have a mind of their own and develop a lethargy where life grows devoid of meaning. The degeneration of the proud self-sufficient savage into the shifty, no-account native is often as tragic as it is inevitable.

If a society is not completely destroyed by the initial cultural shock, it undergoes a second stage, that of rebellion. The primitive culture rebels against both the invaders and their values. This is why so many missionaries ended up in the proverbial cooking pot.

If man resembles an animal, then he resembles a wild animal rather than a domestic one.[22] It is man's destiny to be free, not subject to other men. Thus, the inevitable result of the introduction of a higher culture is to overwhelm a more primitive one.[23]

When a higher culture is introduced, the initial reaction of the natives is to become domesticated, to become like cattle or sheep. If the domestication is complete, the humanity of the native is obliterated, at least, until he assimilates the dominant culture. Otherwise, the natives rebel and reassert their natural humanity.

The same is essentially true of our relationship to God. As long as He is hidden, we can strive toward Him, and attain the Godly. But we do this as a matter of free choice and are not overwhelmed by it. But if God were to reveal Himself, the man would no longer be able to exist as a free entity. He would know that he was always under the scrutiny of his Master, and that would make him into something less than a man. He would become some kind of puppet or robot, with an essential ingredient of his humanness destroyed. The only alternative would be rebellion.

But either alternative could cause more evil and suffering than would be alleviated by God's original intervention. There would be too much light, and the vessels would be shattered.

There was only one time when God literally revealed Himself and visibly stepped in and changed the course of history. This was at the Exodus from Egypt, where He performed miracles both in Egypt and by the Red Sea. This episode was climaxed by the Revelation at Sinai, where an entire nation literally heard the voice of God.

What happened then?

The first reaction at Sinai was one of shock. The people simply could not endure the majesty of God's word, and our sages teach us that their souls literally left them.[24] Their reaction is expressed in the Biblical account of Sinai, where immediately afterward they told Moses (*Ex.* 20:16), "You speak to us and we will listen, but let not God speak with us any more, for we will die."

When the people overcame their initial shock, they proceeded to the second stage, that of rebellion. This took place just 40 days after the Revelation at Sinai. They went against God and all His teachings, reverting to idolatry and worshipping a golden calf. They had heard the Ten Commandments from God Himself just 40 days earlier, and now they were violating every one of them.

We learn a very important lesson from this. For God to reveal Himself to an unworthy vessel can do more harm than good. This is one important reason why God does not show His hand.

Many people say that they would believe if only they could witness some sign or miracle. Sinai showed us that even this is not enough if people do not want to believe.

From all this we can begin to understand one of the most basic restrictions that God imposes upon Himself. He is a hidden God, and does not reveal Himself. This is required by man's psychology as well as God's very purpose in creation. God only reveals Himself to such people whose faith is so great that the revelation makes no difference in their belief. As the Rambam (Maimonides) points out, the only major exception to this rule was the Exodus.[25]

III. The Solutions

Taking into account God's most basic self-restrictions, we can now make some attempt to place ourselves in God's place. Our most basic restriction is that we not reveal our hand.

Taking this restriction into account, we can return to our opening problem, and imagine a microcosm where we are in a position to play God.

This opening problem was discussed in a number of groups, and much of what follows is a result of their conclusions. However, before reading on, you might wish to re-read the problem, and attempt to draw your own conclusions.

Much of the discussion revolved around solutions involving something like a huge chess game with the entire island as the board. There would be moves and countermoves, with a strategy to attempt to maneuver the natives into a desired position. Like a chess grandmaster, you would attempt to keep control of the game at all times. Your "win" would be to achieve the desired result.

While you have enough resources to eventually win, certain problems immediately become apparent. Not the least is the fact that every move may take decades or even centuries. You might achieve results, but it is a very long, drawn-out process. You might have all the time in the world, but each year brings all the more suffering.

There is an even more profound problem. Even more important than influencing events is our ultimate goal of improving the values of the natives. However, even though a lesson may be learned by one generation, it may be equally forgotten by a succeeding generation. To make positive values an integral part of the island's culture is a most formidable task.

A constant thread of suggestion in these discussions involved infiltration. We could try to influence the island through infiltrators. As long as it was not obvious, it would be within the rules.

Such infiltration could serve two purposes. First of all, we could use the infiltrators as an example. They could set up a model society, and if it endured long enough, it might interest people in attempting to emulate it or learn from it.

The infiltrators could also be used to teach the natives directly. Gradually, parts of their culture could be introduced to the island, raising its moral level. This could rapidly accelerate the game's conclusion.

These infiltrators would always be in a position of great peril. Operating on a different value system, they would always be considered outsiders. The more their message diverged from that of the majority, the more they would be resented. Scattered throughout the island to spread their message, they would very likely become a persecuted minority. By the rules of the game, there would be very little you could do to help them. At best, you would play your game in such a way as to protect them as much as possible.

Because of the danger of revealing your hand, communication with your infiltrators would have to be kept to a minimum. They would have to live on this island for many generations, scattered among the natives, and you would have to set up many safeguards to prevent them from assimilating the corrupt values of the island. To some extent, their status as a persecuted minority may also help prevent such assimilation. But essentially, they would have to play their role in ignorance of your overall strategy.

Gradually, the islanders would eventually become aware of your presence. Once the game was ended, you might even be able to reveal yourself. The infiltrators' role would also then be revealed. As part of your organization, they would become the natural leaders and teachers of the island.

IV. The Conclusion

As you might have already guessed, examining this microcosm gives us considerable insight into the way that God interacts with the world. He is working to bring the world to a state of perfection, which in our tradition is the Messianic promise. It is a slow process, whereby God constantly maneuvers the forces of history toward this end. This "game" is essentially all of human history.

You might have also recognized the infiltrators. They are the Jewish people, who were given the basis of a perfect society in the teachings of the Torah. A society living according to these God-given principles can set itself up as an example of a healthy society, free of all the social diseases of its surrounding culture.

When God first gave the Torah, He told the Jewish people (*Lev*. 20:26), "You shall be holy unto Me, for I, the Lord, am holy, and I have set you apart from the peoples, that you should be Mine."[26] It is Israel's mission to set such an example, as the Torah states (*Deut*. 4:6), "You must observe (these commandments) carefully and keep them, for they are your wisdom and understanding in the sight of the nations — when they hear of these statutes, they will say, 'Surely, this great nation is a wise and understanding people.' "

It is our task to bear witness to God's plan for humanity, as we find (*Isaiah* 43:10), "You are My witnesses, says God, and My servant, whom I have chosen."[27] Likewise, God told His prophet (*ibid*. 42:6), "I, the Lord, have called you in righteousness . . . and have set you for a covenant of the people, for a light unto the nations."[28]

We are thus taught that Israel is like the heart of humanity, constantly beating and infusing all mankind with faith in God and His teachings.[29]

It was in this spirit that Judaism gave birth to both Christianity and Islam. Although far from perfection, these religions are a step in the right direction away from paganism.[30] The final step is yet to be made.

More important, however, is the fact that the Jewish people, at least those who keep the Torah, continue to stand as an example of a perfect society designed by God. The Torah and its commandments indeed represent the highest wisdom in perfecting human society. The Tzadik is the closest that we can come to the perfect human being.

Israel's unique position in accepting God's Torah will eventually result in the destruction of all competing cultures. It would also temporarily result in Israel's earning the hatred of these cultures.[31] Our sages teach us that just as an olive must be crushed before it brings forth its oil, so is Israel often persecuted before its light shines forth.[32] Thus, God told His prophet (*Isaiah* 42:3,4), "A bruised reed, he shall not break; a dimly burning wick, he shall not be extinguished; he shall make justice shine forth in truth. He shall not fail nor be crushed, until he has right in the earth, and the islands shall await the teachings of his Torah."[33]

We live in an age of many questions. The newspapers and television bring the horrors of the word onto our front doorstep and into our living rooms. What was once hidden by the barrier of intercontinental distance is now before our very eyes. We see the suffering and killing and starvation, and ask how God can tolerate such evil. For the Jew, the question of the six million always looms in the foreground of any such discussion.

But for one who understands the true depths of Judaism, there is no question. When you have probed into the very reason for existence and purpose of creation, not only do you find answers, but the questions themselves cease to exist.

One of the great Jewish leaders of today is the Klausenberger Rebbe. He lost his wife, children and family to the Nazis, and himself spent two years in the hell of Auschwitz. Yet, he emerged from all this to rally a generation of concentration camp refugees back to Judaism, found a community in

Williamsburg, and eventually build a settlement in Israel.

I often heard this great leader discuss the concentration camps and the six million. There are tears and sadness, but no questions. For here we have a Tzadik, whose great mind can see beyond the immediate. When one's gaze is on the Ultimate, there truly are no questions.

The most important thing to remember is that God is the ultimate good, and therefore, even the worst evil will eventually revert to good.[34] Man may do evil, but even this will be redeemed by God and ultimately be turned into good. The Talmud teaches us that in this world we must bless God for both good and evil, but in the Future World, we will realize that there is nothing but good.[35]

NOTES

1. *Moreh Nevuchim* 3:10.
2. Cf. *Magid Devarab LeYaakov* # 102, *Likutey Moharan* # 64.
3. *Emunos VeDeyos* 1:4 end, 3:0, *Or HaShem* (Crescas) 2:6:2, *Sefer HaYashar* 1, *Pardes Rimonim* 2:6, *Sheur Kuma* (RaMaK) 13:3, *Etz Chaim, Shaar HaKellalim* #1, *Reshis Chochmah, Shaar HaTshuvah* #1, *Shnei Luchos HaBris, Bais Yisroel* (Jerusalem 5720) 1:21b, *Shomrei Emunim (HaKadmon)* 2:13, *Mesilas Yesharim* #1, *Derech HaShem* 1:2:1.
4. *Derech HaShem*, ibid.
5. Cf. *Mechilta* on *Ex.* 14:29, *Bereshis Rabbah* 21:5, *Shir HaShirim Rabbah* 1:46, *Yad, Tshuvah* 5:1.
6. Cf. *Midrash Tehillim* 36:4, *Zohar* 1:23a, 2:184a, *Akedas Yitzchok* 70 (3:145b), *Etz Chaim, Shaar HaMelachim* 5, *Sefer Baal Shem Tov, Sh'mos* #9.
7. *Chulin* 60b.
8. *Zohar* 3:47b.
9. *Bereshis Rabbah* 9:6, *Menoras HaMaor* 237, *Tosefos Yom Tov* on *Avodah Zarah* 4:7, cf. *Ikkarim* 4:12 on *Eccl.* 8:11.
10. *Avodah Zarah* 54b.
11. *Moreh Nevuchim* 2:28 on *Ps.* 148:6. Cf. *Zohar* 1:138b, *Berachos* 60b. Also see *Rashi, Ibn Ezra, Sforno* on *Eccl.* 3:14.
12. *Shabbos* 12:1 (102b).
13. *Sifrei, Haazinu* 306, *Bereshis Rabbah* 8:11, *Rashi* in *Gen.* 2:7.
14. *Chagigah* 16a.
15. *Zohar* 2:94b.
16. Cf. *Ramban* on *Gen.* 2:9; *Kiddushin* 4:14 (82a).
17. *Kisvey HaAri: Shemonah Shaarim, Shaar HaPesukim* on *Gen.* 2:17, *Likutey Torah (HaAri)* on *Gen.* 3:1.
18. *Etz Chaim, Shaar Kitzur ABYA* #3 ff; *Shaarey Kedusha* #1, *Likutey Amarim (Tanya)* #1.
19. *Toras Moshe (Chasam Sofer)* on *Gen.* 2:17, *Tosefos, Sanhedrin* 56b "Lo." See note 17.
20. See note 17. Also see *Bechaya* on *Gen.* 2:9; *Derech HaShem* 1:3.
21. *Etz Chaim, Shaar HaMelachim* 5.
22. See *Kelayim* 8:5, where the *Adney HaSadeh* is found to have an affinity to both a wild animal (*Chayah*) and man. *Meleches Shlema* ibid. 8:6.
23. *Zohar* 1:24b, *Maharal, Beer HaGolah* (Pardes, Tel Aviv) p. 39b. Cf. *Shabbos* 89b, *Sh'mos Rabbah* 2:6.
24. *Zohar* 2:84b.
25. *Moreh Nevuchim* 2:35, from *Deut.* 34:1.
26. See *Rashi* ad loc. Cf. *Lev.* 19:2.
27. *Mahari Kara* ad loc., *Ikkarim* 1:2. Cf. *Isa.* 43:21, 44:8.
28. This is part of the famous "suffering servant" passage in Isaiah. According to *Rashi* and the *Mahari Kara,* this is speaking of Israel. See *Midrash Tehillim* 2:9. However, others, such as the *Targum, Radak* and *Metzudos,* state that it refers to the Messiah. See *Midrash Tehillim* 43:1. *Ibn Ezra,* on the other hand, states that it refers to the prophet himself. For further discussion, see *Abarbanel* ad loc.

29. *Zohar* 2:221b, *Kuzari* 3:36 (51b), 2:12 (13a).
30. *Kuzari* 4:23, *Tshuvos Rambam* 58, *Tshuvos Rivash* 119, *Akedas Yitzchok* 88.
31. See note 23.
32. *Sh'mos Rabbah* 36:1.
33. See note 28. Cf. *Menachos* 53b.
34. Rabbi Moshe Chaim Luzatto, *KaLaCh Pis'chey Chochmah* #2.
35. *Pesachim* 50a.

IMMORTALITY
AND THE SOUL

I. Meet the Real You

Look at your hand. What do you see?

A part of your body, an appendage made of bone and sinew covered with flesh and skin. It is filled with nerves, blood vessels and lymph ducts which run through it and connect it to your body, making it part of you.

You can open and close your hand. It obeys every command that your mind sends to it. It is yours — a part of you. But what are you? Who is the real you? What happens when you tell your hand to open and close? How does your mind will it to obey its commands?

Now point a finger at yourself. If you are an average person, you will point a finger at your chest. You think of yourself as your body. But is your body the real you?

Not too long ago, a person could consider his own body an integral part of himself. You were your body and your body was you. But this is no longer the case. Scientific progress has changed the entire concept of human personality and identity.

Heart transplants are now an almost commonplace occurrence. They do not even make the news anymore. A man can live with another person's heart beating in his breast. If we would ask such a man to point to himself, would he point at his heart? Is this transplanted heart really part of him? Is the heart that beats within your breast the real you? Or is it something else entirely?

Researchers are predicting that within the next decade or two, brain transplants may be possible. This would force us to completely reevaluate the concept of human personality.

Imagine what it would be like to undergo a brain transplant. A man might be suffering from an incurable disease in his body, but still have a healthy brain. The donor, on the other hand, would have suffered irreparable brain damage, but otherwise have a perfectly sound body. The brain is removed from the sick body and placed in the healthy one.

Who is the new man? We have an old brain with all its memories, personality traits and behavior patterns. But it has a brand new body. The old body might have been old and sick, while the new one may be young and full of energy.

Let us ask this man to point to himself. Will he point to his body? Is the real you your body or your brain?

(Actually, an analogous question is raised in the Talmud. As is well known, in the case of an unsolved murder, a special sacrifice, the *Eglah Arufah*, was brought by the city nearest the corpse.[1] The Mishnah raises two questions. What if the head is found in one place and the body in another?[2] And if the body is equidistant from the two cities, from what portion of the body do we measure?[3] In both cases, Rabbi Eliezer states that we measure from the body, while Rabbi Akiba states that we measure from the head. The *Halachah* follows Rabbi Akiba.)[4]

A brain transplant raises enough questions. How about a memory transfer?

The science of cybernetics has discovered many similarities between computers and the human brain. Computer technology allows one to program a memory transfer, taking all the information contained in one computer and transferring it to another. All that passes from one computer to the other is information.

What if this were done with the human brain? This may lie in the realm of science fiction, but even if it will never be possible in practice, it is certainly possible in theory.

Let us try to envision such a memory transfer. Assume we have a person with an incurable disease where neither the body nor the brain can be salvaged. We clone a new body for this individual, brain and all. The possibilities of doing this have already been discussed at length in the literature. This new body has a blank new brain, capable of functioning, but without any memories or thought patterns. As a final step, we accomplish a memory transfer, bringing all the information from the sick person into the brain of the new body.

We now have a fascination situation. If all of a man's

memories, thought patterns and personality traits are transferred to a new body and brain, this person literally exists in his new body. But nothing physical has been transferred. No physical part of him has been placed in the new body. All that has been placed in this new body is information that previously existed in the old brain. Yet this information contains the sum total of this person's personality.

But if this is true, then it offers us tremendous new insight into our original question: Who is the real you?

The real you is not your body or brain, but the information contained in your brain — your memories, personality traits and thought patterns.

(The philosophical Kabbalists write that the spiritual world is a realm whose substance is information. It is an arena where information can interact without being attached to or dependent on matter. Thus, an angel, for example, can interact with another angel, even though they have no connection with anything material. Angels can also interact with material objects. Such a spiritual world would also be able to interact with the information comprising the human persona.)

What happens then when a person dies?

We know that the body ceases to function. The brain becomes inert and the physical man is dead.

But what happens to the real you — the human personality? What happens to all this information — the memories, thought patterns and personality traits? When a book is burned its contents are no longer available. When a computer is smashed, the information within it is also destroyed. Does the same thing happen when a man dies? Is the mind and personality irretrievably lost?

We know that God is omniscient. He knows all and does not forget. God knows every thought and memory that exists within our brains. There is no bit of information that escapes His knowledge.

What, then, happens when a man dies? God does not forget, and therefore all of this information continues to exist, at least in God's memory.

(An allusion to this is also found in the Kaballah. *Gan Eden* or *Paradise* is said to exist in the *sephirah* of *Binah* — the divine understanding.[5] This may well be related to the concept of memory. Souls, on the other hand, are conceived in the *sephirah* of *Daas* — knowledge.[6] One may say that while we live, we exist in God's knowledge (*Daas*), while after death we exist in His memory (*Binah*).)

We may think of something existing only in memory as being static and effectively dead. But God's memory is not a static thing. The sum total of a human personality may indeed exist in God's memory, but it can still maintain its self-identity and volition, and remain in an active state.

This sum total of the human personality existing in God's memory is what lives on even after a man dies.

(This may well be why the Kabbalists speak of this as *Binah* — understanding, rather than memory. For understanding is a dynamic process, where information contained in one's memory interacts in an active manner. The soul is not in a passive memory state, but in a dynamic state of *Binah*.)

The concept of immortality and of the soul may well be outside the realm of human comprehension. "No eye has seen it other than God." However, our limited understanding of both God and man can provide us with some degree of perception into our ultimate future.

(In a Kabbalistic sense, we are here speaking about the lowest level of the soul, the *Nefesh HaBehemis* or "animal soul."[7] This most probably can be identified with the information contained in the human brain. However, this interacts with the higher parts of the soul, *Nefesh, Ruach* and *Neshamah*.)

To speak of a concept such as God's memory is indeed very difficult. It involves a deep discussion of the entire transcendental sphere. We therefore give it names that have meaning to us, such as *Gan Eden*, Paradise, the World to Come, the World of Souls,[8] or the bond of eternal life. However, the Bible speaks of immortality as a return to God Himself (*Eccl*. 12:7): "The dust returns to the dust as it were, but the spirit returns to God Who gave it."

II. Naked Before God

We have seen that our knowledge of the mind and our traditions regarding God can give us some handle on the question of immortality.

But what is immortality like? What is it like to be a disembodied soul? How does it feel to be in the World of Soul?

We know that the human brain, marvelous organ that it is, is still very inefficient as a thinking device. Henri Bergson has suggested that one of the main functions of the brain and nervous system is to eliminate activity and awareness, rather than produce it.

Aldous Huxley[9] quotes Prof. C.D. Broad's comments on this. He says that every person is capable of remembering everything that has ever happened to him. He is able to perceive everything that surrounds him. However, if all this information poured into our minds at once, it would over-whelm us. So the function of the brain and nervous system is to protect us and prevent us from being overwhelmed and confused by the vast amount of information that impinges upon our sense organs. They shut out most of what we perceive and remember. All that would confound us is eliminated and only the small, special selection that is useful is allowed to remain.

Huxley explains that our mind has powers of perception and concentration that we cannot even begin to imagine. But our main business is to survive at all costs. To make survival possible, all of our mind's capabilities must be funneled through the reducing valve of the brain.

Some researchers are studying this effect. They believe that this reducing-valve effect may be very similar to the jamming equipment used to block out offensive radio broadcasts. The brain constantly produces a kind of static, cutting down our perception and reducing our mental activity.

This static can actually be seen. When you close your eyes, you see all sorts of random pictures flashing through your mind. It is impossible to concentrate on any one of them for more than an instant, and each image is obscured by a host of others superimposed over it.

This static can even be seen when your eyes are opened. However, one usually ignores these images since they are so faint compared to our visual perception. However, they still reduce one's perception, both of the world around him and of himself.

Much of what we know about this static is a result of research done with drugs that eliminate it. According to a number of authorities, this is precisely how the psychedelic drugs work.

Now imagine the mental activity of a disembodied soul, standing naked before God. The reducing valve is gone entirely. The mind is open and transparent. Things can be perceived in a way that is impossible to a mind held back by a body and nervous system. The visions and understanding are the most delightful bliss imaginable (as per: "the righteous, sitting with their crowns on their heads, delighting in the shine of the *Shechinah*"[10]).

This is what Job meant when he said (19:26), "And when after my skin is destroyed, then without my flesh shall I see God."

But then, an individual will also see himself in a new light. Every thought and memory will be lucid, and he will see himself for the first time without the static and jamming that shuts out most thoughts.

Even in our mortal physical state, looking at oneself can sometimes be pleasing and at other times very painful. Certain acts leave us proud and pleased with ourselves. Others cause excruciating pains, especially when we are caught.

Imagine standing naked before God, with your memory wide open, completely transparent without any jamming mechanism or reducing valve to diminish its force. You will remember everything you ever did and see it in a new light. You will see it in the light of the unshaded spirit, or, if you will, in God's own light that shines from one end of creation to the other. The memory of every good deed and *Mitzvah* will be the sublimest of pleasures, as our tradition speaks of *Olam Haba*.

But your memory will also be open to all the things of which you are ashamed. They cannot be rationalized away or dismissed. You will be facing yourself, fully aware of the consequences of all your deeds. We all know the terrible shame and humiliation experienced when one is caught in the act of doing something wrong. Imagine being caught by one's own memory with no place to escape. This indeed, may be what Daniel is alluding to when he says (*Dan*. 12:2), "And many of them that sleep in the dust shall awake, some to everlasting life, and some to reproach and everlasting shame."

A number of our great teachers[11] write that the fire of *Gehenom* is actually the burning shame one experiences because of his sins. Again, this may be alluded to in the words of the prophet (*Isa*. 66:24), "And they shall go forth and look upon the carcasses of the men that have rebelled against Me; for their worm shall not die, nor shall their fire be quenched, and they shall be ashamed before all flesh." We find that evil leads to shame, as it is written (*Jer*. 7:19), "Are they angering Me, says God, are they not provoking themselves, to their own shame . . . Behold My anger . . . shall not burn, and shall not be quenched." The main concept of reward is that it be without shame, as we find (*Joel* 2:26), "And you shall eat and be satisfied . . . and my people shall never be ashamed."

The Talmud provides us with even stronger evidence that shame burns like fire. It states, "Rabbi Chanana says: This teaches us that each one (in the World of Souls) is burned by the canopy of his companion. Woe, for that shame! Woe, for that humiliation."[12] We find that shame is a major form of punishment. In the Midrash on the verse (*Ps*. 6:11), "All your enemies shall be ashamed and very confounded," Rabbi Joshua ben Levi says, "God only curses the wicked with shame."[13] This is also alluded to in the Talmudic statement, "It is better for Amram to suffer shame in this world, and not in the World to Come."[14] Similarly, "Blessed is God Who gave him shame in this world and not the next."[15] When the *Zohar* speaks of the future reward, it says, "Happy is he who comes here without shame."[16]

Of course, these concepts of fire and shame, as used by our Sages, may also contain deeper mysteries and meanings. But taken literally, one says that a major ingredient of fire may be shame.[17] How else could one characterize the agony of unconcealed shame upon a soul?

We are taught that the judgment of the wicked lasts 12 months.[18] Even the naked soul can gradually learn to live with this shame and forget it, and the pain eventually subsides. It may be more than coincidence that 12 months is also the length of time required for something to be forgotten in Talmudic law. Thus, one mourns a parent for 12 months,[19] and says a special blessing upon seeing a close friend after this period of time.[20] (Of course, there is an exception to this rule. There are the nonbelievers and worst of sinners reckoned in the Talmud.[21] These individuals have nothing else but their shame and have no escape from everlasting torment.)

But even temporary torment is beyond our imagination. The Ramban (Nachmanides) writes that all the suffering of Job would not compare to an instant in *Gehenom*.[22] Rabbi Nachman of Breslov says the same of a man who suffered for years from the most indescribable torments: It is still better than a single burn in *Gehenom*.[23] Mental torture cannot be compared to the mere physical.

Here again, when we speak of *Gan Eden* and *Gehenom*, we find that we are not discussing mystical concepts, but ideas that are well within the realm of scientific psychology, such as shame. We can now proceed a step further.

III. What the Dead Think of Us

There is another dimension of immortality discussed in the Talmud. It asks: Do the dead know what is happening in the world of the living?[24]

After an involved discussion, the Talmud concludes that they do have this awareness.[25] The Kabbalistic philosophers explain that the soul achieves a degree of unity with God, the source of all knowledge, and therefore also partakes of His omniscience.

When a man dies, he enters a new world of awareness. He exists as a disembodied soul and yet is aware of what is happening in the physical world. Gradually, he learns to focus on any physical event he wishes. At first this is a frightening experience. You know that you are dead. You can see your body lying there, with your friends and relatives standing around crying over you. We are taught that immediately after death, the soul is in a great state of confusion.[26]

What is the main source of its attention? What draws its focus more than anything else?

We are taught that it is the body. Most people identify themselves with their bodies, as we have discussed earlier. It is difficult for a soul to break this thought habit, and therefore, for the first few days, the soul is literally obsessed with its previous body. This is alluded to in the verse (*Job* 14:22), "And his soul mourns for him."[27]

This is especially true before the body is buried.[28] The soul wonders what will happen to the body. It finds it to be both fascinating and frightening to watch its own body's funeral arrangements and preparation for burial.

Of course, this is one of the reasons why Judaism teaches us that we must have the utmost respect for human remains. We can imagine how painful it is for a soul to see its recent body cast around like an animal carcass. The Torah therefore forbids this.

This is also related to the question of autopsies. We can imagine how a soul would feel when seeing its body lying on the autopsy table, being dissected and examined.

The disembodied soul spends much of its time learning how to focus. It is now seeing without physical eyes, using some process which we do not even have the vocabulary to describe. The Kabbalists call this frightening process *Kaf HaKela* — it is like being thrown with a sling from one end of the world to another.[29] It is alluded to in the verse (*I Sam.* 25:29), "The soul of my master shall be bound up in the bundle of life with the Lord your God, and the souls of your enemies shall He sling out, as from the hollow of a sling." The soul perceives things flashing into focus from all over, and is in a state of total confusion and disorientation.

One of the few things that the soul has little difficulty focusing on is its own body. It is a familiar pattern and some tie seems to remain. To some extent, it is a refuge from its disorientation.

Of course the body begins to decompose soon after it is buried. The effect of watching this must be both frightening and painful. The Talmud teaches us, "Worms are as painful to the dead as needles in the flesh of the living, as it is written (*Job* 14:22), 'his flesh grieves for him.' "[30] Most commentaries write that this refers to the psychological anguish of the soul in seeing its earthly habitation in a state of decay.[31] The Kabbalists call this *Chibut HaKever,* [32] the punishment of the grave. We are taught that what happens to the body in the grave can be an even worse experience than *Gehenom*.[33]

This varies among individuals. The more one is obsessed with one's body and the material world in general during his lifetime, the more he will be obsessed with it after death. For the man to whom the material was everything, this deterioration of the body is most painful. On the other extreme, the person who was immersed in the spiritual may not care very much about the fate of his body at all. He finds himself very much at home in the spiritual realm and might quickly forget about his body entirely. This is what we are taught. Tzadikim are not bothered by *Chibut HaKever* at all, since they never consider their worldly bodies overly important.[34]

In general, adjustment to the spiritual world depends greatly on one's preparation in this world. Our traditions teach us that the main preparation is through Torah.

Many of us think of death as a most frightening experience. Tzadikim, on the other hand, have looked forward to it. Shortly before his death, Rabbi Nachman Breslaver said, "I very much want to divest myself of this garment that is my body."[35] If we truly believe and trust in a merciful God, then death has no terror for us.

This is a description of what our tradition teaches us about the soul's existence. Most of these facts are from the teachings of *Chazal* in the Talmud and Midrash as interpreted by the Kabbalists. Here we have synthesized their interpretations with the terminology of modern scientific concepts. The result is a consistent view of soul and human personality as realities which do not possess the body's temporal discontinuity called "death."

NOTES

1. *Deut.* 21:1-9.
2. *Sotah* 9:3 (45b).
3. Ibid. 9:4.
4. *Yad Chazakah, Rotzeach* 9:9.
5. *Shaarey Orah* 8; *Pardes Rimonim* 8:9, 23:3.
6. *Etz Chaim, Shaar MaN U'MaD* 4, *Shaar HaKlipos* 2.
7. Cf. *Zohar* 2:94b.
8. See *Derech HaShem* 1:3:11.
9. Aldous Huxley, *The Doors of Perception* (Harper & Row, N.Y. 1970) p. 22f.
10. *Berachos* 17a.
11. *Ikkarim* 4:33, *Nishamas Chaim* 1:13.
12. *Baba Basra* 75a.
13. *Midrash Tehilim a. l.*
14. *Kiddushin* 81a.
15. *Yebamos* 105b.
16. *Zohar* 1:4a.
17. *Toras HaAdam, Shaar HaGemul* (Jerusalem, 5715) p. 78a.
18. *Eduyos* 2:10.
19. *Moed Katan* 22b.
20. *Berachos* 58b.
21. *Rosh HaShanah* 17a.
22. *Ramban*, introduction to *Job*.
23. *Sichos HaRan* 235.
24. *Berachos* 18b.
25. See *Tosfos, Shabbos* 153a *"VeNishmaso," Sotah* 34b *"Avoi" Maaver Yavek* 2:25, *Nishmas Chaim* 2:22.
26. *Taz, Yoreh Deah* 339:3. Cf. *Avodah Zara* 20b, *Pirkei Rabbi Eliezer.*
27. *Shabbos* 152a, *Midrash Ne'elam, Zohar* 1:122b.
28. *Shabbos* 152b, *Sefer Mitzvos Gadol, Esin DeRabanan* 2 (Vinitzia, 5307) p. 246a.
29. *Shabbos*, ibid., *Maharsha a. l., Zohar* 1:217b, 3:185b, 222b.
30. *Berachos* 18b, *Shabbos* 152a.
31. *Emunos VeDeyos* 6:7, *Tshuvos Rashba* 369, *Sefer Chasidim* 1163, *Tosfos Yom Tov* 2:7, *Tshuvos Sh'vus Yaakov* 2:97, Zvi Hirsh Chayos on *Shabbos* 13b. Cf. *Tanchuma, VaYikra* 8.
32. *Emunos VeDeyos*, ibid., *Nishmas Chaim* 2:24, *Maaver Yavak* 2:7.
33. *Midrash Chibut HaKever* in *Reshis Chochmah, Shaar HaYirah* 12, #3.
34. *Emunos VeDeyos*, ibid. Cf. *Midrash Ne'elam, Zohar* 1:123a.
35. *Sichos HaRan* 179.

A WORLD OF LOVE

The Purpose of Creation

I.

Why did God create the world?

The question is both very simple, and yet, at the same time, involves some of the most sublime mysteries. For the truth is that we do not have the power to understand God, and just as we cannot understand Him, so can we not understand His reasons. But if we cannot understand God, we can try to understand the world, and ask why it exists. We can look and see what God Himself has taught us about the purpose of creation, both in the Bible and in our traditions.

As our sages teach us, there is absolutely nothing positive that we can say about God Himself. He exists — and we can say no more. But we can speak of His relationship with His world.

One of the main things that we can say about God in this manner is that He is good. Not only do we say that God *is* good, but also that He defines good. Every act of God contains the most pure and infinite Good that can exist. His goodness and love are the two most basic of God's qualities as far as we can understand, and they work together to bring about His purpose. The Psalmist sings of this and says (*Psalm* 145:9), "God is good to all, His love rests on all His deeds."[1]

God had absolutely no need to create the world. God Himself is absolute perfection, and has no need for anything, even creation. When He created the world, He therefore performed the most perfect possible act of altruism and love. No matter how selfless a human act may be, there is always some benefit to the doer, even if it is nothing more than a degree of self-satisfaction. But God, on the other hand, has no needs or wants, and therefore, there was nothing about Him that creation could satisfy. It was therefore the most perfect possible act of love. The Psalmist again speaks of this and says

(*Psalm* 89:1), "I have said: 'The world is built of love.' "[2]

We say that God is good because He acts in love. Neither His good nor His love are in any way limited. There is an often-repeated chant that speaks of both God's goodness and His love. It goes (*Psalm* 136:1), "Give thanks to God, His love is infinite."[3]

God was under absolutely no compulsion to create the world.[4] We therefore call His creation an act of pure and infinite love. The litany thus continues (ibid. 136:5-9):

He made the heavens with wisdom	His love is infinite.
Set the earth on the waters	His love is infinite.
He makes the great lights	His love is infinite.
The sun to rule the day	His love is infinite.
The moon and stars by night	His love is infinite.

The Baal Shem Tov explains this in a somewhat deeper manner.[5] We know that God knows the future just as He knows the past. Therefore, even before creation, God knew of mankind. And just as He knew man, He loved man. It was this love of generations yet unborn that brought God to create the universe. God saw the good people of every generation, and His love for them served as a focus for creation. Our sages thus teach us that God perceived the deeds of the righteous before creating the world.[6] He therefore told us through His prophet (*Jeremiah* 31:3), "With an infinite world of love have I loved you, therefore, I have drawn you to Me with affection."

God Himself calls His creation an act of goodness. It is for this reason that at the end of creation the Torah says (*Genesis* 1:35), "And God saw all that He had made, and behold, it was very good."[7] What God is telling us in the Torah is that creation is an expression of His good.

The Talmud tells us a story that expresses this most graphically:[8]

Rabbi Akiba was once traveling. With him, he had a donkey, a rooster, and a torch. He came to a city and sought lodging, but they would not let him stay for the night. Rabbi Akiba did not complain. He merely remarked, "All that God does is for the good."

Having no other choice, he camped in a field. During the

night, a lion came and killed his donkey. Later, a cat came and ate his rooster. Finally, a wind came and extinguished his torch. Again, he said, "All that God does is for the good."

In the morning, Rabbi Akiba walked back to the city where he had sought to spend the night. He found the city sacked and all its inhabitants killed. If he would have spent the night there, he would have been among the dead. If the Romans would have heard his donkey bray, or his rooster crow, or if they would have seen his torch, they would have found him and killed him. Realizing all this, he exclaimed, "Have I not said that all God does is for the good."

What Rabbi Akiba is teaching us is that everything that God does is ultimately good. There are things that may seem to contradict this. There are things that may seem to be bad and evil. But ultimately, everything comes from good and will end up as good.[9] If we have the patience, we will see that everything in the world is ultimately good.

Everything in creation is part of God's plan. God's plan is the ultimate good. The wise Solomon thus teaches us (*Proverbs* 16:4), "God made everything for His purpose, even the wicked for the day of evil." The Talmud comments on this, saying, "Everything that God created in His world, He created for His glory."[10]

Of course, there is a limit beyond which we cannot ask. We cannot ultimately understand God's motive in creation, any more than we can understand anything else about His being. Ultimately, He created for His own purpose, unknown to any being other than Himself. The final statement that we must make is that God created the world for His own reasons, or in His word to His prophet (*Isaiah* 43:7), "Everything that is called by My name, for My glory, I created, formed and made it."[11] When God speaks of His glory, He means that it was for Himself — for His own reason, beyond all human comprehension.[12] With relation to ourselves, we call God's motives "good." But in relation to God Himself, it is totally beyond our understanding.[13]

But God had a plan for the world, and this plan was ultimate Good. The expression of this plan was the Torah, and as such, it served as the blueprint for all creation.[14] Thus, God Himself calls the Torah good, as He told the wise Solomon (*Proverbs* 4:2), "I have given you a good thing, do not forsake My Torah." Our sages explain that this means that the Torah is God's ultimate plan of good for the world, and say, "There is no good other than Torah."[15]

It was this plan that ultimately led God to create the world. Good cannot be given unless there is someone to receive it. There is a Midrash that expresses this quite clearly, teaching us that God asked the Torah if He should create the universe. The Torah replied, "If the King has no camp, then over what is He a King?"[16]

What this Midrash is teaching us is that once God had created the Torah, then it could tell Him to create a world. This means that once God had made His plan to do good, then He had to make a world to receive it. In a sense, we can say that God was drawn to create the world by His own plan.[17] The plan itself could "tell" God, "There is no King without a kingdom," as the scripture itself echoes (*Proverbs* 14:8), "In a multitude of people is a King's glory."[18]

II.

We say that God created the world in order to bestow good to it. But what is this good? What good does God have to offer His world?

First of all, we must realize that any good that God gives must be the ultimate good that His creation can accept. The Psalmist said (*Psalm* 31:20), "How great is Your good, stored up for those who fear You." Our sages interpret this to say that God bestows good in the greatest possible abundance.[19] In another place, they teach us that this verse means that God is telling us, "You according to your strength, and Me according to Mine."[20] In other words, God gives us the greatest good that we can possibly accept.

But what is this ultimate good? What is the greatest possible good that God can bestow?

If we think about it, the answer is really quite simple. The greatest possible good is God Himself.[21] There is no other ultimate true good. The Psalmist thus said (*Psalm* 16:2), "I have no good but You." In the Talmud, Rabbi Acha interprets this to mean that no true good exists in the world, except that of God Himself.[24]

The ultimate good is therefore to partake of God, and it is this good that He planned to give the world. He would create a world where creatures ultimately could partake of His essence. The Psalmist sings of this (*Psalm* 34:9), "Taste and see that God is good, happy is the man who finds refuge in Him."

God therefore created the world in such a way that man could draw close to Him and partake of His essence. Of course, we are not speaking of physical closeness, but of spiritual closeness. Such closeness involves the knowledge and understanding of God, as well as resembling Him to the greatest degree possible. We will later discuss how these two concepts are related, but ultimately, both are spiritual closeness.

Here again, we hear this in the words of the Psalmist (*Psalm* 73:28), "But for me, the nearness of God is good. I have made God my refuge, that I may tell of His works." The Psalmist is teaching us that his ultimate good is nearness to God. This nearness involves "telling of His works" — that is, a deep knowledge and perception of the Divine.[25]

The ultimate good that God offers is therefore the opportunity to perceive Him. In one place, our sages thus teach us that God created the world in order that men may know Him.[26] This is not a separate reason, but the way in which He bestows His good upon us.[27] God thus told us through His prophet (*Isaiah* 48:17), "I am your God, I teach you for your good." The Psalmist expresses the same idea when he says (*Psalm* 119:68), "You are good and You do good: teach me Your statutes."

To know God and understand Him in any way is to have a deep awe and dread of His majesty. All true wisdom is that of God. But such wisdom and knowledge imply the fear and reverence of God. The Psalmist thus said (*Psalm* 111:10), "The beginning of wisdom is the fear of God." The wise Solomon expresses the same idea when he says (*Proverbs* 1:7), "The fear of God is the beginning of knowledge."[28]

We can therefore say that the ultimate goal of creation is that we should come close to God, and therefore both know and fear Him. Again we hear the words of Solomon (*Ecclesiastes* 3:14), "Whatever God does shall be forever . . . God has made it so that man should fear Him." The Talmud comments on this, saying that the world was created for the fear of God.[29] This is man's true purpose in the world, as again we find (ibid. 12:13), "The sum of the matter, when all has been heard: Fear God and keep His commandments, for this is all of man." In the Talmud, Rabbi Eleazar comments on this and says, "Solomon is teaching us that all the world was created for the fear of God."[30]

When our sages say the world was created for the fear of God, they are not contradicting the teaching that it was created as a vehicle for His good. What they are doing is expressing what this good ultimately is. It is a knowledge of God that is most perfectly expressed by the reverence and awe that we call the "fear of God."

The ultimate place where we will be worthy of this vision and perception will be in what we call *Olam HaBa* — the Future World or the World to Come. It is a world of absolute life and goodness. It is of the vision of the Word to Come that·the Psalmist is speaking of when he says (*Psalm* 27:13), "I believe that I will gaze upon God in the land of the living." This "land of the living" is the Future World.[31]

It is this future world that is the goal of all creation. Our sages thus teach us, "This world is like an antechamber before the World to Come. Prepare yourself in the antechamber before you enter the palace."[32]

Since this Future World is the ultimate goal of creation, it is also the place of ultimate good. In the language of the Talmud, it is called, "the World where all is good."[33] It is a good that surpasses anything that this world may possibly have to offer. This is what our sages mean when they say, "One moment of delight in the Future World is more than all the good of this world."[34]

We can obtain some idea of what this Future World will be like from a common saying of Rav, quoted in the Talmud.[35] He said, "In the Future World, there will be no eating, drinking, childbearing or business. Neither will there be jealousy, hatred or strife. The righteous will sit with their crowns on their heads, delighting in the radiance of the Divine Presence."

Our sages teach us that this "radiance of the Divine Presence" is a perception of the Divine.[36] In the Future World, we will perceive and comprehend God in the greatest degree possible.

This perception of God in the Future World is totally beyond our present grasp. That of the least of us will pale the achievements of the greatest sages in this world. Still, of course, it will be impossible to perceive God in His entirety. This is impossible for any being other that God Himself. Although incomparable to anything in this life, our perception will still be less than a drop in an infinite ocean. Nevertheless, it will far exceed anything possible in this world.[37]

In order that we may approach Him, God created a dimension of nearness to His being. By moving through this dimension, we are able to come closer and closer to God, even though we can never actually reach Him. This dimension is what we call the spiritual world. Our sages call the highest spiritual world *Atzilus* — the World of Nearness. All the spiritual worlds were created as vehicles through which we may draw near to God. In a sense, they serve as a filter, allowing us to draw near, and still not be obliterated by His infinite Light.[38]

In a number of places, our sages speak of these worlds as the Celestial Treasuries. Thus, Israel sings of God (*Song of Songs* 1:4), "The King will bring me into His chamber." Our sages comment that God will bring the righteous into His celestial chambers and allow them to probe the treasuries on high.[39]

This is also the meaning of the light that was made on the first day of creation. Our sages teach us that it was not mere physical light, but a wondrous light with which one could see "from one end of the universe to the other."[40] This was the light of perception, shining in all the spiritual worlds, with which one could experience this vision of God. Our sages thus continue, "God set this light aside for the righteous in the World to Come."[41]

This is the light of perception with which we will partake of the Divine — the "radiance of the Divine Presence." Elihu was speaking of this when he told Job (*Job* 33:30) that God will "turn back his soul from destruction, and light him with the light of life." The wise Solomon tells us that this light is the source of eternal life, when he says (*Proverbs* 16:15), "In the light of the King's face is life . . ."[43]

God's ultimate goal in creation was therefore the World to Come, where man could perceive a vision of God. Not God Himself, of course, but a vision. Perhaps through many filters, but still, a vision of God. The Psalmist sings of this vision (*Psalm* 17:15), "In righteousness, I will see Your face, when I awake, I will be satisfied with a vision of You." The Psalmist is speaking of the time when he will awake to the delights of the Future World. Our sages comment on this verse, "God will satisfy the righteous with a vision of the Divine Presence."[44]

The bliss of the Future World will be endless. In His endless goodness, God will give us a world of good without end. The Psalmist is speaking of this when he exclaims (Psalm 16:11), "In Your presence is fullness of joy, in Your right hand is bliss forever."[45]

Of course, everything about this Future World is totally beyond our powers of description. Even the visions of the greatest prophets will pale in comparison. It is something that no human mind can possibly imagine in this life. It cannot come through human understanding, but only as a gift from God, and when He gives it, we will understand. The prophet therefore says when speaking of the World to Come (*Isaiah* 64:3), "Never has the ear heard it — no eye has seen it — other than God: what He will do for those who hope in Him."[46]

III.

The creature destined by God to bring about this ultimate purpose is man. It is man who will enjoy this ultimate closeness to God in the Future World, and thereby fulfill God's purpose in creation. He therefore tells us through His prophet (*Isaiah* 45:12), "I have made the earth, and have created man upon it."

Every man must personally look upon himself as a partner with God in fulfilling this purpose. Creation exists for the sake of man, and it is man's duty to work toward fulfilling God's goal. Our sages thus teach us that every man should say, "The world was created for my sake."[47]

The Talmud provides us with an excellent example. A king once built a lavish palace, decorating it beautifully, and stocking it with the best food and drink. When it was all finished he invited his guests, saying, "If there are no guests, then what pleasure does the king have with all the good things that he has prepared?"[48]

It is for this reason that God made man last in the order of creation. All the world had to be prepared for its special guest. After everything had been prepared, the guest — man — was brought into the world.[49]

One may wonder how God can consider man. God is King over the entire universe, billions of light years in diameter, containing hundreds of billions of galaxies and quadrillions of suns. How can such a God care about man? How can he place His goal of creation on a mere speck of cosmic dust that we call our planet earth?

This question was actually first raised by the Psalmist. It might have been on a clear night, and as he gazed at the heavens, he saw them illuminated with a myriad of stars, and realized how small man really is. He then burst forth in song (*Psalms* 8:4-6):

> When I look at Your heavens,
> The work of Your fingers,
> The moon and stars
> That You have established —
> What is man that You think of him?
> Mortal man that You remember him?
> Yet, You have made him little less than God,
> You have crowned him with glory and splendor.

We know that God exists independent of space. It is therefore not too difficult to imagine that size alone is of little consequence to Him.

However, we also know that man is among the most complex things in all the universe. There is nothing that we know that is more complex than the human brain. It is infinitely more complex than even the largest galaxy. The brain of the smallest infant is vastly more wonderful than all the visible stars. It is little wonder that the Psalmist introduces his question with the remark (ibid. 8:3), "From the mouths of babes and sucklings, You have founded strength." He is providing the answer even before he asks the question. The heavens and stars may be awe inspiring, but a single word uttered by a child is vastly more wonderful.

Besides being complex, man is also the most aware thing in the universe. He is both perceptive and introspective. Even the stars and galaxies cannot match him in this. Since these are things that really matter to God, it is not so very surprising that He thinks of us.[50]

Beyond this, man is unique in creation because of his Divine soul. In one place, Job says (*Job* 31:2), "What is a portion from God on high?" He is here speaking of the human soul, which is called "a portion from God on high." Man's soul comes from the highest possible of Godly levels, and is therefore a portion of the Divine.[51]

The Torah describes the creation of man with the words (*Genesis* 2:7), "God formed man of the dust of the earth, and He breathed into his nostrils a living soul." Our sages tell us that the Torah uses the expression "He breathed" for a very special reason. Just as human breath comes from the inner recesses of the body, so the human soul comes from the innermost depths of the Divine. Man's soul is therefore nothing less than a breath of God.[52]

The deeper meaning of this is that man's soul was God's very first thought and ultimate goal in creation. As such, it is closer to Him than anything else. In order to express this closeness, we call the soul a breath of God.

More than anything else, it is this soul that makes man unique in creation.[53] It is closer and more meaningful to God than any star or galaxy. In a spiritual sense, we may say that a single human soul is even greater than the entire physical universe. This is what the Talmud means when it says, "The deeds of the righteous are greater than the creation of heaven and earth."[54]

IV.

In order to make man a vehicle to accept His good, God created him with the capacity to enjoy. There are many things that give man pleasure. There are bodily pleasures, such as eating and drinking. There are mental pleasures, such as looking at beautiful art, reading a good book, or listening to fine music. But above all these is the pleasure of accomplishment. There are few human pleasures greater than those of accomplishment — of completing a job well done. Whether it is in doing good to others, solving a difficult problem, or simply doing the right thing, man experiences a certain glow of pleasure that is beyond comparison. The only thing that might come close is the spiritual pleasure of the mystic vision. Indeed, we find that many people are willing to forego the greatest physical pleasures in order to pursue a meaningful goal.[55]

For most of us, there is a glow of accomplishment that accompanies a meaningful act itself. If we are praised for it, the pleasure is all the greater. If an important person were to tell us that we had done something good, we would experience an even greater pleasure in accomplishment. To win, for example, a Nobel prize and be recognized by the world, is indeed one of the great pleasures of life, and there are people who would work a lifetime toward this end.

Accomplishment and recognition are among the natural pleasures of man. They are not physical pleasures, but delights of the spirit. The wise Solomon spoke of them when he said (*Proverbs* 13:12), "Desire fulfilled is a tree of life." He reiterates this several verses later, saying (ibid. 13:19), "Desire accomplished is sweet to the soul."

If the President were to summon you and tell you that you

had done something good, you would feel great pride in accomplishment. How then would you feel if you were told this by One much greater? What if God Himself were to tell you that you were doing something good and beneficial? How great would be your feeling of accomplishment?

In a sense, man's ultimate reward for doing good is this sense of accomplishment. God Himself tells us what is good, and the reward is in ultimately knowing that one has obeyed God's direct command. What greater accomplishment can there be than to act as a partner in the very purpose of creation?

It is for this reason that God revealed His will to man. He revealed the Torah to us, telling us what is good. When man then lives by the Torah and does what God Himself has defined as good, he can feel that he has accomplished one of the most meaningful things possible. God teaches us the way in order that we may achieve this everlasting bliss. This is what the Psalmist means when he says (*Psalms* 16:11), "You make me know the path of life; in Your presence is a fullness of joy, in Your right hand, everlasting bliss."[56]

The very fact that God revealed what is good to us provides us with the essence of its reward. Our sages thus teach us, "Greater is one who does something that he is commanded to do than one who does what he is not commanded to do."[57] The very fact that it is commanded by God makes it all the more valued.

Our sages also explain this concept in a somewhat different light, teaching us that one who gives a gift to another must tell him about it. They derive this from the fact that God told us how great were the commandments that He was giving us. Rashi explains the reason for this, saying that when one is informed about a gift, then he both realizes its importance and is not ashamed to accept it.[58] Both of these concepts also apply here. The fact that God Himself tells us that certain things are good makes us realize their importance. Furthermore, as we shall see, it also prevents us from being ashamed of the good that God will give us.

The vehicle through which God defined what is good and beneficial is the Torah. When we obey the commandments of the Torah, we know that we are doing something that God commanded. In this way, we are then able to accept God's own goodness and fulfill His purpose in creation. The Torah is therefore the prime vehicle of God's purpose, and our sages thus teach us that the world was created for the sake of the Torah.[59]

The pleasure in accomplishment is not something that God gives us, but essentially something that we create ourselves. We ourselves therefore generate the good that God gives us. Our sages therefore teach us that virtue is its own reward.[60] The Prophet expresses this idea when he says (*Isaiah* 3:10), "Say to the righteous that it shall be good, for he shall eat the fruit of his deeds."[61] In another place our sages put it this way: "Today to act, tomorrow to receive reward."[62]

This concept is expressed most clearly by the words of Rabbi Chiya in the Talmud. He says, "Enjoying the fruits of your labor is better than the fear of heaven. It is thus written (*Psalms* 128:2), 'You shall eat the fruit of your effort — you shall be happy, and it shall be well with you.' 'You shall be happy'— in this world — 'and it shall be well with you' — in the World to Come."[63]

What Rabbi Chiya is saying is that the main good of the Future World is the enjoyment of the fruits of one's labor. This is what he means when he says that "it shall be well with you in the World to Come." This, he says, is greater than mere "fear of heaven." As we discussed earlier, "fear of heaven" refers to our knowledge and perception of God. This perception may be a great thing, but it is all the greater when it comes as the fruit of our own efforts.

The opposite of pleasure is pain. Here again, we have both physical pain and mental anguish. Among the worst possible kinds of psychological pain are the feelings of guilt and shame. In one place, our sages say that the pain of shame is as great as that of death.[64]

A number of our great teachers write that the fire of *Gehenom*, the ultimate punishment for evil, is actually the burning shame that one experiences when he stands naked before God with all his sins revealed.[65]

Imagine standing before God, with your memory wide open

and with no way to escape. We all know the terrible shame and humiliation of being caught doing wrong. Imagine what it is like when the One who catches you is God Himself. This is shame without comparison.

It is of this shame that Daniel is speaking when he says (*Daniel* 12:2), "Many who sleep in the dust shall awake, some to everlasting life, and some to everlasting shame." The Prophet also speaks of this, saying (*Isaiah* 66:24), "They shall go forth and look upon the carcasses of the men who have rebelled against Me. For their worms shall not die, neither shall their fire be quenched — they shall be ashamed before all flesh."[66]

But there is another kind of shame that is even more basic. This is the shame of having to accept a free gift. This is a very primeval shame, deeply seated in man's psyche. Our sages thus teach us, "One who eats another's bread is ashamed to look in his face."[67] From the context of this saying, we see that it not only applies to human psychology, but even to the most primitive things in nature.

Our sages repeat this lesson any number of times. They teach us that "when a man must depend on gifts, his face changes."[68] In another place, they say, "When one depends on the gifts of others, the world appears dark to him."[69] Elsewhere they proclaim, "One who eats at another's table is never satisfied."[70]

God wanted the good that He would give to be perfect good, not tinged by any shame. If it were given as a free gift, however, it would always be accompanied by the shame that results from accepting a free gift. The only way to avoid this would be for the good to be earned, so that it would no longer be a gift. It is for this reason that the good that God gives us is only bestowed as a reward for our own actions.

When the Zohar speaks of the ultimate world of good, it says, "Happy is he who comes here without shame."[71] This is actually echoing the words of the Prophet, who said (*Jeremiah* 2:26), "And you shall eat and be satisfied . . . and my people shall never be ashamed."

V.

In order that man enjoy the pleasure of his accomplishment, it is imperative that he know that he acted as a matter of free choice, rather than through compulsion. It is for this reason that God gave us free will. We bear full responsibility for our action and full credit for the good we do. We are free to choose between good and evil. This is what makes the choice of good a true accomplishment.[72]

If man did not have free will, then he would be little more than a puppet or a robot. Both a robot and a puppet can accomplish things, but they cannot have any feeling of accomplishment. They are mere machines. In a sense, it is free will that makes us more than a machine. If man did not have free will, his accomplishment would be no more than that of a robot. There would be no feeling of pride or pleasure in it at all.

We can therefore say that free will is required by God's justice.[73] In a deeper sense, we must say that it is required by God's very purpose in creation. For the good that God desired to grant to His world is essentially bestowed as a result of our free will. We can therefore say that free will is one of the most essential ingredients of all creation.[74]

But there is a much deeper way of looking at the concept of free will, and it follows as a direct result of our previous discussion. As discussed earlier, the greatest good that God could give is Himself. The purpose of creation was therefore to give man a chance to come close to God.

When we speak of coming close to God, we are not speaking of physical closeness. God exists in a realm far beyond the mere physical. When we speak of closeness to God, we are speaking of spiritual closeness.

We said earlier that this spiritual closeness involves knowledge and perception of God. But on a deeper level, this is really a result of our closeness to Him. For we cannot know God by looking at Him. We cannot even know Him by meditating or contemplating about Him. There are no symbols in our minds which we can use to even think of God. Philosophy is equally futile, and for the same reason. We can only extend our thoughts beyond the immediate, using symbols and concepts that we can conceive. But God is utterly beyond our conception. Therefore, the only way in which we can know God and perceive Him is by coming close to Him in a spiritual sense.

But what is closeness in a nonphysical sense?

We find a hint in the words of our sages. The Torah states (*Deuteronomy* 13:5), "You shall follow the Lord your God, fear Him and keep His commandments, obey Him and serve Him, and bind yourself to Him." The Talmud asks, "How can one bind himself to God? Is it not written (*Deuteronomy* 9:3), 'The Lord your God is a consuming fire?' " The Talmud answers that we bind ourselves to God by imitating His attributes.[75]

What the Talmud is teaching us is that in a spiritual sense, closeness is resemblance. Two things that resemble each other are close in a spiritual sense. Things that differ are distant. The more two things resemble each other, the closer they are spiritually.

This is expressed even more clearly in the Midrash,[77] commenting on the verse (*Leviticus* 19:2), "You shall be holy, for I, the Lord your God, am holy." The Midrash tells us that this passage explains two other passages: (*Deuteronomy* 4:4,) "You, who have bound yourselves to God, are all living today," and (*Jeremiah* 13:11), "As a loincloth clings to a man's waist, so shall the whole house of Judah cling to Me."

Although the Midrash does not openly state it, it is asking the same question as the Talmud did above. What does the Torah mean when it says that "you have bound yourselves to God," or that the people shall "cling" to Him? The Midrash therefore tells us that these passages are explained by the verse, "You shall be holy, for I am Holy." We bind ourselves to God by working to resemble Him in His holiness. For in a spiritual sense, the more two things resemble each other, the closer they are.

We can now understand the reason for free will in a deeper sense.

As we discussed earlier, the good that God's plan has destined for His world is the ultimate good, namely God Himself. His plan is to give a creature, namely man, the opportunity to draw close to Him.

But when we speak of giving such good, we immediately face a dilemma. God is the giver and man is the receiver, and as such, they are two opposites. In a spiritual sense, they are as far from each other as north and south. Giver and receiver are exact opposites. As long as man is a mere receiver, he stands at the opposite pole away from God, the Giver. In a spiritual sense, man and God would then be ultimately distant from each other.

Therefore, God arranged things so that man himself would be the creator of good.

God made man in such a way that he too can create good. Man does so every time he obeys God's commandments. In doing so, he draws God's light to his own being, and thus, rather than being a mere receiver, he becomes a partner with God. The good that man ultimately receives is therefore as much the result of his own efforts as it is a gift of God.

Man therefore receives God's good by himself doing good, thereby resembling God in the greatest degree possible. For man draws close to God by imitating Him, and when he does so, he can be a recipient of God's good. This is what the Psalmist meant when he sang (*Psalm* 125:4), "God is good to the good." In order to receive God's goodness, one must himself be good. Our sages interpret this verse by saying, "Let he who is good, come and accept good, from He who is good to the good."[78]

In order for this resemblance to be in any way complete, man had to be created with free will. Just as God acts as a free Being, so does man. Just as He operates without prior restraint, so does man. Just as God does good as a matter of His own choice, so does man. According to many commentators, this is one meaning of man having been created in the "image of God."[79]

We can experience a glimmer of this closeness to God, even in the physical world. The pleasure of accomplishment that we experience when doing good is a touch of this closeness. It is a pure spiritual pleasure, and as such is a reflection of the ultimate spiritual pleasure, namely, closeness to God. When we accomplish good, we are imitating God and bringing Him close to us, and therefore feel an inkling of this pleasure.[80]

On the other hand, the ultimate spiritual pain is being separated from God. This explains the psychological pain experienced when one is forced to accept charity from others. When one is a taker rather than a giver, then he is ultimately far from God, the Giver.

Our sages therefore describe this feeling as shame. They say that if God were to give us His good as a free gift, then we would experience shame in accepting it. For what is shame? Most often, it involves being caught in an improper situation. A person experiences shame when he is caught doing something that he should not or when he finds himself in an improper place. But for a mere receiver to be close to God is also an improper place. Therefore, we describe this feeling as one of shame.

VI.

As we have said, one of the ultimate goals of man is the imitation of God. We do this in every good act, paralleling God's own creation of good. The most direct way that we can do this, however, is in our actions toward our fellow man.

God's purpose in creation could have been fulfilled with the creation of a single creature to accept His good. Such a creature, however, could never truly resemble God. God Himself is a bestower of good, and if only one creature existed, then to whom would it do good? Certainly not to God, for God has no needs. It is for this reason that God created the world as an arena for an entire species of man.

When God first created man, Adam was one. God then said (*Genesis* 2:18), "It is not good for man to be alone; I will make him a helper as his counterpart." As long as man was alone, he could not really be good. For to be good is to imitate God, the giver of good. A man alone would have no one to whom to bestow good, and therefore, could not be called "good." This is what God meant when He said, "It is not *good* for man to be alone."

God then created woman as a counterpart of man. The relationship between man and woman would be very much the same as that of God to the world. It is for this reason that we always refer to God in the masculine gender, since He is the active creative force in the world.[81] God is the archetype of the masculine and His creation is that of the feminine. Woman was therefore created from man, just as the world came from God.

Man can become a partner of God in the procreation of children. Just as God is a creator, so man also becomes a creator of life. Our sages therefore teach us that there are three partners in the procreation of a child: his father, his mother and God.[82] The sexual act is the vehicle through which man displays this aspect of his partnership with God, and this is one reason why its perversion is considered among the worst of sins.[83]

In a spiritual sense, the good that man does also benefits every other human being. Thus, in doing good, one is at least indirectly benefiting his fellow man, even in the case of ritual laws that do not directly do so. Our sages thus teach us that every single Jew is morally responsible for every other.[84] The author of *Reshis Chochmah*[85] explains that all souls are bound together, as with a rope, and the movement of one is reflected in every other. This is what the Torah means when it says (*Numbers* 16:22), "One man sins, and anger is directed against the entire community." The Midrash provides us with an excellent example illustrating this:[86] A number of people are sitting in a small boat. All of a sudden, one man begins to drill a hole under his seat. When the people complain, he retorts, "What complaint do you have? After all, I'm drilling the hole under my own seat." Finally, a wise man answers him, "We are all in the same boat. The hole may be under your seat, but the water that comes in will make the boat sink with all of us."

In a spiritual sense, we are all in the same boat. Every good thing that we do affects all mankind, and the same is true of all evil. In every good act that we do, we imitate God insofar that we ultimately bring good to all humanity. This is indeed one reason why God put us all in the same spiritual boat.

Of course, we do this more directly when we do good toward our fellow man. This is the archetype of all good. There is no way of imitating God more closely than in doing good to others.

In the previous section, we quoted the Talmud as saying that we bind ourselves to God by imitating His ways. But in what ways does the Talmud say that we imitate God? Look at its words carefully:[87]

Just as God clothes the naked, so shall you.
Just as God visits the sick, so shall you.
Just as God comforts the bereaved, so shall you.

In another place, the Talmud says that we must also imitate

God in His mercy and compassion.[88] The general lesson is that we resemble God most in our relationship with our fellow human beings.

This concept is best exemplified by the famous story of Hillel.[89] The Talmud tells us that a non-Jew once came to Hillel and said, "I wish to convert to Judaism, but only if you teach me the entire Torah while I stand on one foot."

Hillel replied, "What is hateful to you, do not do to your fellow man. This is the core of Judaism. The rest is mere commentary."

Many of the commentators find this story very perplexing. The commandments dealing with our relationship toward our fellow man are certainly very important. But there are also many other important commandments that apparently have nothing at all to do with other people. How could Hillel have dismissed these as mere commentary?

What Hillel was teaching us, however, was that the main reason for all the commandments is the imitation of God, and that this is exemplified by our relations with our fellow human beings. We must deal with our fellows just as God deals with us. In doing so, we fulfill His purpose in creation. This imitation of God is ultimately the purpose of all the commandments.

This is also the meaning of what God told His prophet (*Jeremiah* 22:16), "He judged the cause of the poor and the needy, and it was well. Is this not to know Me?" As discussed earlier, we can only know God by drawing close to Him through imitating Him. God is telling us that the main way in which we know Him is by imitating Him in doing good to others.

There is a commandment in the Torah (*Leviticus* 19:18), "You shall love your neighbor like yourself." One of our foremost leaders, Rabbi Akiba, said, "This commandment is the core of the Torah."[90] Rabbi Akiba is teaching us the same lesson as Hillel. We imitate God's love for the world through our love toward our fellow man. In this way, we draw ourselves close to God and fulfill His purpose in creation.

In a deeper sense, the concept of love itself is the archetype of spiritual closeness. Where a bond of love exists between two people, they are close — even though they may be separated by vast distances.[91] On the other hand, people who hate each other are far apart, even when they are sitting right next to each other. Love and hate exist in a spiritual, rather than a physical dimension. Love between two people implies a harmony and complementarity between them. It is this harmony that makes them close, irrespective of physical distance. In obeying God's commandments, we seek to bring a similar harmony and closeness between ourselves and God. "You shall love your neighbor as yourself" is therefore indeed the prime rule of the Torah. It not only leads us to a closeness to God, but also teaches us the meaning of such closeness.[92]

Following a similar line of reasoning, we can understand what our sages mean when they teach us, "He who denies the doing of kindness (Gemilus Chasadim) is like one who denies the most fundamental principle (God Himself)." God is the ultimate bestower of kindness, and one who divorces himself from such deeds, places himself poles apart from God. God is the ultimate doer of good, and this man denies doing good. He is therefore said to be like one who divorces himself from God.

God is the source of all life, and therefore, the more one resembles God, the more he partakes of life. One who clings to God is said to be truly alive, as the Torah says (Deuteronomy 4:4), "You who have clung to God are all alive today." One who divorces himself from God, on the other hand, is considered dead.

This is the meaning of what the wise Solomon said (Proverbs 15:27), "He who hates gifts shall live." For God is a giver, never a receiver. When one refuses to become a receiver, he resembles God in this respect, and is thus considered alive. The more one gives, the more he resembles God in this respect. We thus find (Proverbs 10:2), "Charity saves from death." When one gives, he resembles his Creator, the source of all life.

One who does not resemble God, on the other hand, is counted among the dead. Thus, for example, our sages teach us that the poor man who lives off charity is counted among the dead.[93] In this sense, such a man is poles apart from God, since God is a Giver, and this poor man only takes. The same is true of one who does not have any children.

In a similar vein, our sages teach us, "The wicked are called dead, even during their lifetime."[94] In being wicked, they are ultimately separated from God, the source of all life. They are therefore considered dead, even while they are still walking and breathing. They may be alive in a physical sense, but in a spiritual sense, they are no longer among the living.

VII.

One of the fundamental principles of creation is therefore free will, where man can choose good as a matter of his own choice. God's purpose in creation does not allow man to be a robot or a puppet. But if God's purpose does not allow man to be a robot, neither does it permit him to be a prisoner.

Just as man must have free will, so must he have the opportunity to make use of it. A man locked up in prison may have the same free will as anyone else, but there is little that he can do with it. If man is to do good as a matter of free choice, he must also have the possibility of doing that which is not good. For man to resemble his Creator to the greatest possible extent, he must exist in an arena where he has the maximum freedom of choice. The more that man resembles God in His omnipotence, the closer he can resemble Him in his free choice to do good.

It is for this reason that God created the possibility of evil.[95]

God therefore told His prophet (*Isaiah* 45:7), "I form light and create darkness, I make peace and create evil. I am God, I do all these things." In keeping himself from evil, man takes the first step toward good.[96] Job thus said (*Job* 28:28), "The fear of God is wisdom, and to depart from evil is understanding."[97] God created evil in order that it may be conquered.

If nothing but good were possible, it would produce no benefit. To use the Talmudic metaphor, it would be like carrying a lamp in broad daylight.[98] The *Zohar* states, "The advantage of wisdom comes from foolishness, just as that of light would not be discernible, and would produce no benefit. Thus, it is written (*Ecclesiates* 7:14), 'God has made one thing opposite the other.' "[99]

Ultimately, there is one Source of everything that exists, even evil. It is not that God actually created evil, but it is through His will that the possibility of evil exists.[100] Everything comes from God and must return to Him.[101] In the meanwhile, however, evil exists in order to be conquered.

The Zohar gives us a very excellent example explaining this.[102] A king once wanted to give his son greater responsibility. Before doing this, however, he wanted to test his loyalty. What did the king do? He hired a temptress to try to persuade the son to rebel against his father. She was to use all her wiles to tempt the boy to go against his father.

Whether or not this temptress succeeds, she is still a servant of the king, doing his will. Even if she succeeds in persuading the son to go against his father, she is still doing what the king bid her. The same is true of evil. Ultimately it exists to fulfill God's purpose.

As discussed earlier, the closeness to God resulting from our good deeds is reflected in our satisfaction of accomplishment accompanying such acts. However, such satisfaction is enhanced according to the difficulty of the accomplishment. Our sages thus teach us, "The greater the suffering, the greater the reward."[103]

The Midrash illustrates this with another example.[104] A king once wanted to know which of his subjects really loved and respected him. He built an iron wall around his palace. He then proclaimed, "Let those who really love and respect the king come to the palace." Those who were truly loyal scaled the iron wall and thus showed their loyalty.

This wall of iron represents the forces of evil in the world. God makes it all the more difficult for us to approach Him in order to increase our ultimate reward. This is expressed quite well in another Midrash:[105]

Another king wanted to test the loyalty of his subjects. He built a high wall around his palace, and then placed a very narrow opening in it. All those who wanted to see the king had to squeeze themselves through this very narrow opening.

Of course, there is one major difference between God and the earthly king in the example. God knows and does not have to find out. The reason why He creates these barriers, however, is to bring out our own good potential into action.[106] In this way, He enhances our feeling of satisfaction of accomplishment, and ultimately, our reward.

This world was therefore created as a place of maximum challenge. For the greater the challenge, the greater the reward. This of course may result in many who do not overcome the challenge. Still, even they will receive reward for the good that they do. Ultimately, however, the world was created for the sake of those who overcome their challenge. Our sages thus teach us that the universe was created for the sake of the righteous.[107] As the *Sefer HaYashar* puts it, the good are like the fruit, while the evil men are like the husks. Both may grow on the same tree, but only the fruit fulfills its purpose.[108]

This is the meaning of a question disputed in the Talmud:[109] For two and a half years, there was a dispute between Shammai's school and that of Hillel. Shammai's school contended that it would have been better for man never to have been created. The school of Hillel said that it was better for man to have been created. After two and a half years, they finally agreed and decided that man would have been better off if he had not been created. But now that he is created, let him be very careful what he does in this world.

It is indeed a gamble for man to have to descend to this world of temptation. One might argue that it would have been better for God to grant man a less complete good and not make him earn it. This is the dispute between the schools of Shammai and Hillel. The good that man receives is greatly enhanced by virtue of his having earned it. Still, coming to this world is a great gamble. It is a place of the greatest of temptations. If a man was given an initial choice, perhaps it would be best for him to choose a lesser good, without taking the gamble of coming to this world of evil. This was the contention of Shammai's school. The school of Hillel, on the other hand, maintained that the good realized makes the gamble worthwhile.

Ultimately, we are taught that one cannot depend on a wager.[110] They therefore finally decided that it would have been better for man not to have taken the gamble of having been born into this world. This contention is supported by the words of the wise Solomon (*Ecclesiates* 4:2-3), "I count the dead happy because they are dead, happier than the living who are still in life. Happier than both is the man yet unborn, who has not seen the evil that is done under the sun."[111]

When a man dies, he no longer faces the challenge of evil in this world. Better yet, however, is he who is not yet born. It would be better for him never to have to take the gamble, struggling against the evil of this world. Solomon therefore concludes (ibid. 4:6), "Better a handful of repose than two hands full of effort and chasing the wind."

VIII.

There are two basic concepts in human existence. First, man must earn the good that God has prepared. Secondly, he must receive this good.

There is, however, a basic difference between the environment needed for these two concepts. While earning the reward, we must have the maximum possible challenge. This in turn gives us the greatest possible satisfaction in accomplishment. Such an environment must therefore be one where neither God Himself, nor the divine nature of our good deeds, is obvious. It must be a world where God is hidden, and where good is only accomplished with the greatest difficulty.

The place where man receives good, on the other hand, must be the exact opposite. In order for man to enjoy the maximum possible satisfaction from the good that he has done, the true nature of his deeds must be as obvious as possible. The existence of God must also be as apparent as possible in such a world. It must be a place where man realizes the goodness of his deeds and their relationship to God.

It is for this reason that God created two levels of existence.[112] First there is this world — *Olam HaZeh* — a place of accomplishment and maximum challenge. Secondly, there is the World to Come — *Olam HaBa* — the world of ultimate reward, where both God's existence and the nature of one's deeds are totally apparent.

IX.

Both this world and the World to Come exist on a physical plane. This is obvious in the case of the physical world. However, according to most authorities, the Future World will also be physical. This is the reason for our belief in the resurrection of the dead. It is a foundation of our faith that God will ultimately bring the dead back to life, or at least provide the souls of the dead with bodies like their previous ones.[113] It will be in these resurrected bodies that man will partake of his ultimate reward in the World to Come.[114]

But why is a physical world necessary at all? Since both God and His ultimate good are spiritual, what need is there for a physical body?

Before we can answer this question, we must first ask another question. What is the difference between the material and the spiritual?

We speak of the material and the spiritual as two different concepts.

We know that the spiritual is not material. But precisely what is the difference?

The answer should be obvious. The main difference between the material and spiritual involves space. Physical space only exists in the physical world. In the spiritual, there is no space as we know it.

As discussed earlier, the concept of distance and closeness also exist in the spiritual world. They do not refer to physical distance, since this does not exist in the spiritual realm. As we have mentioned earlier, however, closeness in a spiritual sense involves resemblance. Two things that resemble each other are said to be spiritually close. Two things that differ, on the other hand, are far apart in a spiritual sense.

This has very important implications. In the spiritual world, it is utterly impossible to bring two opposites together. Because they are opposite, they are by definition, poles apart.

Thus, for example, God and man are worlds apart — "as the heavens are higher than the earth." On a purely spiritual plane, it would be totally impossible for the two ever to be brought together.

It was for this reason that God created the concept of space. Spiritual things can be bound to the material, just as for example the soul is bound to the body.

Two opposites can then be brought together by being bound to physical objects. In the physical world, space exists, and two opposites can literally be pushed together. Furthermore, two spiritual opposites can even be bound to the same material object.[115]

Thus, for example, man has both an urge for good and an urge for evil, the *Yetzer Tov* and the *Yetzer HaRa*. In a purely spiritual sense, these are poles apart. Without a physical world, they could never be brought together in a single entity.

The archetype of the spiritual being is the angel. Since an angel has no body, it can never contain both good and evil in its being. Our sages therefore teach us that angels have no *Yetzer HaRa*. [116]

It is only in a physical being that both good and evil can exist together. Although they are at opposite poles spiritually, they can come together in the physical man. One reason why God created man in a physical world was therefore to allow him to have full freedom of choice, with both good and evil as part of his makeup. Without a physical world, these two concepts could never exist in the same being.[117]

The fact that good and evil can exist in the same physical space also allows good to overcome evil in this world. Here again, this is only possible in a physical world. In a purely spiritual arena, good could never come close enough to evil to have any influence over it. In the physical world, however, good and evil can exist together, and good can therefore overcome evil. Our sages thus teach us that one of the main reasons why man was placed in the physical world was to overcome the forces of evil.[118] The *Zohar* expresses it by stating that we are here "to turn darkness into light."[119]

The entire concept of the nonphysical is very difficult to comprehend, and may be clarified by a remarkable teaching of our sages. The Midrash tells us, "One angel cannot have two missions. Neither can two angels share the same mission."[120]

This teaching brings our entire discussion into focus. The angel is the archetype of the nonphysical being. When we speak of an angel, we are speaking of an entity that exists purely on a spiritual plane. Angels can be differentiated only by their mission, that is, by their involvement and attachment to some physical thing.

Two angels therefore cannot share the same mission. It is only their different missions that make the two angels different entities. They cannot be separated by space like physical objects.[121] Therefore, if they both had the same mission, there would be nothing to differentiate them, and they would be one.

Similarly, one angel cannot have two missions. On a purely spiritual plane, two different concepts cannot exist in a single entity. If an angel had two missions, then it would be two angels.

We can also understand this in terms of the human mind. In a sense, the mind is a pure spiritual entity, bound to man's physical brain. Many thoughts and memories may be bound together by man's physical brain, but the mind can only focus on one of them at a time. In simple terms, a person can only think of one thing at a time. A thought is a spiritual entity, and as such, can only contain a single concept. Since both a thought and an angel are basic spiritual entities, this is very closely related to the fact that an angel can only have a single mission.[122]

For a similar reason, angels have no way of knowing anything that does not pertain to their particular mission. An angel may be created initially with a vast storehouse of knowledge, but it has no way of increasing it, at least, not beyond its own sphere of activity. Thus, for example, we find one angel asking another a question (*Daniel* 12:6): "And one [angel] said to the Man dressed in linen . . . 'How long shall it be until the end of these wonders?' " One angel had to ask the other, because he himself could not know something outside of his own domain.[123]

In the physical world, we can learn things through our five senses. We can see, hear, feel, smell and taste. Our knowledge of things comes from our physical proximity to them. In the spiritual world, however, this does not exist. The only way that one can learn about a thing is to come into spiritual proximity with it. An angel cannot do this outside of his own realm.

Man therefore has an advantage over an angel. The very fact that he exists in this lower world enables him to reach up ever higher.

There are concepts of good decreed by God, and as His decrees, they are intimately bound to Him. When a man physically involves himself with these good concepts, he literally binds himself to God. He thus achieves a closeness that no angel could ever hope to reach.

This is a major difference between a man and an angel. An angel is assigned to one spiritual station, and has no way to rise any higher. Thus, when the Prophet speaks of angels, he says (*Isaiah* 6:2), "Around Him, the seraphim stood." Angels are described as standing and stationary. But when God speaks to man, He tells him (*Zechariah* 3:7), "If you walk in My ways . . . then I will give you a place to move among those who stand here." God was showing the Prophet a vision of stationary angels, and telling him that he would be able to move among them. Man can move from level to level, but angels are bound to their particular plane.

There are may different levels in the spiritual world. The Talmud thus speaks of angels called *Chayos*, and says:

> The distance between heaven and earth
>   is five hundred years.
> The width of each heaven
>   is five hundred years.
> This is true of each of the seven heavens.
> The feet of the Chayos are as great as them all.
> The ankles of the Chayos are as great
>   as everything below them.
> The shins of the Chayos are equally great.
> The thighs of the Chayos are equally great.

The hips of the Chayos are equally great.
The body of the Chayos is equally great.
The neck of the Chayos is equally great.
The head of the Chayos is equally great.
The horns of the Chayos are equally great.
The legs of the Throne of Glory (*Kisey HaKavod*)
   are as great as everything below them.
The throne itself is equally great.

Here we see the many levels of the spiritual world, and the Kabbalists speak of many other levels. In a purely spiritual sense, there is no way for these to come together. The only thing that in any way unifies them is their relationship to the physical world.

In order to reach the highest levels of holiness, man must therefore become part of the physical world. When he obeys God's commandments, he attaches himself to the same physical objects as the One who commanded them. In obeying the commandments, man therefore attaches himself to God to the greatest possible degree. He is thus able to scale the highest spiritual levels.

This is the symbolism of the ladder in Jacob's dream. The Torah tells us that Jacob saw (*Genesis* 28:12), "A ladder standing on earth, whose top reached the heavens." It is only through earthly deeds that we climb to the loftiest heights. The different levels of the spiritual world — the rungs of the "ladder" — can only be bound together when they are "standing on the earth."

The *Zohar* therefore gives an interesting example explaining why the soul must descend to the physical world: "A king once had a son. He sent him to a faraway village to grow and thereby learn the way of the king's palace. The same is true of the soul. It is sent far away to this world to learn the way of the King's palace."

In the light of our discussion this example becomes very clear. For it is only in this physical world that we can achieve any true closeness and perception of God.

In obeying the commandments, man brings God's light down to this world. The Midrash thus tells us that the reason that God created the physical world is because "He wanted to have a dwelling place below." It is through the physical that God's light becomes connected with lower levels of creation.

Just as there are different levels in the spiritual world, so are there different levels in the human soul. These levels extend to the highest spiritual domains. It is only through the body, however, that these different levels are united. Without the body, each would remain separated in its own level.

The main concept here is that spiritual unity is mainly a result of the physical. The *Zohar* expresses this concept, saying, "One who wishes to understand the concept of the holy unity should look at the flame rising from a coal or from a burning lamp. The flame is only unified when it is attached to a physical object."

A flame also contains numerous levels. As in the case of the human soul, these parts can only be united when they are attached to a physical entity.

When a person dies, the different levels of the soul therefore separate. Death not only involves the separation of body and soul, but also the separation of the various parts of the soul. When they are not bound together by the body, each level acts as a separate entity.

This is one reason why the World to Come will bring body and soul back together. A soul alone has no connection to its higher parts, and moreover, has no way of elevating itself. As such, it is no better than an angel. Between death and the resurrection, it remains in the "World of Souls" in what is primarily a static state.[133] It is only when it is reunited with the body that it can once again elevate itself. Of course, there is no challenge in the Future World, and therefore this elevation is more tenuous than in this physical world. It therefore depends to a very large extent on the individual's previous preparation.

The Talmud therefore teaches us that the righteous have no rest, neither in this world nor in the next. They are constantly rising from one level to the next, as it is written (*Psalm* 84:8), "They go from strength to strength, every one appearing before God . . ."

X.

Although all this may seem very deep and complex, it is all really something very simple. It is merely a simple expression of God's love for us. It is for this reason that He gave us the Torah and its commandments. These too are an expression of His love. Our sages thus teach us that "God wanted to do good to Israel, and therefore gave them Torah and Commandments in abundance."

When we realize this, we also know that our ultimate goal in life is to fulfill God's purpose. We must study God's Torah, and then follow its teachings. Only then can we find meaning in life.

This entire concept is expressed most beautifully in the prayer *Ahavas Olam,* part of the evening service:

> With an infinite world of love,
> You loved Your people Israel;
> You taught us Your Torah, Your Mitzvos,
> Your code, Your way.
> Therefore, O Lord our God,
> When we lie down and wake up
> We will think of Your teachings —
> Find happiness in Your Torah's words.
> For they are our life and length of days;
> We will follow them day and night,
> And Your love will never be taken from us.

NOTES

1. Cf. *Sanhedrin* 39b, *Rashi* ad loc. *"Oder."*
2. *Zohar* 1:10b, 1:230b, 2:166b, *Sefer HaBris* 2:1:3. Also see *Emunos VeDeyos*, 1:4 end, 3:0, *Or HaShem* (Crescas) 2:6:2, *Sefer HaYashar* #1, *Pardes Rimonim* 2:6, *Etz Chaim, Shaar HaKelallim* #1, *Reshis Chochmah, Shaar HaTshuvah* #1, *Shnei Luchos HaBris, Bais Yisroel* (Jerusalem, 5720) 1:21b, *Shomrei Emunim (HaKadmon)* 2:3, *Derech HaShem* 1:2.1, *Likutey Moharan* #64.
3. Also see *Psalms* 106:1, 107:1, 118:1, *I Chronicles* 16:34, *2 Chronicles* 20:21. From this, we see that it was a much-repeated praise.
4. *Likutey Moharan* 52, *Akedas Yitzchak* 4 (35b). Also see *Yad, Yesodey HaTorah* 1:3. Cf. *Bemidbar Rabbah* 10:1.
5. See *Sefer Baal Shem Tov, Bereshis* 6; *Magid Devarav LeYaakov* #102. Cf. *Bereshis Rabbah* 1:5, *Sh'mos Rabbah* 38:5.
6. *Bereshis Rabbah* 2:7.
7. *Moreh Nevuchim* 3:25.
8. *Berachos* 60a.
9. Rabbi Moshe Chaim Luzzatto, *KaLaCh Pischey Chochmah* #2.
10. *Yoma* 38a.
11. See *Avos* 6:11.
12. See *Moreh Nevuchim* 1:64, from *Exodus* 33:18.
13. *Moreh Nevuchim* 3:13; *Shamayim Chadishim (Abarbanel)* 4:6, quoted in *Shevil Emunah* (on *Emunos VeDeyos*) end of 1, #9; *Shomer Emunim* 2:13.
14. *Bereshis Rabbah* 1:2.
15. *Avos* 6:3, *Berachos* 5a, *Kallah* 8, *Yerushalmi Rosh HaShanah* 3:8, *Tanchuma Re'eh* 11, *Tana DeBei Eliahu Zuta* 17, *Pesichta Eicha Rabbah* 2.
16. *Pirkey DeRabbi Eliezer* 3.
17. *Likutey Moharan* 52. See *Zohar* 3:257b, *Etz Chaim, Drush Egolim VeYashar* #1; *Shevil Emunah*, beginning of #3.
18. *Sefer HaYashar* 1.
19. *Esther Rabbah* 10:14.
20. *Midrash Tehillim* 31. See *Derech HaShem* 1:2:1.
21. Ibid. 2:6:4; *Shiur Kumah* 13:3.
24. *Yerushalmi Berachos* 6:1 (41b). Cf. *Targum* ad loc.
25. *Moreh Nevuchim* 1:18.
26. *Zohar* 2:42b, *Emunos VeDeyos*, end of chapter 1, *Etz Chaim, Shaar HaKelallim* #1.
27. *Shiur Kumah* 13:3.
28. *Reshis Chochmah*, introduction. Cf. *Rabenu Yonah* on *Proverbs* 2:5.
29. *Shabbos* 31b.
30. *Berachos* 6b.
31. *Yad, Tshuvah* 8:7. Cf. *Berachos* 4a.
32. *Avos* 4:16.
33. *Kiddushin* 39b, *Chulin* 142a.
34. *Avos* 4:17.
35. *Berachos* 17a.
36. *Yad, Tshuvah* 8:3, *Toras HaAdam, Shaar HaG'mul* (Jerusalem, 5723) p. 307.

37. *Daas Tevunah* (Tel Aviv, 5726) p. 9.
38. *Pardes Rimonim* 2:6, *Shefa Tal,* end of #2, *Etz Chaim, Shaar Derushey ABYA* #1.
39. *Midrash,* quoted in *Shaar HaG'mul,* p. 296. See also *Zohar* 2:166a, *Likutey Moharan* 275, *Sichos HaRan* 134.
40. *Bereshis Rabbah* 12:5, *Chagigah* 12a.
41. Ibid., *Bereishis Rabbah* 3:6; *Rashi* on *Genesis* 1:4.
42. *Bahir* 160, *Shaar HaG'mul* p. 306; *Avodas HaKodesh* 2:25.
43. *VaYikra Rabbah* 20:7, *Zohar* 1:135a.
44. *Baba Basra* 10a.
45. *Emunos VeDeyos* 9:5, *Ibn Ezra* ad loc., *VaYikra Rabbah* 30:2.
46. *Berachos* 34b, *Sanhedrin* 99a, *Rashi, Metzudos* ad loc., *Yad, Tshuvah* 8:7.
47. *Sanhedrin* 4:5 (37a).
48. Ibid. 38a, *Bereshis Rabbah* 8:5, *Emunos VeDeyos,* introduction to #4.
49. See *Bereshis Rabbah* 8:1, 19:4, *Tikuney Zohar* 6a, *Levush Techeles* #1, *Ikkarim* 1:11.
50. See *Emunos VeDeyos* 4:2, *Akedas Yitzchak* 5 (43a).
51. *Shefa Tal,* beginning of introduction; *Nishmas Chaim* 2:9, *Nefesh HaChaim* 1:15, *Likutey Amaram (Tanya)* 1:2 (6a); *Shaarey Kedushah* 3:2, *Likutey Torah HaAri* on *Exodus* 33:5; *Pischey Chochmah VoDaas, Biur Olom HaNikudos* (with *KaLach Pischey Chochmah,* Jerusalem, 5721) p. 23a.
52. *Zohar* 1:27a, 3:123b, *Zohar Chadash* 10c, *Likutey Amaram* loc. cit., *Ramban* on *Genesis* 2:7; *idem, D'rashash Toras HaShem Temimah* (in *Kisvey HaRamban,* Jerusalem, 5723) p. 159, *Shefa Tal* (Brooklyn, 5720) p. 4c in *Hagah, Shiu Kumah* 51.
53. For the question whether or not there is intelligent life on other worlds, see my article, "On Extraterrestrial Life," in *INTERCOM* 14:1, December 1972.
54. *Kesubos* 5a.
55. See *Rambam* on *Sanhedrin* 10:1, *Ikkarim* 4:33.
56. *Ibn Ezra* ad loc., *Emunos VeDeyos* 1:4 end, 3:0.
57. *Kiddushin* 31a.
58. *Shabbos* 10b.
59. *Bereshis Rabbah* 1:1, *Rashi* on *Genesis* 1:1.
60. *Avos* 4:2; *Ohav Yisroel (Re'eh)* on *Deuteronomy* 8:16, *Shnei Luchos HaBris, Bais Chochmah* 1:22a, *Nefesh HaChaim* 1:12, *Avodas HaKodesh* 2:18, *Amud HaAvodah* (Chernowitz 5623) 101b.
61. *Nishmas Adam* #1 (Pieterkov, 5671) p. 16b.
62. *Avodah Zarah* 3a.
63. *Berachos* 8a. See *Nishmas Adam* loc. cit.
64. *Baba Metzia* 59a, *Shaarey Tshuvah (Rabenu Yonah)* 3:141.
65. *Ikkarim* 4:33, *Nishmas Chaim* 1:13. See *Shaar HaG'mul* p. 289.
66. See my article, "Immortality and the Soul," in *INTERCOM* 13:2, May 1972, p. 6.
67. *Yerushalmi Arlah* 1:3 (6a), quoted in *Rabenu Shimshon (Rash), Tosfos Yom Tov,* on *Arlah* 1:5, *Tosfos, Kiddushin* 36b *"Kol Mitzvah," Turey Zahav, Yoreh Deah* 294:25, and more specifically in this context in *Daas Tevunah* p. 5, *Pischey Chochmah VoDaas* #1, *Kinas HaShem Tzevakos* 5,

KaLaCh Pischey Chochmah 4, Avodas HaKodesh (Chida) Moreh BeEtzba
319; Nishmas Chaim 2:6.
68. Berachos 6b.
69. Betza 32b. Cf. Sh'mos Rabbah 14:2.
70. Avos DeRabbi Nathan 31:1.
71. Zohar 1:4a.
72. Yad, Tshuvah 5:1, Moreh Nevuchim 3:17, Emunos VeDeyos 4:4 (64b), cf.
Pirkey DeRabbi Eliezer 15 (35a), Menachos 29b.
73. Yad, Tshuvah 5:4.
74. Zohar 1:23a, Emunos VeDeyos 3:0, Reshis Chochmah 3:1 (101b).
75. Sotah 14a.
76. See Amud HaAvodah, Hakdamah Gedolah #31; Rabbi Yitzchok Ashlag,
Hakdama LeSefer HaZohar (in Sulam) #9, idem., Talmud Eser Sefiros,
Histaklus Penimis, part 1, 1:4 (p. 15).
77. Tanchuma, Kedoshim 5, according to Reshis Chochmah 2:3 (59d).
78. Menachos 53b.
79. Yad, Tshuvah 5:1.
80. See Gan Ravah on Deutoronomy 7:10 (143b).
81. Ikkarim 2:11, Akedas Yitzchak 4 (36b), Shiur Kumah 18. Cf. Berachos 32a,
Bereshis Rabbah 13:14.
82. Kiddushin 30a.
83. Derech Mitzvosecha (Chabad) "Aroyos" p. 29b f.
84. Shavuos 32a.
85. Reshis Chochmah 1:14 (41d).
86. VaYikra Rabbah 4:6.
87. Sotah 14a, Yad, Deyos 1:8. See above, note 75.
88. Shabbos 153b.
89. Ibid. 31a.
90. Sifra ad loc., Yerushalmi Nedarim 9:4 (30b), Bereshis Rabbah 24:8.
91. Amud HaAvodah 119a, 131a. Our Sages thus teach us, "Love breaks all
barriers," cf. Bereshis Rabbah 55:11.
92. Amud HaAvodah 136d.
93. Nedarim 64b. Cf. Tikuney Zohar 22 (66b).
94. Berachos 18b.
95. Cf. Midrash Tehillim 36:4, Zohar 1:23a, 2:184a, Akedas Yitzchak 70
(3:145b), Etz Chaim, Shaar HaMelachim 5, Sefer Baal Shem Tov, Sh'mos
#9.
96. Makkos 3:15 (23b).
97. Cf. Emunos VeDeyos, end of 4:1.
98. Chulin 60b.
99. Zohar 3:47b.
100. Cf. Moreh Nevuchim 3:26.
101. KaLaCh Pischey Chochmah #2.
102. Zohar 2:163a. Cf. Baba Basra 10a, Rabbi Yaakov Emden (Maharibatz) ad
loc.
103. Avos 5:23.
104. Tana DeBei Eliahu Zuta 12 (17a).
105. Tana DeBei Eliahu Rabbah 16 (78a). Cf. Menachos 29b.
106. Kuzari 5:20 (48b), Ramban on Genesis 22:1, 22:12, Exodus 16:4,

Deuteronomy 31:1, *Shaar HaGemul* p. 272, *Radal* on *Pirkey DeRabbi Eliezer* 31:2. See also *Bereshis Rabbah* 32:3, 34:2, 55:2.

107. *Sifri Ekev* 47, *Yalkut* 1:872.
108. *Sefer HaYashar* #1.
109. *Eruvin* 13b, according to *Avodas HaKodesh* 2:22, *Ikkarim* 4:29, Cf. *Yaaros Devash* 1:14, *Bachya* on *Genesis* 6:6.
110. *Sanhedrin* 24b.
111. *Ibn Ezra* ad loc. Cf. *Zohar* 2:89b.
112. *Derech HaShem* 1:3:4.
113. *Thirteen Principles of Faith*, #13; *Sanhedrin* 10:1. See *Bereishis Rabbah* 4:5.
114. This is the majority opinion, see *Emunos VeDeyos* 7:8, *Shaar HaGemul* p. 310, *Avodas HaKodesh* 2:41f., *Shnei Luchos HaBris, Bais David* (30a f.), *Derech HaShem* 1:3:9, *Derech Mitzvosecha, Tzitzis* 14b. The *Rambam*, however, holds that the World to Come is for souls only, see *Yad, Tshuvah* 8:2, *Moreh Nevuchim* 2:27, *Iggeres Techiyas HaMesim*. Also see *Kuzari* 1:114, 3:20,21, *Chovos HaLevavos* 4:4:6.
115. See *Moreh Nevuchim*, introduction to part 2, #16; *Amud HaAvodah, Vikuach Shoel U'Meshiv* #99.
116. Cf. *Shabbos* 89a, *Bereshis Rabbah* 48:11.
117. *Pischey Chochmah VoDaas* #3, *Shefa Tal* 3:1 (48a).
118. *Toldos Yaakov Yosef, VaYereh* 17a.
119. *Zohar* 1:4a.
120. *Bereshis Rabbah* 50:2, *Targum*, *Rashi* on *Genesis* 18:2, *Zohar* 1:127a.
121. *Pardes Rimonim* 6:6. See note 115.
122. *Amud HaAvodah* p. 83c.
123. *Sefer Chasidim* 530. Cf. *Zohar* 1:101b.

THE
REAL
MESSIAH?

*A Jewish Response
to Missionaries*

Very often, in an attempt to respond to a missionary challenge, one can make a number of seemingly logical moves which, in fact, play directly into the hands of the missionaries. Therefore, a number of Jewish communal leaders have prepared these guidelines for dealing on the spot with missionaries and their followers.

A Practical Guide To The Missionary Problem

1. You will not win hearts to Torah by trying to convince people that the claims of Christianity are false. Spend your time learning, teaching and explaining the meaning of the Torah and its Mitsvos. Better still, invite a person who is in search of religious values to a Shabbaton, or to your home for Shabbat. Let the truth and beauty of Torah and its way of life restore people to the right path.

2. Do not argue with missionaries; do not lend credence or dignity to their efforts at soul snatching. There are tens of millions of non-practicing Christians in this country who are better targets for their efforts.

3. Missionaries are usually closed-minded fanatics. They are trained to respond to your arguments with pat, almost memorized answers. If they can't handle your objection, they will deflect it by raising another, and still another point. Even if you win — you lose.

4. Do not debate, dialogue or argue with missionaries. Missionaries often seek to engage Jews in public discussion. Do not be drawn into this utterly fruitless exercise. Above all, do not invite missionaries or their followers to address meetings under Jewish auspices. Such hospitality only gives the missionary cause institutional dignity and legitimacy. On the other hand, do not publicly attack or abuse the

missionaries; this merely serves to surround them with an aura of martyrdom, to our loss. Our essential obligation is to shore up our Jewishness.

5. Do not be taken in by the "Jewish Christian" ploy. Some missionary groups appeal specifically to Jews with the specious notion that those joining them are thereby "completed" or "fulfilled" as Jews. This is patently incompatible with Jewish tradition and conviction. Conversion to Christianity or any other faith is an abandonment of Judaism. We must strive, with loving concern, to restore erring individuals to their own faith and community.

6. Do not lose your "cool." The style of the missionaries is likely to be cool and affable. Emulate it. When they come smiling to the door, respond politely — firmly but with no recrimination — "No, thanks, I'm not interested," or some brief and definitive equivalent.

7. Get the facts. Fact-finding is a "must." This is an indispensable step. Until the actual situation in the community has been established, planning cannot proceed intelligently. Are Jews, as Jews, being missionized? By whom, from what centers or sources? In what settings and by what means — in schools, through coffee houses, "drop-in" centers, via the communications media, prayer meetings, home study groups, bookmobiles?

8. Plan strategy and approaches. Assuming the fact-gathering process indicates a problem requiring action:

> (a) Survey the available resources — knowledgeable and experienced personnel, appropriate literature, suitable facilities.

> (b) Priority should go to marshalling individuals — young and old. Set up a task force of peer-to-peer as well as adult resource people with some forte or expertise in this area.

> (c) *Very carefully* study *at first hand* the needs of those Jewish young people who are flirting with or have been drawn into other religious movements,

and what they are seeking. *Make no prejudgments* on these matters. The Jesus Movement is very complex.

(d) With equal care, plan how to offer a positive Jewish response to their need and search. Only then will it be possible to reach out to them and to share the needed knowledge and understanding with others to be trained for further intensive outreach.

9. Focus on the teenager. Not only college students, but those in the high schools and even in the junior high schools must be deemed vulnerable. Many missionaries may concentrate on teenagers, deliberately using a peer-group approach, exploiting the unsettled state that marks the adolescent years particularly in these times, and the readiness of young people to challenge any traditional accepted values.

These areas demand our greatest scrutiny and innovative planning. Our caution against overreaction bears repeating here. "Crash programs," counter-crusades, or resort to gimmickry must be avoided.

10. Create opportunities for youth participation. Unfortunately those who are confused Jewishly and troubled personally will not always avail themselves of the programs conducted in synagogues, or youth organizations. Additional ways need to be developed for reaching out with approaches that truly enable young people to shape the content, directions and policies of the programs that *are regarded by them* as not controlled by the "establishment." Some recently initiated youth and teen programs reflect this approach, utilizing informal settings such as storefronts and coffee houses, providing opportunity for "rapping" and for making contacts with other youth. Such programs are consistent with the long-range goals of reaching youth, providing a Jewish setting in which they can relax, meet other Jewish youth, "shmoos" and talk seriously with warm, sensitive, responsive and skillful people — including members of their own peer-groups. Experimentation with innovative and creative approaches to opening channels of participation by our youth must be given high priority.

Most of all, remember that most people drawn to the missionaries have never experienced real Torah living — just suggest, "Before you go to the gentiles, why not see what our own tradition has to offer." But follow through by making positive Torah experiences available to them.

For almost 2,000 years, Christian missionaries have been trying to convince the Jew to accept their beliefs, and for just as long, the Jew has resisted. The ones who resisted most strongly were those who sought G-d with the most fervor. What was their motivation? Why did we never give in to the missionaries?

Why Aren't We Christians?

by
ARYEH KAPLAN

We hear quite a bit today about a movement called "Jews for Jesus." A small number of Jews seem to be finding the teachings of Christianity very attractive. The vast majority of Jews, however, still reject these teachings in the most emphatic terms.

For almost two thousand years, the Christians have been trying to win over the Jew. And for the same period of time, the Jew has resisted all such overtures. But why? Why don't we accept Jesus? In short: Why aren't we Christians?

In order to understand this, we must look at the origin of Christian beliefs. Christianity began with a Jew. Jesus lived as a Jew, around the same time as many of our greatest Talmudic sages. The great Hillel lived just a generation earlier, and Rabbi Akiba, a generation after. Our own sources, however, record very little about Jesus' life. Everything that we know about him is found in the Gospels of the New Testament, a book written by and for the early Christian church. This book, however, was written primarily to further the cause of Christianity, and it is therefore impossible to separate the historical person of Jesus from the "Christ" required by early Christian theology.

Soon after the death of Jesus, we find a marked change in the teachings of his followers. Christianity as we know it began during this period in the work of Paul of Tarsus. Paul, or as he was earlier known, Saul, was a disciple of the great Talmudist Rabbi Gamliel, and he began his career by actively opposing the early Christians. In a dramatic incident on the road to Damascus, Paul converted to Christianity, and later became one of its foremost leaders. Although he had never seen Jesus alive, he claimed to have spoken to him in spirit. Under Paul's leadership, many of the distinctive doctrines of Christianity were first proclaimed, and, for the most part, they have never changed. His teachings are recorded in his Epistles, which form the second part of the New Testament.

Among Paul's major teachings, we find the following:

1. Jesus was the Messiah or Christ predicted by the Prophets of the Bible and awaited by the Jews. He is also the Son of G-d, and like any son, is essentially the same as his Father.

2. Man is evil and sinful. All mankind is damned because of Adam's sin. The Torah cannot save man, since its many commandments make it too difficult to keep. The only thing that can prevent man's utter damnation in hell is the belief in Christ.

3. The Jews were originally G-d's chosen people, but they were rejected when they refused to accept His son, Jesus. The name "Israel," G-d's chosen people, is no longer carried by the Jew, but by those who accept Jesus as the Messiah. Only these share G-d's love. Everyone else is damned in hell.

4. There is only one law now that Christ has come, and that is love. One must follow the example of Christ's sacrifice, and patiently hope that G-d will be gracious in return.

It is enough to state these articles of Christian faith to see why the Jews could not accept them. Taking them one by one, the Jewish viewpoint would be:

1. Jesus could not have been the Messiah. The Prophets predicted a world of peace and love after the Messiah's coming, and this certainly does not exist today. Furthermore, any talk of the Messiah as being the "son of G-d" is totally unacceptable. In no place do the Prophets say that he will be anything more than a remarkable leader and teacher.

2. Although the Torah does speak of Adam's sin, it teaches that man can rise above it. Man might not be able to perfect himself, but it was for this reason that G-d gave us the Torah. It is absurd to think that G-d would give a Torah that was impossible or too difficult to follow. In no place does Judaism teach that one can be saved from damnation by mere belief. Any true belief in G-d must lead a person to also follow His commandments.

3. It is impossible to imagine that G-d would ever reject the Jewish people. In many places, the Bible clearly states that His covenant with them will be forever.

4. In many places, the Bible says that the Torah was given forever. It is therefore impossible to say that it has been replaced by a new law or testament. Love alone is not enough, for one must know how to express it, and for this, we need the Torah as a guide. Love is only one of the Torah's commandments, and good deeds are its necessary expression.

Why do we believe these ideas rather than the ones expressed by Paul and Christianity?

For one thing, we see no evidence that Jesus was indeed the Messiah expected by Israel. The Messianic promise included such things as perfect peace and unity among men, love and truth, universal knowledge and undisturbed happiness, as well as the end of all evil, idolatry, falsehood and hatred. None of these things have been fulfilled by Christianity.

The Christian answer to this is the simple assertion that all things have indeed changed by the coming of Jesus. If the change is not visible, it is because man is evil and has not truly accepted Jesus and his teachings. Thus, the Messiah or Christ will have to return in order to prove his victory.

The Jew refuses to accept the excuse that the major prophecies concerning the Messiah will only be fulfilled in a "second coming." He expects the Messiah to complete his mission in his first attempt. The Jew therefore believes that the Messiah is yet to come.

But there is also another more important issue at stake than the mere identity of the Messiah. Christianity teaches that

Jesus was also G-d in human form. The Jew sees this as a totally mistaken idea about G-d. It makes G-d too small, for in stating that He can assume human form, it diminishes both His unity and His divinity.

We disagree with Christianity not only with regard to belief, but also with regard to what man must do. Christianity tends to deny that man's actions are ultimately very useful. The only thing that can save man is his utter despair in his own sinfulness, and total dependence on G-d. The Jew, on the other hand, believes that man can come close to G-d by obeying Him and keeping His commandments.

Christianity thus starts with one idea about man, while Judaism starts with the exact opposite idea.

Judaism starts with the idea that man is created in the "likeness of G-d." He therefore does not have to go very far to discover the divine, both in himself and in others. There is always the opportunity to awaken the divine in oneself by obeying G-d's commandments. The Jew begins with this opportunity.

Christianity, on the other hand, begins with the basic assumption that man is depraved and sinful. Left to himself, man is utterly damned. He is naturally involved in evil, and must therefore do something to be saved from it.

The first question that the Christian asks is, "What have you done to be saved?" To the Jew, this question is almost meaningless. This is not the Jewish way of thinking at all. The Jew asks, "How can I serve G-d? How can I keep His commandments?" The central focus of Judaism is obeying the commandments of the Torah. We look at man and see his greatness, for he can obey these commandments and fulfill G-d's will.

Christianity teaches that man is so evil that he can never really serve G-d. The Torah is too difficult for man. The only thing that man can do is believe in Christ and wait for salvation.

The Jew replies that the very fact that G-d Himself gave us commandments and told us to obey them teaches us that we can indeed serve G-d and fulfill His will. It is unthinkable that G-d would give His people a Torah if it were impossible to keep it.

Although all of Jesus' disciples were Jews, they could not convince their fellow Jews of their teachings. The early dogmas of Christianity seemed closer to those of the pagan gentiles than to those of the Jews. More and more, Christianity was rejected by the Jews and accepted by the gentiles. It thus gradually developed into a gentile church, and its attitude toward the Jews became more and more unfriendly. It may have constantly appealed to the Jews to convert, sometimes even resorting to cruelty and force, but the Jew stood firm. Christianity may have changed human history, but it could never win over the Jews. The Jew stood by his Torah and walked his own way.

In essence, there were two Christian teachings that the Jew could never accept. Christianity taught that G-d had assumed human form in Jesus, and that the Torah no longer mattered. The Jew rejected these two dogmas, even under pain of death.

In rejecting Christianity, Judaism therefore did not reject anything that it needed spiritually. There was nothing in all the teachings of Jesus that would have added even one iota to the strength of the Torah. If Christianity made any contribution at all, it was to the non-Jewish world.

The Jew knew that his Torah provided him with a unique relationship with G-d. Everything that he saw in Christianity seemed to contradict this relationship. It is for this reason that throughout the centuries, the Jew has found it impossible to accept the teachings of Christianity. He believed with perfect faith that G-d had shown him the way, and he had no intention of ever leaving it.

For the Jew, accepting Christianity involved much more than merely accepting a false Messiah. Aside from its belief in Jesus as the Messiah, Christianity has altered many of the most fundamental concepts of Judaism. Here, we explore the Halachic consequences of a Jew who embraces Christianity.

When A Jew Becomes A Christian

by
ARYEH KAPLAN

The sign shouts, "Jews for Jesus!"

You look at the sign and wonder what's going on. You might have heard of them or read about them in the papers. Your curiosity is aroused.

You decide to find out more about it, and speak to one of these strange people. You strike up a conversation. He tells you that he is a Jewish Christian — one of the "Jews for Jesus."

Before you know it, he is asking you how you feel about your Jewishness. You might admit that you find your Judaism spiritually unfulfilling. You both agree that the typical liberal synagogue in which you grew up seemed to offer everything but a religious experience.

You admit that deep down you realize that there is a spiritual dimension missing from your life. He sympathizes and tells you the reason why Judaism does not fulfill this need is because you have left out an essential ingredient.

Then he gives you the punch line: What you need is Jesus. He tells you that to be a true Jew you must believe in Jesus. Only then, so he says, can Judaism provide you with that dimension you are seeking.

Do not be deceived.

For the past two thousand years, Christians have been trying to convert Jews to their beliefs. This is a central goal of their religion. Jesus, the central object of their belief, was a Jew. He taught and preached to Jews. Yet, he was rejected by them. How can Christians justify their belief, when Jesus' very own people refused to accept him? To get the Jews to accept Jesus is therefore one of their most important goals. However, in our generation, some enlightened Christian leaders have called for an end to such active missionary activity. Sadly enough, these leaders are ignored by the growing missionary "cult."

But you might ask, "So what's that terrible? At worst I'll be believing in a false Messiah. What do I have to lose?"

The truth is that you have a lot to lose.

Let us begin by examining the basic beliefs of Christianity.

Beside its basic creed that Jesus was the Messiah, the fundamental doctrines of Christianity are:

The Trinity: According to most Christians, G-d consists of three persons, the Father, the Son, and the Holy Ghost.

The Incarnation: Christians believe that the Son, the second part of the godhead, came down to earth in human form in the person of Jesus.

Mediation: According to their creed, no man can approach G-d directly. Everyone must go through Jesus, the Son.

Let us carefully examine these beliefs.

A basic foundation of most Christian sects is belief in the Trinity. Christianity teaches that G-d consists of three persons, the Father, the Son, and the Holy Ghost. The Father is the one who created the world, the Son is the one who redeems man, and the Holy Ghost is the member of the godhead that speaks to the prophets.[1]

Jesus himself alluded to the doctrine of the Trinity. The Gospel of Matthew tells us that his final words to his disciples were, "Go ye therefore, and teach all nations, baptizing them in the name of the Father, and of the Son, and of the Holy Ghost."[2] This belief in a three-part god is a basic doctrine of Christianity.

Christians claim that this three-part god that they worship is the same as the G-d worshipped by the Jews.

This is not true.

The Bible states (Deut. 6:4), "Hear O Israel, the Lord is our G-d, the Lord is *One*."

Twice every day, the believing Jew cries out these words. They are the first thing a Jew learns as a child and the last words he utters before he dies. On every Jewish doorpost there is a Mezuzah proclaiming these words. They are again found in the Tefillin, bound daily next to a Jew's heart and mind, proclaiming this most basic principle of Judaism.

Worship of any three-part god by a Jew is nothing less than a form of idolatry.[3]

Idolatry does not necessarily mean worshipping a god of stone or wood. Even if a Jew worships the highest angel, it is also a form of idolatry.[4] G-d is the infinite One, Creator of all things. Anyone who worships anything else is guilty of idolatry.[5]

The three-part God of Christianity is not the G-d of Judaism. Therefore, in the Jewish view, Christianity may very well be a variation of idolatry.

Although Christianity began among Jews, it was rapidly adopted by the pagans of the ancient world. These pagans believed in an entire pantheon of gods. It was just too much for them to give up all these gods in favor of the One True G-d. So early Christian missionaries compromised with these pagans by introducing the Trinity, a sort of three-in-one god. Even many contemporary Christian scholars see the Trinity as the result of pagan influence on Christianity.

This might represent an improvement for the pagan. But for the Jew it is a regression, representing a step backwards towards idolatry.

This might not seem to be in the Jewish spirit of never attacking other faiths, but when missionaries are spreading lies about Judaism, it is time to unmask these lies. Indeed, several contemporary Christian leaders have denounced the missionaries who prey on Jews.

Let us now examine a second basic belief of Christianity, that of the Incarnation. According to this doctrine, G-d in the person of the Son assumed human form in the person of Jesus.

It is best expressed in the Nicene Creed, recited every Sunday in most churches. In it, the Christian declares:

"I believe in one Lord, Jesus Christ, the only-begotten Son of God. Born of the Father before all ages. God of God, Light of Light, true God of true God. Begotten, not made, of one substance with the Father. By whom all things were made. Who for us men and for our salvation came down from heaven. And he became flesh by the Holy Spirit of the Virgin Mary: and was made man."

Christians really believe that Jesus was G-d, and this is one of the most fundamental beliefs of Christianity.

If we accept the testimony of the Gospels, then this belief originated with Jesus himself.

Among other things, Jesus said:

"All things that the Father (i.e. G-d) hath are mine."[6]

"My father worketh hitherto, and I work."[7]

"For the Father judgeth no man, but hath committed all judgment unto the Son; that all men should honour the Son, even as they honour the Father."[8]

"I and the Father are one."[9]

"He that hath seen me hath seen the Father."[10]

From these quotes, it seems obvious that Jesus himself claimed to be G-d. The missionaries and "Jews for Jesus" do not tell you about this. They wait until you have fallen into their net. But this is one of the most basic beliefs of Christianity.

If belief in the Trinity is idolatry, then, from the Jewish point of view, this concept is perhaps even more objectionable. The pagan gods came down in human form, copulated with mortals, and bore human children. Many Christian historians attribute it to the early Christians who were attempting to win over pagans to their new religion, and therefore adopted this pagan concept.

But what does the Bible say about the unity of G-d?

It says:

"Know this day, and lay it in your heart, that the L-rd is G-d, in the heavens above and on the earth below, there is none else" (Deut. 4:39).

"Do I not fill heaven and earth, says G-d" (Jer. 25:24).

"The whole earth is filled with his glory" (Isa. 6:3).

"Great is G-d, highly praised, His greatness is unfathomable" (Psalms 145:3).

G-d is the Ultimate, the Infinite, the All Powerful Creator of all things. To say that any man was G-d is — to the Jew — the height of absurdity.

The Bible says (Numbers 23:19), "G-d is not a mortal that He should lie, nor a man, that He should change His mind." G-d does not suddenly decide to visit the earth in a human body. A G-d who fills and sustains all creation does not have to visit our planet in human form. The Jerusalem Talmud flatly states the Jewish view, "If a man claims to be G-d, he is a liar!"[11]

The third basic belief of Christianity is that of Mediation. This states that man cannot approach G-d except through Jesus. All prayer must be in the name of "Jesus Christ our Lord."

Here again, it was Jesus himself who is alleged to have proclaimed this doctrine. He openly said, "I am the way, the truth, and the life, no man cometh unto the Father but by me."[12]

This Christian doctrine goes against the very opening statement of the Ten Commandments.

The Ten Commandments begin with the words, "I am the L-rd your G-d, Who brought you out of the Land of Egypt, from the house of slavery. You shall have no other gods *before Me*."

When G-d says, "Before Me," He is stressing that you should not believe in any other deity, even if you believe in G-d as well. One who sets up a mediator between G-d and man is guilty of violating this Commandment.[13]

If a man believes in G-d, then why should he need any other deity? But a person might think that G-d is so high as to be unapproachable without a mediator. The opening statement of the Ten Commandments teaches us that this is also idolatry.

G-d is infinite and all-knowing. To say that He needs a

mediator to hear our prayers is to deny His infinite wisdom.

If Jesus actually made these statements recorded in the Gospel, then he was advocating idolatry, with himself as the deity. If this is true, is there any wonder that Jews never accepted him either as a prophet, rabbi or teacher?

Judaism is unique among the religions of the world. Almost without exception, the world's religions begin with a single individual, be he Jesus, or Buddha, or Mohammed, or Confucius, or Lao-tze. This individual gradually gathers a following, either through "miracles" or through sheer charisma. But from the beginning the entire foundation rests on a single individual.

Judaism is the one exception to this. It did not begin with any individual. An entire nation stood at the foot of Mount Sinai and heard G-d introduce Himself.

Only G-d, speaking to an entire nation, could reveal a true religion. And once G-d speaks, He does not "change His mind," or revise the truths He proclaimed as absolute and eternal.

Our most basic beliefs were taught by G-d Himself at Sinai. The Bible says (Deut. 4:35), "Unto you it was shown, that you might know, that the L-rd is G-d, there is none else besides Him. Out of heaven He made you hear His voice, that He might instruct you."

No matter how many miracles a prophet might produce, he cannot change this basic principle. If a man tells us to commit idolatry, he is a false prophet, no matter how many wonders he pulls out of a hat.

G-d warned us about this in the Bible (Deut. 13:2):

"If there arise among you a prophet, or a dreamer, and he gives you a sign or a miracle. And the sign or miracle comes to pass, and he calls on you, saying, 'Let us go after other gods, whom you have not known, and let us worship them.' You shall not listen to that prophet or dreamer. For G-d is testing you, to see whether you love the L-rd your G-d with all your heart and with all your soul."

G-d Himself was warning us about movements like Christianity. Even if all the miracles recorded in the Gospel were true, we do not pay any heed to them. G-d has already warned us.

When A Jew Becomes A Christian □ 269

This brings us back to our original question. What can a Jew lose by embracing Christianity?

The answer is: Everything.

Christianity negates the fundamentals of Jewish faith, and one who accepts it rejects the very essence of Judaism.[14] Even if he continues to keep all the rituals, it is the same as if he abandoned Judaism completely. The Talmud teaches us, "Whoever accepts idolatry, denies the entire Torah."[15]

A Jew who accepts Christianity might call himself a "Jewish Christian," but he is no longer a Jew.[16] He can no longer even be counted as part of a Jewish congregation.[17]

Conversion to another faith is an act of religious treason. It is one of the worst possible sins that a Jew can commit. Along with murder and incest, it is one of the three cardinal sins which may not be violated even under pain of death.[18]

The missionaries tell you, "Believe in Jesus and be saved."

The truth is that one who falls into their net is eternally cast away from before his G-d.

A Jew must give his life rather than embrace Christianity.[19]

This is not mere rhetoric. Throughout our history, millions of Jews were given this choice: The Cross or death. Invariably, they chose death.

The missionaries now come and preach love and peace. But Jesus himself said, "Think not that I come to send peace on earth. I come not to send peace, but the sword."[20]

It was this sword that the Crusaders used to wipe out hundreds of Jewish communities in the name of Jesus, the Jew.

It was this sword that they used when they entered Jerusalem in 1215. Their first act was to round up all the Jews to the central synagogue and burn them to death.

It was this sword used by the Spanish Inquisition, when they tortured Jews to death in the name of "Christian Love."

Remember all this when the "Jews for Jesus" speak of peace and love.

These "Jews for Jesus" may arouse your curiosity. But they should also arouse your pity. For they are in an inherent paradox. A Jew for Jesus is a contradiction in terms.

* * *

But what about the Jew who has embraced Christianity? What about the one who has already taken Jesus as his "savior?"

Is he eternally cut off from Judaism? Is he lost without hope of redemption? Is he totally cut off from his people and his G-d?

Judaism teaches that there is always hope.

No matter how far one strays from G-d and Torah he is always accepted back.

The Bible says:

"As I live, says G-d, I have no pleasure in the death of the wicked, but that they turn from their way and live" (Ezek. 33:11).

"When the wicked turns from his sin, and does what is lawful and right, he shall live thereby" (*Ibid*. 33:19).

"That every man shall return from his way, and I will forgive him" (Jer. 36:3).

"If they return to You, and confess Your Name, and pray . . . then You will hear in Heaven, and forgive their sin" (I Kings 8:33, 34).

Even a Jew who has embraced another religion is given a second chance. He can still return to Judaism and be reaccepted by G-d.

He must completely disavow Christianity for all time and commit himself totally and without reservation to Judaism. He need not be formally "converted" back to Judaism, but a definite commitment is in order.[21]

Christianity for a Jew is a form of idolatry, and must be repented as such. Our sages teach us that keeping the Sabbath is particularly effective for such atonement.[22]

* * *

If you find your life spiritually empty, devoid of religious experience, then you need Torah Judaism all the more. You might have been turned off by the pseudo-intellectual substitutes offered by certain "liberal" rabbis. You may never have been exposed to the true depths of Judaism. But it is there, and millions of Jews are inspired by it.

I can gaze at a beautiful sunset, and try to describe it to you. But until you open your eyes and see it for yourself, my words are in vain. You must see it to appreciate it.

I can describe the most delicious fruit. But you must taste it to appreciate it.

The same is true of Judaism. The Bible tells us (Ps. 34:9), "Taste and see, that G-d is good, happy is the man who embraces Him."

You must actually live Torah Judaism to appreciate its beauty and wisdom. Only when you immerse yourself in it totally will you discover its full spiritual dimension.

NOTES

1. Nicene Creed.
2. Matthew 28:19. All quotations are from the King James' Version.
3. *Emunos VeDeyos* 2:5-7, *Moreh Nevuchim* 1:50, Beginning of *Maamar Techiyas Ha-Mesim* (Rambam); *Tshuvos Meil Tzedakah* 22, *Tshuvos Shaar Ephraim* 24, Chasam Sofer on *Orech Chaim* 156:1.
4. *Yad, Avodas Kochavim* 2:1.
5. *Kesef Mishneh, Lechem Mishneh,* on *Yad, Tshuvah* 3:7.
6. John 16:14.
7. *Ibid.* 5:17.
8. *Ibid.* 5:22.
9. *Ibid.* 10:30.
10. *Ibid.* 14:9.
11. *Yerushalmi, Taanis* 2:1 (91). Cf. *Moreh Nevuchim* 3:15.
12. John 14:6.
13. *Yad, Avodas Kochavim* 1.
14. *Ibid., Yesodei HaTorah* 1:6.
15. *Sifri* on *Num.* 15:22 and *Deut.* 11:28; *Yad, Avodas Kochavim* 2:4. Cf. *Horios* 8a.
16. *Yad, loc. cit.* 2:5.
17. *Pri Megadim, Eshel Avraham* 55:4.
18. *Sanhedrin* 74a.
19. *Tshuvos Rivash* 4,11, *Tshuvos Rabbi Yosef ben Lev* 1:15.
20. Matthew 10:34. Cf. Luke 12:49, 51.
21. It is recommended that such a penitent undergo the ritual of immersion like a convert. See *Nimukey Yosef, Yebamos, Rif* 16b "*Kedusnav,*" *Yoreh Deah* 268:12 in *Hagah, Turey Zahav ibid.* 267:5; *Magen Avraham* 325:8. Cf. *Avos DeRabbi Nathan* 8:8.
22. *Shabbos* 118b; *Tur, Orech Chaim* 242.

To the Jew, the Messiah has a most important mission, namely to bring the world back to G-d, and make it a place of peace, justice and harmony. When Jesus failed to accomplish this, the early Christians had to radically alter the very concept of the Messiah. This, in turn, transformed Christianity from another Jewish Messianic sect into a religion that is quite alien to many basic Jewish teachings.

From Messiah To Christ

by
ARYEH KAPLAN

Belief in the coming of the Messiah has always been a fundamental part of Judaism. Thus, for example, Maimonides counts the belief in the Messiah as one of the thirteen cardinal principles of Judaism. It is a concept that is repeated again and again throughout the length and breadth of Jewish literature.

There have been many people in Jewish history who have claimed to be this Messiah. The most famous, of course, was Jesus. His followers therefore gave him the title Christ. *Mashiach* — the Hebrew word for Messiah — literally means the "anointed." The Greek word for "anointed" is Christos, and thus, Christ is really just another word for Messiah.

Although Christians claim that Jesus was the Messiah of the Jews, there are a number of important differences between the way the Jew looks at the Messiah, and the way the Christian does. It is most important to know these differences.

◦§ The Jewish Messiah

The Jewish concept of the Messiah is that which is clearly developed by the prophets of the Bible. He is a leader of the Jews, strong in wisdom, power and spirit. It is he who will bring complete redemption to the Jewish people, both spiritually and physically. Along with this, he will bring eternal peace, love, prosperity, and moral perfection to the entire world.

The Jewish Messiah is truly human in origin. He is born of ordinary human parents, and is of flesh and blood like all mortals.

As described by the Prophet (*Isaiah* 11:2), the Messiah is "full of wisdom and understanding, counsel and might, knowledge and the fear of G-d." He has a special feeling for justice, or, as the Talmud put it (*Sanhedrin* 93b), he "smells and judges." He can virtually sense a man's innocence or guilt.

The Prophet (*Isaiah* 11:4) goes on to say that the Messiah will "smite the tyrant with the rod of his mouth, and slay the wicked with the breath of his lips." Evil and tyranny will not be able to stand up before the Messiah.

Still, the Messiah is primarily a king of peace. Our Sages therefore teach us (*Derech Eretz Zuta*:1): "When the Messiah is revealed to Israel, he will only open his mouth for peace. It is thus written (*Isaiah* 52:7), 'How beautiful upon the mountains are the feet of the messenger who announces peace.' "

The first task of the Messiah is to redeem Israel from exile and servitude. In doing so, he will also redeem the entire world from evil. Oppression, suffering, war and all forms of godless-ness will be abolished. Mankind will thus be perfected, and man's sins against G-d, as well as his transgression against fellow man, will be eliminated. All forms of warfare and strife between nations will also vanish in the Messianic age.

Most important, the Jewish Messiah will bring all peoples to G-d. This is expressed most clearly in the *Alenu* prayer, which concludes all three daily services:

"May the world be perfected under the kingdom of the Almighty. Let all humans call upon Your Name and turn all the world's evildoers to You. Let everyone on earth know that every knee must bow to You . . . and let them all accept the yoke of Your kingdom."

We find a very similar thought in the High Holy Day *Amidah*, where we pray, "Let all creatures bow before You. May they form a single band and do Your will with a perfect heart."

The Jewish Messiah will thus have the task of perfecting the world. He will redeem man from servitude, oppression and his own evil. There will be great material prosperity in the world, and man will be restored to an Eden-like existence, where he can enjoy the fruits of the earth without toil.

In the Messianic age, the Jewish people will dwell freely in their land. There will be an "ingathering of the exiles," when all Jews return to Israel. This will eventually bring all nations to acknowledge the G-d of Israel and accept the truth of His teachings. The Messiah will thus not only be king over Israel, but, in a sense, ruler over all nations.

Ultimately, redemption comes from G-d alone, and the Messiah is only an instrument in His hands. He is a human being, consisting of flesh and blood like all mortals. He is, however, the finest of the human race, and as such, must be crowned with the highest virtues that mortal man can attain.

Although the Messiah may achieve the upper limit of human perfection, he is still human. The kingdom of the Jewish Messiah is definitely "of this world."

Judaism is a religion based on a people serving G-d. It is from the Jew that G-d's teachings emanate to all humanity. The redemption of Israel must therefore precede that of the rest of mankind. Before God redeems the world, He must redeem His oppressed, suffering, exiled and persecuted people, returning them to their own land and restoring their status.

The ultimate promise, however, is not limited to Israel alone. The redemption of the Jew is closely linked to the emancipation of all humanity as well as the destruction of evil and tyranny. It is the first step in man's return to G-d, where all mankind will be united into a "single band" to fulfill G-d's purpose. This is the "Kingdom of the Almighty" in the Messianic Age.

Although the Messiah may occupy a central place in this "Kingdom of Heaven," he is still not the primary figure. This position can only belong to G-d Himself.

This, in brief, is the concept of the Jewish Messiah.

◆§ The Christian Messiah

The primary figure in Christianity is its Messiah. Its very name indicates that Christianity is completely based on the personality of the Messiah. As mentioned earlier, the name "Christ" comes from *Christos*, the Greek word for Messiah. The Christians are thus those who make the person of the Messiah central to their teachings.

The first major difference between the Jews and the early Christians was that the Christians believed that the Messiah had already come, while the Jews believed that he was yet to come. At first, this was the main point of controversy.

The Jews had one minor objection to the Christian Messiah, and that was the fact that he had been unsuccessful. Judaism had always taught that the Messiah would redeem Israel in a political sense, and Jesus had failed to accomplish this. Instead, he had been scourged and humiliated like a common rebel, and finally crucified along with two ordinary thieves.

How could the career of Jesus be reconciled with the glorious picture of the Messiah as taught by the Prophets of Israel? The early Christians faced this dilemma, and, in justifying Jesus as the Messiah, readily altered the entire concept. These new Messianic ideas were developed in the writing of John, and even more so in the Epistles of Paul.

If we look in these sources, we find a gradual transition. The Messiah of the Jew progressively becomes transformed into the Christ of the Christian. This can be traced in a series of logical steps.

1. Jesus was totally unsuccessful in redeeming the Jews politically, and therefore the early Christians could no longer look upon this as the task of the Messiah. His redemption had to be given a new meaning. They therefore taught that his mission was not to redeem man from political oppression, but only to redeem him from spiritual evil.

2. Once the Messiah's mission was redefined, it could also be expanded. Political oppression was a special problem of the Jews, but spiritual evil is worldwide. The early Christians therefore began to teach that Jesus had come to redeem the whole world. They rejected the view that he would come to redeem the Jewish people and their land first, and only then redeem the rest of the world. The Messiah's reign is therefore

universal, but only spiritual. The kingdom of Jesus is thus "not of this world."

3. Jesus had been scourged and humiliated like a common rebel. His followers felt, however, that he had only preached repentance and good works, and therefore could not be a common rebel. They were then faced with an important and difficult question. If Jesus was the true Messiah, then why did G-d allow him to undergo such frightful suffering? Why was he subjected to crucifixion, the most painful and shameful death of all? Why did G-d not save him from all this?

For his followers, there could only be one answer. The fact that Jesus was scourged, humiliated and crucified had to be the will of G-d. But still, another question remained. If Jesus did not sin, what purpose could there be in his suffering and death? For this, the early Christians found a most ingenious solution. The only answer could be that he suffered and died because of the sins of mankind.

But the question was still not completely answered. Had there not been suffering and death before this? Why did Christ himself have to suffer and die? What sin was so great that it required his sacrifice?

The early Christians answered that this was required to atone for the sin of Adam. All mankind is descended from Adam, and therefore, all inherit his sin. This "original sin" cannot be erased with good works, or even with ordinary human suffering. The only thing that could eliminate it was the death of Jesus.

The Messiah of the Christians therefore willingly went to a disgraceful and painful death in order that humanity might be redeemed from this "original sin." Mankind is therefore redeemed from evil, sin, suffering, death and the powers of Satan only by the blood of Christ.

Support for this belief was found in the 53rd chapter of Isaiah, where the Prophet speaks of G-d's suffering servant, who "bore the sin of many." Instead of interpreting it to refer to the persecuted people, Israel, the early Christians claimed that it referred to Jesus.

4. But still the question remained, how could the career of

the Redeemer end in such a shameful death? The story had to be given a sequel. Such an epilogue was found in another traditional Jewish belief, namely, that of the Resurrection of the Dead. The early Christians therefore taught that Jesus had risen from the dead, and furthermore, that he was the first one to do so. Therefore Jesus was not mortal like other men.

5. Jesus' followers could not bring themselves to say that G-d had forced this suffering and death upon His Messiah. Therefore, they had to say that the will of the Messiah was exactly the same as the will of G-d, even when it came to his crucifixion. But how could a mere mortal undertake such suffering? The early Christians replied that Jesus was not a mere mortal. Since his will was so uniquely related to that of G-d, he had to be related to G-d in some special way.

6. During his lifetime, Jesus often spoke of G-d as "my Father in Heaven." For the Jews, this was a common poetic expression, and one that is still used in Jewish prayers. For the pagan gentiles, however, it had a much more literal connotation. The Greeks already had legends about men who had been fathered by gods who had visited mortal human women. Legends like these had even sprung up about such eminent men as Plato, Pythagoras, and Alexander the Great. Why should Jesus be any less? They therefore interpreted his poetic expression quite literally, to mean that he had an actual genetic relationship with G-d. Jesus therefore became the "son of G-d," conceived when the Holy Ghost visited Mary. As the "son of G-d," Jesus was not susceptible to sin or even death.

The death of Jesus was therefore only temporary. The only reason why it was needed at all was to atone for the sin of Adam. His followers taught that Jesus was resurrected for eternity and ascended to heaven. There he sits at the "right hand of G-d," even higher that the angels.

This was the first step toward the deification of Jesus, and it was not very difficult for the pagan world to take the second step. Jesus was credited with such statements as (*John* 10:30), "I and the Father are one." He had also spoken of (*Matthew* 28:19), "The Father, the Son, and the Holy Ghost." It was easy for the paganized Christians to look at the three as equal and identify Jesus with the "Son."

Jesus therefore became G-d-man — one person with two natures. He is G-d and man at the same time. Christians therefore soon found themselves speaking of Mary as the "mother of G-d."

7. Still, there were many Messianic prophecies that Jesus had failed to fulfill. The early Christians therefore taught that he would return to the world again in a "second coming." The Day of Judgment will then occur, and Jesus, having taken his seat at the "right hand of his Father," will judge every man who has ever lived. Those who believed in him will be delivered, while those who did not will be eternally damned to hell.

It is only after this judgment that Satan will be conquered. Evil will then end, sin will vanish, and death will pass away. The powers of darkness will thus be eliminated, and the kingdom of heaven established.

8. In this world, meanwhile, all prayer must be addressed to Jesus. The Christian therefore concludes every prayer "in the name of Jesus Christ our Lord." In this sense, Jesus is the mediator between G-d and man.

* * *

This, in essence, is what the early Christians did to the Jewish concept of the Messiah. The Messiah ceased to be a mere man, and passed beyond the limits of mortality. They taught that man cannot redeem himself from sin, and therefore G-d, clothed in the form of the Messiah, had to freely shed his own blood to redeem mankind. Since Jesus did not fulfill the most important Messianic prophecies, they expected him to return to complete this task in a "second coming."

At first, Christians expected that this "second coming" would come very shortly, and prayed that they would see it in their lifetime. When their prayer was not answered, they began to hope that it would come a thousand years after Jesus' death. This was the millennium or "thousand year kingdom." Finally, after a thousand years passed and Jesus still had not returned, they postponed his "second coming" to an indefinite time.

We therefore see that the early Christians were forced to radically alter the Jewish concept of the Messiah in order to explain Jesus' failure. This, compounded with the pagan influence in the early church, gave birth to a Messianic concept totally alien to Judaism.

◆§ Jewish Reaction

It is not very difficult to understand why the Jews totally rejected the contentions of Christianity.

First of all, the Jews had a tradition, well supported in the teachings of the Prophets, that the Messiah would bring about major changes in the world. The "spiritual kingdom" did not in any way fulfill these prophecies. The Jews were furthermore unconvinced by the answer of the "second coming" since it was not even hinted at in Biblical literature.

Thus, first of all, the Jew found absolutely no evidence to support Jesus' claim to having been the Messiah. On the other hand, Jesus' lack of success appeared to repudiate it.

Even more important, however, was the fact that the Christians had logically developed their belief in Jesus in such a manner that they radically altered many of the most basic Jewish beliefs. Even such a basic concept as G-d's unity was threatened by their teachings. Even if the evidence of Jesus' Messiahship was more concrete, its logical consequences would have to be rejected.

The early Christians tried to justify their contention by finding hints of it in the Jewish scriptures. They went over the entire Bible with a fine tooth comb, looking for any evidence, however flimsy, to prove that Jesus was the Messiah, and that their entire logical structure was in accord with ancient Jewish teachings. In many cases, they were not above using verses out of context, changing texts, and even mistranslating them, in order to prove their point. One needs no further evidence than the fact that most modern Christian Bible scholars totally reject almost all the "proofs" of the early Christians. Indeed, some of the best refutations of these "proofs" may be found in contemporary Christian Bible commentaries.

Most important, Christianity tried to set itself up as the new

"Israel," and looked upon the Jews as utterly rejected by G-d. It therefore taught that Judaism was a corrupt and dying religion, with little hope of growth or success.

The Jews, on the other hand, did much more than argue this point with words. They refuted it by embarking upon one of the most creative periods in their history. The entire scope of Talmudic literature was developed essentially during early post-Christian times.

Thus, to the Jews, the strongest refutation of Christianity was the fact that Judaism itself remained alive and vital. The Jew has found that he can both exist and flourish without accepting Christian beliefs. He believes that the Messiah is yet to come, and that at that time, the truth will become known and the Jew will be justified before all the world.

Although the Jews for Jesus movement is a relatively recent development in its present form, the groundwork for it was laid by the "ecumenical" movement. "Ecumenicism," however, does have ancient and, for the Jew, dangerous precedents.

Ecumenicism and Dialogue 1263 C.E.

by
BEREL WEIN

The winds of change that Vatican II unloosed into the Christian world are beginning to be felt. And even though the position of the Catholic Church vis-a-vis Jews and Judaism has yet to show any substantive, meaningful change, the new methodology of the Church regarding the treatment of the problem of the people of Israel has begun to emerge. The main bridge that the Church hopes to use in expanding a positive relationship with the Jewish people, particularly in the United States, is that of the open forum or dialogue. The Church is now much interested to foster open public discussion between Jews and Christians of the differences and similarities of the two major religions of Western man. In so doing, the Church has struck a responsive chord in certain Jewish circles, once again, particularly here in the United States. Unlike Orthodox Jewry, the agencies representing the Conservative, Reform and secular wings of Jewry have committed themselves to participation in this dialogue. (The exception of Orthodoxy is notable for two reasons. First, it is one of the few policy decisions that *all* of Orthodoxy is in accord with. Secondly, Orthodoxy's position is disturbing to both Christian and non-Orthodox Jewish participants; not to have the cooperation and blessing of the traditional Jew, whose participation, all feel, would give such an exchange real substance, lends a certain quality of hollowness to the dialogue.)

However, the idea of a "dialogue" between Jews and Christians is not a 20th-century thought but was already explored centuries ago, albeit in a different environment and under other circumstances.

The most famous example of an exchange of this order is the debate that took place in the city of Barcelona, Spain, in the year 1263. James I of Aragon sat on the throne of northern Spain, and the spirit of Christian dominance of the civilized world was wafted in the air. Seven hundred and four years have passed since then, but in the record of that dialogue written by Rabbi Mosheh ben Nachman (commonly called the Ramban, and, in the non-Jewish world, Nachmanides), and preserved by both Jewish and non-Jewish sources, one senses yet the grandeur and terror of that moment in Barcelona and a feeling of immediacy and relevancy overtakes the reader of that record. For here are our modern-day problems, differences, disputes, and bitterness poured out on an ancient canvas and curiously, the positions of the antagonists have changed very little in the seven centuries that have since swept by. It will be the attempt of this article to reflect some of the thoughts and words of this debate and thereby emphasis that the cascading dash to dialogue may perhaps be merely the foolish pursuit of an unattainable and ephemeral illusion.

◆§ The Historical Background

James I, who was destined to reign 63 years over the province of Aragon, was, as medieval monarchs went, a friend of the Jews. During the period of his reconquest of Catalonia and Aragon from the Moors, he consistently displayed a tolerance and sympathy towards the Jewish residents of those countries. He encouraged Jewish emigration to those lands, appointed Jews to vital governmental positions, and generally did nothing to interfere with the Jews' ability to practice and worship in the tradition of their fathers.[1]

However, then as now changes were being felt in the structure of the Roman Catholic Church, particularly in Spain.

The reforms in the church initiated by Innocent III and continued by Gregory IX reached Spain and rested in the province of Aragon, where the "Holy Office" of the Inquisition was to reach dominance. The Dominican confessor to James I, Raymond de Penaforte, was noted for his zeal to punish, persecute, and/or convert the Jews in Aragon, and his influence over the king was notable.

From 1228 to 1250, a series of anti-Jewish economic edicts were issued by the king which helped foster a climate of anti-Jewish feeling in the land. In 1254, the famous trial of the Talmud in Paris occurred, and the Talmud was found guilty of stating calumnies against Christianity, and cartloads of Talmudic manuscripts were burned by the order of Louis IX of France. When this coercion had little or no effect on the Jews or on their reverence for the Talmud, the Dominican friars of Spain, benefiting by the lesson of their French colleagues, changed their strategy.

No longer was the Talmud criticized, it was rather extolled. The Midrash now became an accepted source book of accurate portrayals, and Jewish scholarship was no longer publicly reviled. The reason for this was ingeniously simple — the truth of Christianity would now be proven, not from Christian or other non-Jewish sources, but rather from the Talmud and the Midrash themselves! It was their obstructionism that prevented the Jews from seeing the light of Christianity emanating from their own holy books. This new approach was spearheaded by an apostate Jew who had become a leader in the Catholic church of Aragon, Pablo Christiani. Because of his zeal to convert his fellow Jews, he goaded Raymond, the king's confessor, to convince James to order a public debate regarding the proofs from the Talmud as to the veracity of Christianity. The burden of defending the Talmud and the Jews fell upon the venerable shoulders of one of the greatest of all Talmudists, Rabbi Mosheh ben Nachman. On the 20th of July in 1263, at the Court of James I of Aragon, this dialogue began. It was to last until the 31st of July, though actual debating sessions occupied only four days of this time. The shock of this debate was to leave scars on the memories of both protagonists which have lasted to this day.

❧ The Debate

The record of the debate that forms the basis for this article is one written by one of the protagonists himself — the Ramban.[2] Written in a clear and lucid Hebrew style, it presents a picture of the debate and a record of the polemics as seen and heard by the Ramban.

At the outset, Mosheh ben Nachman insisted that he be granted the right of free speech throughout the debate. This right was guaranteed to him by the king, and because of this right, the Ramban at all times spoke boldly, incisively, and openly. It was the presence of this guarantee that made this medieval debate in reality a modern one wherein both sides speak their minds without intimidation. Such an open debate was a rarity in Christian Europe until our own times. Later events proved to the Ramban how costly the exercise of this freedom would prove to him personally. I would presume to state that this freedom of expression is what uniquely characterizes and ennobles this discussion and precludes any comparison with the earlier debate of Rabbi Yechiel of Paris[3] or the later encounter at Tortossa.[4] For here, perhaps for the only time in the annals of medieval Christian European history, Jew meets gentile as equal, and for the majority of the debate is not the defendant or apologist but rather presses home his criticism and disbelief of Christian concepts and principles.

Rabbi Mosheh ben Nachman summarized one main historical argument against the acceptance of Christianity by the Jews of Aragon and, in so doing, he attempted to entirely avoid the necessity of debating Talmudic or Midrashic references to Jesus. "It has been proposed to me that the wise men of the Talmud themselves believed that Jesus was the Messiah, and that he was a man and a god, and not merely a mortal man alone. But is it not a well-known fact that the incidents and events of Jesus occurred at the time of the Second Temple and that he was born and died before the destruction of that Temple (70 C.E.)? And the Rabbis of the Talmud, such as Rabbi Akiva and his colleagues, died after the destruction of the Temple . . . and the editor of the Talmud, Rav Ashi, lived almost 400 years after the Temple's destruction. If it would be true that the wise men of the Talmud believed in Jesus and in the truth of his religion, how then did they themselves remain faithful to the religion and practices of the Jews? For they lived and died as Jews, they and their children and their disciples unto this very day. And they are the ones who have taught us the faith of Judaism, for we are all Talmudic Jews . . . And if they believed in Jesus, as you are trying to impute from their words, why did they not behave as Friar Paul (Pablo Christiani), who evidently understands their words better than they (and themselves convert)?"

His argument resounds through the halls of time — the classic answer of Jewish tradition: "If our forefathers, who witnessed Jesus, saw his works, and knew him, did not hearken unto him, how should we accept the word of our king (James I), who himself has no first-hand knowledge of Jesus, and was not his countryman as were our forefathers?" Here the Ramban puts into awful clarity the basic point of contention between Jews and Christians. The stubbornness of the Jew stems not from his "perfidy" but rather from the fact that he is convinced of the truth of his own belief and not the slightest convinced of the truth of Christian belief. The current Vatican schema on the Jews remains unclear as to whether Christianity has yet come to grips with this fact. For it does not yet specify the cause of the Jew's affirmation of the one and denial of the other — it merely hopes through better social relations to soften, if not to reverse, that affirmation and denial.

The Dominicans were not deterred from their purpose by the Ramban's onslaught. They brought numerous passages from Talmudic and Midrashic literature to prove the truth of their faith. The Ramban stated that he did not consider himself bound by the "agadoth" of the Talmud,[5] and therefore no proofs could be deduced from them. However, he said that even if he granted their accuracy, they in no way agreed with Christian thought or belief. His strength in swimming in the sea of the Talmud easily refuted his antagonists who were nearly as erudite in the subject matter as he. And he used every opportunity to return to the offensive against his opponents. "Does not the prophet say regarding the Messiah 'that he shall reign from sea to sea and from the river to the ends of the earth' (Psalms 72:8) — and has not your empire (the Roman empire) declined since it accepted Christianity? Do not your enemies, the Moslems, rule over a greater empire than yours? And does not the prophet also say that at the time of Messiah 'they shall not teach their friends war, etc.' (Jeremiah 31:33) and is it not written (Isaiah 11:9) that then 'the world shall be full of knowledge of the Lord as the waters cover the sea' . . .? And from the days of Jesus till now, the entire world is full of robbery and pillaging, and the Christians have spilled more blood than any of the other nations, and they are also sexually immoral. How hard it would be for you, my great king, and for your knights, to survive if there would be an end to warfare!"

This indictment of the status of the Christian, or, as we call it today, the Western world, is even sharper in our time when over fifty million people have been destroyed by war in the past century alone, and when all of the economies of the great powers of the world rest on a foundation of defense spending and war preparation.

The Ramban further stated that the basic dispute between Christianity and Judaism is not regarding the messianic mission of Jesus himself as much as it is regarding the entire Christian concept of Divinity and belief. "Listen to me, my master, my king," said the Ramban. "Our contention and judgment with you is not primarily concerning the Messiah,[6] for you are more valuable to me than the Messiah. You are a king and he is a king. You are a gentile king and he is a king of Israel, for the Messiah will only be flesh and blood as you are. When I serve my Creator under your sovereign rule, in exile, poverty, oppression and humiliated by the nations that constantly insult us, my reward for this service is indeed great: For I bring forth a voluntary sacrifice to G-d of my own being, and through this shall I merit a greater portion of the world to come. However, when there will be a king of Israel, abiding by my Torah, who shall rule over all the nations, then I shall be involuntarily compelled to retain my faith in the Torah of the Jews, and therefore my reward shall not be as great (as it is now). However, the main dispute and disagreement between the Christians and the Jews is in that you have some very sorry beliefs regarding the essence of Divinity itself." Thus did the Ramban emphasize clearly that the fundamental differences between Judaism and Christianity are not those of detail and history but rather those of definition and understanding of the nature of Divinity and His relation to man.

The question of Original Sin was also touched upon in this debate. Both Pablo and King James asserted that all men had been condemned to Hell because of the original sin of Adam, but that the advent of belief in Jesus had released man from this state of eternal damnation. To this the Ramban retorted with bitter irony: "In our province we have a saying — He who wishes to lie should be sure that the witnesses to the transaction are far away. There are many punishments mentioned in regard to Adam and Eve — the earth was cursed, thorns and thistles shall grow therefrom, man shall earn his bread by the sweat of his brow, that man shall return to the dust, and that woman shall suffer the pain and travail of childbirth. All of these conditions yet exist to this day, and anything tangible that can be evidenced, as the alleviation of any of these conditions, has yet to appear, even since the advent of your messiah. But the curse of damnation to Hell, which Scripture nowhere records, this is the punishment which you say was relieved (by Jesus coming), for this is the one matter which no one can disprove. Send from your midst someone, and let him return and report to us! G-d forbid that the righteous should be punished in Hell for the sin of the first man, Adam. For my soul is as equally related to the soul of the wicked Pharaoh as to the soul of my father, and I shall not be punished by the damnation of my soul because of the sins of that Pharaoh. The punishments that accrue to mankind because of the sin of Adam were physical, bodily punishments. My body is given to me by my father and mother, and therefore if it was ordered that they be mortal and die, so will their children forever be mortal and die, for such is the law of nature." But, he stated, the soul of man, which is given to him by the Eternal Creator, is not damned because of the sins of others, even of his ancestors themselves, unless he himself continues in their evil ways.

The Ramban thereupon entered into a theological disputation regarding the theories of the Virgin Birth and the Trinity. He proved them not to be Jewish in origin and that therefore "the mind of no Jew could understand or accept them." He stated that "your words (regarding the Talmud and the Messiah) are there for naught, because this is the kernel of our disagreement, but if you wish to discuss the concept of Messiah, I will bow to your wishes." He told the king that "you believe this bitter thing regarding divinity (the Virgin Birth and the concept of the Trinity) because you are born a Christian, the son of Christian parents, and you have been indoctrinated your entire life by priests who have filled your mind and marrow with this belief, and you now accept its truth, by basis of habit alone." His criticism of these tenets of the Roman Catholic faith placed in sharp focus the reason for the Jew's refusal to accept Christianity from its very onset. Its notion of G-d was, and is, foreign to Jewish tradition and logic. Nothing has yet occurred to change this status either for the Jew or the Christian.

The debate ended rather abruptly. It was never formally closed, but the king recessed it, apparently out of fear of rioting by fanatical mobs stirred up by emotional sermons of certain Dominican friars.[7] The king himself took an active part in the debate and one is struck by the fairness and tolerance of James I. It was only the deceitful friars who distorted the teachings of the Talmud. He is quoted by the Ramban as having told him that "I have yet to see such a man as you, who, though being wrong, has yet made an excellent presentation of his position."[8] The Ramban also notes that he received a gift of three hundred coins from James, evidently as reimbursement for his expenses. The Ramban states that "I departed from [the king] with great affection." Mosheh ben Nachman remained in Barcelona for over a week, and was present for a sermon in the Synagogue on the following Sabbath delivered by a Dominican priest, in the presence of King James, calling on the assembled Jews to convert to Christianity.[9]

The Dominicans, angered by the Ramban's successful defense, turned their wrath against him personally. He was sentenced to temporary exile from Aragon and had to pay a fine for speaking blasphemy. In his old age, broken by the ordeal of his persecution and by a vision of the sorrows that would yet befall the Jews in Spain, Rabbi Mosheh ben Nachman emigrated to the Land of Israel in the year 1267 and on its holy soil he expired shortly thereafter.

⊸§ Conclusion

The importance of this encounter between the Jews and the Christian world is not to be minimized. It would be many centuries before Jews dared to speak so openly to their Christian fellow countrymen about the fundamental differences that separate them. To our very day, no other Jewish religious leader of the caliber of the Ramban, responsible and responsive to his faith and tradition, has ever presented our case. Those who presume to speak for Judaism in today's dialogues would do well to read the record of this dialogue seven centuries ago. I do not believe that the case for Jews and Judaism can be better stated, with as much candor, compassion and truth, than the manner in which it is reflected in the words of Rabbi Mosheh ben Nachman. Both Jew and Christian would profit by a study of that record from Barcelona before plunging headlong into any new dialogue or ecumenical discussion. The issues and the world itself has changed little from the days of James I of Aragon. Neither has the people of Israel.

> *The mountain of His holiness, His Holy Temple*
> *standing on the heights of eternal hills,*
> *That is Sinai, the glory of G-d that dwelled*
> *upon it, thrills,*
>
> *Let the nations proclaim His majesty and awe,*
> *The voice of the Red Sea, never ending,*
> *where His flock saw,*
>
> *All of His wonders, miracles, beauty,*
> *Cleanse yourselves, O ye nations and states,*
> *Raise up your son,*
> *give glory and honor to the Lord!*[10]

NOTES

1. Yitzhak Baer, "A History of the Jews in Christian Spain," Volume I, pp. 138-147.
2. *Vikuach HaRamban* — Found in *Otzar Havikuchim* by J. D. Eisenstein, Hebrew Publishing Society, 1915 and *Kithvey HaRamban* by Rabbi Charles D. Chavel, Mosad Horav Kook, 1963.
3. Rabbi Yechiel of Paris, one of the leaders of the school of the Tosafists, defended the Talmud against the accusations of Nicholas Donin, a Jewish apostate, before Louis IX of Paris in 1254.
4. Tortossa was the locale of a series of debates carried on by many Jewish Rabbis, foremost among them being Rabbi Yoseph Albo, against Dominican theologians and a Jewish apostate, Joshua Halorki, in the years 1413-1414, which ended in disaster for the Jewish cause.
5. The Agadoth — literally, Tales — are the parables and traditional legends of the Talmud —usually with a moral or ethical message woven into their fabric. The term "Agadah" is used in contradistinction to "Halachah" which is the law or legal system of Torah. Whether or not the Ramban's point in this connection was actually his belief, or was merely a tactic used for this discussion, has been a matter of conjecture among Jewish scholars for considerable time.
6. See Rabbi Chavel's note in his *Kithvey Ramban*, wherein he quotes the statement of the Ramban in the *Sefer Hageulah*, that "even if we admit to ourselves that our sins and those of our fathers are so enormous that all hope of comforting us be lost, and that our exile will last till eternity — all of this will still not damage our belief in the fundamental precepts (of our Torah), for the ultimate reward to which we look forward is only in the world to come — the pleasure of our soul in Paradise, and our salvation from Hell; yet we still believe in our redemption (the Messiah), because it is a well-known truth among those of great stature in Torah and prophecy."
7. Baer, "A History of the Jews in Christian Spain," Vol. I, p. 153. Also see the *Vikuach HaRamban* where the Ramban himself makes mention of the "preachers who stir up the mob and bring terror to the world, and of many great priests and knights of the king's court, who have advised me not to speak evil against their religion. Also the Jews of this sector reported that they were told to warn me not to continue to do so."
8. An alternative reading of this statement in the Hebrew original is: "I have yet to see such a man as you, who though not being a legal advocate, has yet made an excellent presentation of his position."
9. The Ramban himself delivered a sermon-lecture in rebuttal, entitled, "The Torah of G-d Is Perfect," a copy of which is printed in the *Kithvey HaRamban* mentioned in note 2 above.
10. The last stanza of a poem "From Thy Hand, Lord, Give Forth Honor," written by the Ramban in honor of the Pesach festival.

The missionaries claim that Jesus fulfilled all the prophecies pertaining to the Messiah. The truth, however, is that he did not fulfill even one of the important prophecies. All the things that he fulfilled were in reality quite trivial.

Was Jesus The Messiah? Let's Examine The Facts

by
PINCHAS STOLPER

If Christians merely believed that Jesus was *their* messiah, this belief would be of little concern to us as Jews. Their claim, however, is not that he is the Christian Messiah, but *our* Messiah, the Messiah of the Jews, the Messiah foretold by the Jewish Prophets. Christians then attempt to prove this belief by quoting *our* Bible.

Certain Christian missionary groups have now set up a front organization called "Jews for Jesus," through which they entice naive Jews to Christianity with an old and discredited argument. "Don't become a Christian," they will argue, "remain a Jew, — however, while you remain a loyal Jew, accept Jesus as your 'Messiah.' "

In view of the confusion created by the many false claims of missionary groups, Jews must be armed with the facts to substantiate our conviction that everything Christians claim for Jesus as the *Jewish* Messiah is false.

The following few "items" will point our some of the glaring discrepancies and inconsistencies in the missionaries' arguments: —

Item: The Jewish Messiah is to be a human being born

naturally to husband and wife. He is not to be a god, nor a man born of supernatural or virgin birth, as the Christians claim.

Nowhere does our Bible say that the Messiah would be a god or G-d-like. The very idea that G-d would take on human form is repulsive to Jews because it contradicts our concept of G-d as being above and beyond the limitations of the human body and situation. Jews believe that G-d *alone* is to be worshipped, not a being who is His creation, be he angel, saint, or even the Messiah himself.

Nowhere does the Bible predict that the Messiah will be born to a virgin. In fact, virgins never give birth anywhere in the Bible. This idea is to be found only in pagan mythology. To the Jewish mind, the very idea that G-d would plant a seed in a woman is unnecessary and unnatural. After all — what is accomplished by this claim? What positive purpose does it serve? The claim that Mary did not have natural relations with her husband must have made the Jews of that time suspect her of wrongdoing. The New Testament (the Christian Bible) admits as much when it says (Matthew 1, 19), "Then Joseph her (Mary's) husband, being a just man, and not willing to shame her in public, decided to divorce her quietly." The whole idea of virgin birth serves no purpose, except to attract pagans to Christianity.

Item: The Jewish Messiah is expected to return the Jews to their land. Jesus was born while the Jews still lived in their land, before they had gone into exile. He could not restore them to their land because they were still living in it!

Item: The true Messiah is to rebuild the Temple in Jerusalem — but Jesus lived while the Temple was still standing.

Item: The Jewish Bible says that the Messiah will redeem Israel. In the case of Jesus, the very opposite took place. Not long after his death, the Holy Temple in Jerusalem was destroyed, Jerusalem was laid to waste, and the Jews went into exile to begin a 1900-year-long night of persecution — largely at the hands of the followers of this self-styled "Messiah!"

Item: The Prophets in the Bible foretold (Isaiah 45 and Zafania 3) that when the Messiah comes, all the nations of the world will unite to acknowledge and worship the one true G-d. "The knowledge of G-d will fill the earth. The world will be filled with the knowledge of G-d as the waters cover the seas" (Isaiah 11,9). Nothing of this nature took place following the death of Jesus. On the contrary, Islam developed and became the religion of the Arabs and many other nations, Christianity broke up into many conflicting sects which were constantly at war with each other, and a large part of the world continued to worship idols. Even today the world is far from the worship of one G-d.

Item: When the true Messiah comes, his influence will extend over all peoples who will worship G-d at the Temple in Jerusalem. The Prophet says, "For My House will become the House of Prayer for all the Nations." This has obviously not yet taken place, and, therefore, the Messiah has not yet come.

Item: During the time of the Messiah a new spirit will rule the world, and man will cease committing sins and crimes; this will especially apply to the Jews. The Torah (in Deuteronomy 30,6) says that "G-d will circumcise your heart and the heart of your children to love G-d." The Prophets taught: "And your people are all righteous, they will inherit the earth forever" (Isaiah 60,21); "In that day I will seek the sins of Israel and there will be none" (Jeremiah 50,20); "I will give you a new heart and a new spirit — and you will obey My laws and commandments and do them" (Ezekiel 36,26,27). Soon after the time of Jesus, ignorance of G-d and even ignorance of science and philosophy filled the earth, as the "Dark Ages" overtook the world.

Item: The true Messiah is to reign as King of the Jews. Jesus' career as described in the New Testament lasted all of three years, at the end of which he was crucified by the Romans as a common criminal. He never functioned as anything but a wandering preacher and "faith healer"; certainly, he held no official position or exercised any rule of any kind.

Item: During the time of the Messiah, prophecy will return to the Jewish people and the presence of G-d will dwell amongst us. (Joel 3,1) "And after that I will pour my spirit on all of mankind and your sons and daughters will prophesy." These predictions, too, are yet to be fulfilled.

Item: One of the Messiah's major tasks is to bring peace to the entire world. In the time of the Messiah, there are to be no more wars, and the manufacture of arms will cease. The Prophet Isaiah (2,4) says, "And they shall beat their swords into plowshares and their spears into pruning hooks. Nation shall not lift up sword against nation, neither shall they learn war any more." Yet, Christian nations are very war-like, and wars have been going on almost non-stop since the time of Jesus up to and including today.

Item: The New Testament itself claims that the prophecies concerning the Messiah were to be realized in Jesus' own generation. Mark (13,30) clearly says, "Truthfully I say unto you that this generation shall not pass till all these things be done." In Matthew 4, Jesus is quoted as saying that "the Kingdom of Heaven is at hand." 2,000 years have passed and still nothing has been accomplished.

Item: Nowhere does the Jewish Bible say that the Messiah would come once, be killed, and return again in a "second coming." The idea of a second coming is a pure rationalization of Jesus' failure to function in any way as a messiah, or to fulfill any of the prophecies of the Torah or the Prophets. The idea is purely a Christian invention, with no foundation in the Bible.

Item: The Bible says that the Messiah would be descended in a direct line from King David. However, if G-d was Jesus' "father," is it not somewhat ridiculous to claim that he is descended from King David on his father's side?

Item: Why do some missionaries insist on distorting the meaning of the words of the prophets in order to substantiate their claims? (An example: The Hebrew term in Isaiah "almah" which means a "young woman" is mistranslated as "virgin.") Honest Christian scholars now acknowledge that this is "a pious fraud" and now (see the new Protestant "Revised Standard Version" of the Bible) translate the word correctly. This is but one of many mistranslations or forced translations.

Item: While on the cross Jesus is quoted as saying, "Forgive them, Father, for they (the Jews) know not what they do." Why do some Christians insist on persecuting the Jews if Jesus *himself* gave instructions to forgive them?

But further — if his rising from the dead was so crucial to demonstrate who he was, why did this take place in secret and not in the presence of his "thousands" of devotees?

Item: Jesus claimed that he did not intend to change the Laws of Moses — "Think not that I have come to abolish the Law (Torah) and the Prophets, I have come not to abolish them but to fulfill them. For truly, I say to you, till heaven and earth pass away, not an iota, not a dot, will pass from the Law until all is accomplished. Whoever then breaks one of the least of these commandments and teaches men so, shall be called least in the Kingdom of Heaven" (Matthew 5). Later on, he himself abrogated some of the laws, while his followers eventually abolished or changed nearly all of them.

However, the Torah itself clearly states in many places that its laws are eternal, never to be abolished. And even the Christians acknowledge that the Jewish Bible is the word of G-d. If the Torah is eternal and Jesus himself claims to have no intention of abolishing or changing it, why do the Christians celebrate the Sabbath on Sunday when G-d clearly calls the Saturday-Sabbath an Eternal Covenant? Why do Christians eat pig when the Torah forbids it? What reason can Christians give for not celebrating Rosh Hashana and Yom Kippur which are clearly spelled out in the Torah? This same argument applies to hundreds of other Torah laws that are ignored by Christians.

On the other hand, Christians and Easter are not mentioned in either the Jewish Bible or the Christian "New Testament" — these festivals are pagan in origin, adapted for Christian use. But Pesach, Sukkos and Shavuos are clearly spoken of in the Bible. On top of which, Jesus nowhere requests that the Biblical festivals no longer be observed.

Item: Christians teach the philosophy of "turning the other cheek" and "loving your enemy." Do you know of any Christian nations that live by this impractical ethic, or even take it seriously?

Item: The many Christian statements about G-d being "Love" have been borrowed from the Jewish Bible and the Jewish religion. Among many such quotations from our Torah are: "Love thy neighbor as thyself"; "Love the stranger, for you were strangers in the land of Egypt"; "And you shall love the L-rd thy G-d with all your heart and with all your soul and with all your might."

If G-d is "Love," how can Christians explain the silence and indifference of the Church and most Christian nations while six million Jews were being gassed and burned by the Germans? Why the stone-like silence during the Six Day War? Where was Christian love during the Spanish Inquisition and the hundreds of pogroms inspired by priests and monks?

Item: Judaism believes that G-d is eternal, above and beyond time. G-d cannot be born, He cannot die, He cannot suffer, He can not "become flesh," nor can He be divided into sections ("Father, Son, and Holy Ghost"). These are pagan notions. Certainly no "G-d" or "Son of G-d" could have called out on the cross, as Jesus is supposed to have said, "My G-d, my G-d, why have you abandoned me?" If he was G-d's son, he would at least have said, "My father. . ."

Item: If Jesus was really the Messiah, why does the New Testament admit that all the rabbis of the time, without one exception, rejected his claim? Why was there not one man of learning, nor one prominent leader who accepted him?

Item: If Jesus was the Messiah, why did the overwhelming majority of his own people, the Jews living at that time, reject him? Why did his followers consist of a handful of people, almost all of whom were poorly educated? Why did his own family turn against him?

Who was in a position to judge if he was or was not the Messiah — his own people, who anxiously awaited the arrival of the Messiah, or pagan peoples who had no understanding of what the concept really meant?

Item: Jesus commanded his disciples to preach to the Jews only and not to the gentiles (Matthew 10), yet his disciples disobeyed him and did just the opposite. He clearly thought of himself as the Messiah of the Jews and of no one else. Yet, he was accepted by foreign nations and not by the Jews.

Item: If God has "rejected" the Jews for not "accepting Jesus" as Christians claim, why have we managed to survive

2,000 years of Christian persecution? How do Christians explain the miracle of Jewish survival? Why has G-d restored the city of Jerusalem and the Land of Israel to His "rejected" people?

How do they explain the fact that the Jewish people has re-established its national life in its ancient homeland, and is in possession of the City of Jerusalem? These are living historic facts without parallel. Must not the Christians now acknowledge that the re-emergence of a Jewish State is indeed an unfolding and realization of Bible prophecy in our day? Does this not demonstrate that the many Biblical prophecies that speak of the return of the Jew to his land refer to the Jews and not to anyone else? (The Christians often refer to themselves as the "real Jews" — the "New Israel," i.e. G-d chose them because the Jews rejected Jesus.)

Isn't this theological "slap in the face" the reason for the Pope's refusal to recognize Israel, and for Christian silence during the Six Day War?

Item: The Prophets contain many prophecies concerning the end of days and the time of the Messiah that have not yet taken place. These *will* all take place when the Messiah comes.

Why do we need a Messiah in the first place? In order to teach the Torah to the world and to establish "The Kingdom of G-d on Earth." If the Christians have done away with the laws of the Torah, if they no longer regard the Torah as valid, what is left to teach mankind? Nowhere does the Torah suggest that it is to be abolished by the Messiah. On the contrary, the Torah is eternal, and the purpose of the Messiah is to bring us to the day when all of the Jewish people will observe the Torah and all of mankind will acknowledge its truths.

Item: Nowhere does the Torah state that someone else's death can bring forgiveness to a person's sins. On the contrary, each man will be punished for his sins, and each man must repent for his sins alone. "The soul that sinneth, it shall die"; "Sons will not be punished for the sins of their fathers." The idea that someone else's death 1,900 years ago can somehow bring forgiveness from G-d for my sins is absurd and unfounded. Each person must return to G-d, each sinner must change his own ways and seek G-d's forgiveness.

* * *

Jews firmly believe that the Messiah will come. We believe that man will not self-destruct, that we will not disappear in a gigantic atomic blast. Man is basically good, and G-d's Kingdom will be established. However, it is not enough to believe in G-d. Faith alone is not adequate — G-d demands deeds and action. G-d's revelation on Mount Sinai demands obedience to the 613 commandments spelled out in the written and unwritten Torah. G-d wants discipline, loyalty, and practice; not pious statements and magical formulas. Jews wait for the day when "G-d will be King over all the earth and on that day He will be One and His name One" (Zacharia 14,9).

Maimonides put our belief into words — and we firmly stand by these words, "I firmly believe, in complete faith, in the coming of the Messiah, and although he may tarry, I daily wait for his coming." Indeed, the Messiah is coming . . . we can almost hear his footsteps.

In the First Corinthians (9:20), the apostle Paul says, "Unto the Jews, I come as a Jew, that I might convert the Jews. To those who believe in the Law, I come like one who follows the Law, that I might convert those who follow the Law." When the missionaries approach us, they come as Jews, quoting from our Bible. It is both interesting and instructive to carefully examine a few of their "proofs."

Jesus And The Bible

---

by
ARYEH KAPLAN

For almost two thousand years, Christians have been trying to convince the Jews that they are right.

After all, Jesus was a Jew, and it seems strange that his own people refused to accept him.

One of the favorite ploys of the missionaries is to attempt to use the Jewish Bible to prove that Jesus was the Messiah of the Jews.

It takes a lot of nerve for outsiders to tell us how to interpret *our* Bible, written in *our* language.

Jews also know how to read the Bible. It was originally given in Hebrew, which is our language. When the Christians translated the Bible, they often slanted their translations to suit their own purposes. A close look at the original Hebrew is enough to destroy a good portion of their "proofs."

In many cases we do not even have to go to the original Hebrew. Merely taking the passages in context does away with all their "proof."

Let us take a few examples:

Missionaries claim that Jesus fulfilled the prophecy of the Messiah being born in Bethlehem.

They base this on the verse (Michah 5:1), "But you, Bethlehem Ephratah, which are little among the thousands of Judah. Out of you shall one come forth unto Me, to be a ruler in Israel."

Both Matthew (2:6) and John (7:43) attempt to use this as proof that Jesus was the Messiah.

Of course, this does not prove anything, since thousands of children were born in Bethlehem.

Furthermore, if this is really speaking of Jesus, why was he never accepted as a "ruler in Israel?"

The verse continues to say (Michah 5:4), "And there shall be peace."

This means to say that the Messiah will bring peace to the world, as we find elsewhere in the Bible (Isaiah 2:4).

If this is speaking of Jesus, why did he not succeed in bringing peace to the world?

He himself said that he is not coming to bring peace but the sword (Matthew 10:34).

But if this verse (Michah 5:1) is actually speaking of the true Messiah, then it is really referring to a descendant of King David. Since David came from Bethlehem (1 Samuel 17:12), the Bible speaks of Bethlehem as the Messiah's place of origin.

The true Messiah, who Jews are still waiting for, will be a ruler and will bring lasting peace to the world.

* * *

Missionaries claim that Jesus fulfilled a prophecy that the Messiah would be born of a virgin.

They attempt to prove this from a verse, which even many contemporary Christian editions of the Bible translate to read (Isaiah 7:14), "Therefore, the Lord Himself shall give you a sign: Behold a young woman shall conceive and bear a son, and shall call his name Immanuel."

The idea of gods and demigods being born of virgins occurs

in many places in pagan mythology.

When Matthew (1:23) quoted this passage and translated it into the Greek of the New Testament, his anxiety to prove a point led him to actually mistranslate this passage.

He translates the Hebrew word *Alma*, which actually means "young woman," as "virgin." Thus, we suddenly have an instant prediction of the virgin birth of the Messiah.

But the proper Hebrew word for virgin is *Besulah*, and *Alma* is never translated as "virgin."

More honest recent Christian Bible translations, such as the Revised Standard Version, the Jerusalem Bible, and the New English Bible, have corrected this original error.

Furthermore, there is absolutely no evidence that this prophecy speaks of the Messiah at all. It was directed at King Ahaz, and, according to most Biblical commentators, speaks of the birth of King Hezekiah rather than of the Messiah.

* * *

Missionaries claim that Jesus fulfilled the prophecy of being a prophet like Moses.

G-d says in the Bible (Deuteronomy 18:18), "I will raise them up a prophet among their brethren, like unto you (Moses)." What this verse means in context is that any prophet must be similar in qualifications to Moses, i.e. Jewish, a scholar, righteous, and of highest personal character.

But John (1:45) and the book of Acts (3:22, 7:37) take this quote out of context, claiming that this verse refers to Jesus, and gives him the right to contradict the Torah of Moses.

However, this is an obvious distortion, since the Bible openly states that there would never be another prophet like Moses (Deuteronomy 34:10), "And there shall not arise a prophet in Israel like unto Moses."

G-d Himself attested to Moses, as we find (Exodus 19:9), "And G-d said to Moses: Behold, I come to you in a thick cloud, that the people may hear when I speak with you, and may believe in you forever."

At Mount Sinai, G-d attested to the prophecy of Moses by publicly speaking to him in the presence of millions of people.

He never did the same for Jesus.

Indeed, there is no evidence that Jesus was a prophet at all, in Jewish terms.

The Bible (Deuteronomy 18:22) says that one of the signs of a true prophet is when his prophecy comes true exactly. There is no evidence that Jesus fulfilled this condition (See John 9:29).

Furthermore there is no evidence that the original passage (Deuteronomy 18:18) speaks of the Messiah at all. The verse merely states that the future prophets of Israel in general would share Moses' saintly qualities.

* * *

Missionaries claim that Jesus fulfilled the prophecy of living a sinless life.

They base this on the verse (Isaiah 53:9), "And they made his grave with the wicked, and with the rich his tomb, although he had done no violence, neither was any deceit in his mouth."

This is the famous "Suffering Servant" passage in Isaiah.

Some commentators indeed state that this passage is speaking of the Messiah. Others, however, say that it is speaking of the entire Jewish people. A careful reading of the entire passage may well convince you that it is speaking of the Six Million Jews killed by Hitler. Other commentators say that it is speaking of the Prophet Isaiah himself.

In any case it cannot be proven that this passage is speaking of the Messiah at all.

Furthermore, Jesus himself was far from being sinless as the Gospel claims.

Speaking to the entire Jewish people, G-d commanded us to keep the Sabbath in the Ten Commandments. Since G-d Himself gave this commandment, no one can abrogate it.

Yet, the Gospel records that Jesus violated the Sabbath.

As expected, the people's reaction was one of outrage. The Gospel records that the people said (John 9:16), "This fellow is no man of G-d, he does not keep the Sabbath." They realized that "miracles" alone do not give anyone the right to go against G-d, as G-d Himself warned in the Bible (Deuteronomy

13:2). Only the gullible and superstitious are taken in by "miracles" and magic alone.

Beyond this, the Gospel records many instances where Jesus claimed to be G-d (John 10:30, 14:9, 16:15). If so, from the Jewish point of view, he was guilty of idolatry, one of the worst possible sins.

* * *

Missionaries claim that Jesus fulfilled the prophecy that the Messiah would be killed by crucifixion.

They quote a Biblical verse, which, correctly translated, reads (Psalms 22:17), "For dogs have encompassed me, a company of evil-doers have enclosed me, *like a lion,* they are at my hands and feet."

"Like a lion" in Hebrew is *KeAri.* The fundamentalist Christian interpreters actually changed the spelling of the word from *KeAri* to *Kari.* If one then totally ignores Hebrew grammar, one can twist this to mean "He gouged me." Then, as in the King James' Version, they make this verse read "they pierced my hands and feet."

However, this bears no relation to the original meaning of the verse. Even with the change in spelling, it is a forced translation.

This is but one more example of the lengths missionaries go to prove that they are right.

Furthermore there is absolutely no evidence that this Psalm is speaking of the Messiah. From the opening verse, it would seem that King David, the author of this Psalm, was actually speaking of himself.

* * *

Missionaries claim that Jesus fulfilled the prophecy of dying for our sins.

The Bible says (Isaiah 53:11), "He shall see the travail of his soul . . . who by his knowledge did justify the Righteous One to the many, and their iniquity he did bear."

We are again in the famous "Suffering Servant" passage.

Missionaries claim that it teaches that our sins can only be forgiven through Jesus. This is a basic Christian doctrine.

However, the Bible clearly states (Deuteronomy 24:16), "The fathers shall not die for the children, neither shall the children die for the fathers; every man shall die for his own sin."

Every man is responsible for his own actions, and he himself must make them good. This is a most basic theme repeated over and over in the Bible.

According to the commentaries who say that the "Suffering Servant" is the Messiah (or the prophet Isaiah), a more precise translation would indicate that he did not suffer *to atone* for our sins, but suffered *because of* our sins.

The Messiah's mission is to perfect mankind. The more we sin, the more difficult we make his task. Thus, our sins will cause the Messiah great anguish.

According to the commentators who contend that the "Suffering Servant" is the entire Jewish people, it is not very far fetched to say that the prophet is speaking of the Six Million who died for the sins of mankind.

Missionaries lay great stress on the fact that the Bible prescribes blood as atonement (Leviticus 17:11). They therefore claim that without the blood of Jesus, there can be no remission of sin (Hebrews 9:22).

However, there is no place where the Bible says that blood is the *only* means of atonement. Furthermore a close reading of the chapters on sacrifices shows that the sacrificial blood was only prescribed for a small category of transgressions.

There is one way of atonement, however, repeated again and again in the Bible. This is repentance. (See Ezekiel 33:11, 33:19, Jeremiah 36:3, etc.) The prophet said (Hosea 14:3), "Take with you words, and return to G-d." The main way back to G-d is through words of prayer. The sacrificial blood might have helped in some cases, but the most important part of atonement was always repentance and prayer.

It is not overly difficult to approach G-d. But it does involve effort on the part of the individual.

*   *   *

There are many other "proofs" offered by the missionaries. Every one is as twisted as those presented above, but to refute each one would require an entire book.

The main thing is that a clear reading of the Jewish Bible offers absolutely no support to the "proofs" of Christianity. In most cases, all you need is a good translation (or better still, the Hebrew original), and all those "proofs" fall away. Many contemporary Christian scholars admit as much.

However, the missionaries never mention the most important prophecies concerning the Messiah that Jesus *did not* fulfill.

The main task of the Messiah was to bring the world back to G-d, and to abolish all war, suffering and injustice from the world. Clearly, Jesus did not accomplish this.

In order to get around this failure on the part of Jesus, Christians invented the doctrine of the "Second Coming" (Hebrews 9:29, Peter 3). All the prophecies that Jesus did not fulfill the first time are supposed to be taken care of the second time around. However, the Jewish Bible offers absolutely no evidence to support the Christian doctrine of a "Second Coming."

Anything that they can twist to prove that Jesus was the Messiah is exploited to the fullest. All the embarrassing prophecies that he did not fulfill are swept under the rug of a "Second Coming."

The prophecies that Jesus is said to have fulfilled are, for the most part, trivial. It really does not make much difference in G-d's plan if the Messiah is born in Bethlehem or conceived by a virgin. His really important mission is to perfect the world. This, Jesus failed to do.

Jesus, therefore, was not the Messiah of the Jewish tradition.

We still await the true Messiah who will accomplish all this in his first attempt.

But, many argue, even if Jesus was not the Messiah, he was still a perfect human being, and one that we may take as an example. A closer look at his career, however, raises many questions about his "perfection."

Behold The Man:
The Real Jesus

by
ARYEH KAPLAN

Many people are fascinated by the person of Jesus. Even when they find it impossible to accept Christian theology, they still feel that they can identify with Jesus the person. They see him as someone who preached love and peace, and whose life embodied the greatest ideals.

When we look at Jesus in such idealized terms, many of the things done in his name seem very strange. How could the Crusaders have pillaged and destroyed entire communities in his name? How could the Inquisition have tortured people to death in the name of a man who taught that the foremost commandment was "love your neighbor as yourself?" How are such contradictions possible?

It is much less surprising that his followers did not live by Jesus' teachings when we realize that even Jesus himself did not abide by them. Christians like to present us with an idealized picture of Jesus the man, but a careful reading of the Gospels dispels this picture very quickly.

Let us look at a few examples.

One of the best-known teachings of Jesus is (*Luke* 6:29), "If someone smites you on one cheek, turn the other cheek." This might have been a beautiful ideal, but Jesus himself did not live up to it. When one of the High Priest's officers struck him, Jesus did not turn the other cheek at all. Instead, the Gospel tells us that his response was (*John* 13:23), "If I spoke amiss, state it in evidence at my trial. If I spoke well, then why did you smite me?" He did not meekly and quietly submit, as he himself is alleged to have preached.

Throughout history, it seems that the only one who ever "turned the other cheek" was the Jew.

In the Sermon on the Mount, Jesus instructed his followers (*Matthew* 5:43), "Love your enemies, bless those who curse you, and do good to those who hate you." This might have been a fine lesson if Jesus himself lived up to it. But when it came to his own enemies, Jesus declared (*Luke* 19:27), "Take my enemies, who would not have me rule over them, bring them here, and kill them before me."

Jesus might have preached against vindictiveness, but he did not practice as he preached, when he said (*John* 11:39), "I come to the world for judgment. I may give sight to the sightless, but I will blind those who see."

Some of us may have a picture of Jesus preaching love and peace, as when he said (*Matthew* 5:22), "Anyone who nurses anger against his brother must be brought to judgment . . . If he even sneers at him, he will have to answer for it in the fires of hell." The picture, however, changes very rapidly when Jesus himself is put to the test. We then find him declaring (*Matthew* 10:34), "Think not that I have come to send peace to the world. I come not to send peace, but the sword."

Jesus subjected anyone who dared oppose him to the most awful abuse, curses and threats of dire punishment. When the Jews tried to defend their ancient faith, Jesus answered them by saying (*Matthew* 23:33), "You snakes, you generation of vipers, how can you escape the damnation of hell?"

Jesus did not limit himself to his immediate opponents, such as the Rabbis and teachers. He spoke against all those who dared not believe in him, branding them as outcasts subject to divine punishment. We thus hear his pronouncement (*John* 3:36), "He who believes in the Son has everlasting life. But he who does not believe in the Son shall not see life, but shall suffer the everlasting wrath of G-d." He may have preached love, but it was a very restricted love. He thus said (*John* 3:5), "I surely say to you: Unless a man is born of water and the Spirit, he cannot enter the Kingdom of G-d."

In contrast to this, the Rabbis, whom Jesus hated so much, did not place any such limitations on G-d's love. It was the Rabbis of the Talmud who made the statement (*Tosefta, Sanhedrin 13*), "The righteous of all nations have a share in the World to Come." They saw G-d's love as available to all people, and not only to Jews.

An even stronger statement can be found in our Midrashic literature, where a rabbi declares (*Tana DeBei Eliahu Rabba 9*), "I call heaven and earth as witnesses: Any individual, whether gentile or Jew, man or woman, servant or maid, can bring the Divine Presence upon himself in accordance with his deeds."

The Jewish attitude toward non-Jews is most clearly expressed in King Solomon's prayer, where he says (*I Kings* 8:41-43), "When a stranger, who is not of Your people Israel, but comes from a distant land . . . turns in prayer toward this Temple, then listen to his prayers."

Jesus, however, was not so broad minded. When he sent out his twelve disciples, he charged them (*Matthew* 10:5,6), "Do not take the road to gentile lands, and do not enter any Samaritan city. Go only to the lost sheep of Israel."

The Rabbis who lived in Jesus' time taught (*Avos* 4:3), "Do not despise any man." They likewise declared (*Baba Kama* 38a), "Even a gentile who studies Torah is equal to a High Priest." These Rabbis saw G-d's salvation freely available to all men. Contrast this with the terrible sentence proclaimed by Jesus (*John* 15:16), "He who does not abide in me is thrown away like a withered branch. Such withered branches are gathered together, cast into the fire and burned." This terrible statement was later used by the Catholic Church to justify their practice of burning non-believers at the stake.

In the Sermon on the Mount, Jesus preached (*Matthew* 5:43:44), "You have been previously taught to love your neighbor and hate your enemy. But I say to you: Love your enemies and bless those who curse you." Jesus may have said this, but the Gospels are aflame with his own words of hatred toward those who did not accept him. Time after time, he displays the same appetite for revenge as any other mortal.

One of the basic teachings of Judaism is (*Leviticus* 19:18), "You shall love your neighbor as yourself." This commandment is so important that Rabbi Akiva declared that it was the fundamental principle of the Torah. Even though this is openly stated in the Torah, written over a thousand years before Jesus' birth, many people still think of it as one of Jesus' teachings.

But even in explaining this commandment of love, Jesus was not above displaying his vindictiveness. The Gospel (*Luke* 19:29) records that he was asked, "But who is my neighbor?" Jesus replied with one of the best-known parables in the Gospels:

A man traveling from Jerusalem to Jericho is attacked by robbers. They plunder and beat him, leaving him half dead by the roadside. A priest comes along and sees the injured man, but he promptly crosses the road to avoid him. A Levite then happens to pass by, and he also crosses the road to avoid him. Finally a Samaritan comes by and is touched by pity. He binds the stranger's wounds, carries him to a secure spot, and tenderly cares for him. Thus, the Samaritan becomes a perfect example of the good neighbor.

At first glance, this looks like a most beautiful story. But when we look beneath the surface we see Jesus' vindictiveness only too clearly.

Let us carefully note the three persons who saw the unfortunate victim. They are a priest (*Cohen*), a Levite and a Samaritan. Anyone familiar with the three classes of Jews called to the Torah knows that they are Cohen (priest), Levite and Israelite. We would therefore expect that after the Cohen and Levite passed up the victim, the story would tell us that the third person was an Israelite, an ordinary Jew.

Instead, however, Jesus substitutes a Samaritan, a member of a tribe who had been enemies with the Jews for almost five hundred years. This Samaritan then becomes the example of moral love. The Priests and Levites, who were the religious leaders of the Jews, were thus downgraded, while the hated Samaritan was praised. What Jesus is implying is that every

Jew, even a religious leader, is incapable of even a simple act of mercy.

Even in his parable about love, Jesus was not above demonstrating his spite toward the Jewish leaders who rejected him. "Good Samaritan" is a byword among Christians to this very day. Many churches even bear the name, "Church of the Good Samaritan." But Jesus' vindictiveness assured that there would never be a church with the name, "Church of the Good Israelite."

Jesus was even able to be vindictive against a tree. When he found himself hungry, he was not able to restrain his too-human emotions. The Gospel thus records (*Matthew* 21:18, 19), "In the morning, on his way to the city, Jesus felt hungry. Seeing a fig tree near the road, he went up to it, but found nothing on it but leaves. He said to the tree, 'May you never bear fruit anymore.' The tree then withered and died." The Gospel of Mark (11:13) makes it plain that it was not even the season for figs.

Did this innocent tree deserve such cruel punishment? It was not even the season for figs, and the tree was merely fulfilling its nature. If Jesus merely wanted to show his miraculous powers, as the Gospel seems to indicate, why did he not command the tree to bring forth fruit?

Indeed, the Talmud (*Taanis* 24a) brings a very similar incident, but with a very different ending. Rabbi Yosi's son once wanted to provide his father's field hands with food. All he could find was a fig tree, but it was not the season, and the tree was bare. He cried out, "Fig tree, fig tree, send forth your fruit so that my father's workers may eat." The Talmud tells us that the tree produced fruit before its time and the men were able to fill themselves.

If Jesus were truly capable of miracles, he could have done the same. Instead, he chose to display his vindictiveness.

A primary teaching of Judaism is expressed by the Psalmist many generations before Jesus. He declared (*Psalm* 145:9), "G-d is good to all, and his love extends over all His works." No distinction is made between a Jew and gentile.

Contrast this with the following even in Jesus' career (*Mark* 2:25-27): "A woman whose daughter was possessed by an unclean spirit heard of Jesus, and came in, falling at his feet. She was a gentile, a Phoenician from Syria. She begged Jesus to drive out the spirit from her daughter. Jesus replied, 'Let the children be satisfied first. It is not right to take the children's bread and cast it to the dogs.' "

From the context, it is obvious that the "children" mentioned by Jesus refer to the Jews, while the "dogs" were the gentiles. These "dogs" must be satisfied with scraps from the table.

Now compare this narrow view with a teaching of the much-maligned Pharisees (i.e. rabbis). They declare in the Talmud (*Gitten* 61a), "We are obliged to feed the gentile poor in exactly the same manner as we feed the Jewish poor."

We can bring many such contrasts between Jewish and Christian ethics. In every case, the margin seems to be on the side of Judaism. Jesus may have taught many beautiful ideals, but unfortunately, he never seemed to be able to live up to them himself.

Apparently, it was difficult even for "Christ" to be a Christian.

Belief in the Messiah is one of the basic tenets of Judaism. We believe that the Messiah will yet come, and hopefully anticipate the Messianic Age. But what sort of person will the Messiah be? What sort of age will he usher in?

The Real Messiah

---

by
ARYEH KAPLAN

What is the future bringing?

There are some pessimists who say that mankind is approaching its end. They predict that we will either pollute ourselves off the face of this planet or overpopulate to the barest marginal existence. Others see man doing the job more quickly, bringing his civilization crashing down on his head in a nuclear war.

On the other hand, there are optimists who predict a utopian future for mankind. They see unlimited energy being generated by thermo-nuclear furnaces, the conquest of man's most dread diseases, and the solution of all our social problems, leading to a world beyond our fondest present dreams.

Never before has mankind been faced with such a wide range of possibilities. Never before has it had such tremendous power at its disposal, to use for good or evil.

We live in an accelerated age. A man of 2000 years ago would not find the world of two hundred years ago very different. But the man of two hundred years ago, if transported to today's society, would find himself in a world beyond his wildest imagination.

He would find himself in a world where reaching for the moon is not a metaphor for the impossible, but a well-financed government project; where atoms are smashed and the secrets of life are being exposed; where the dread plagues that decimated entire civilizations no longer exist; where man communicates instantaneously with all parts of the world, and flies in hours to the most distant lands; where beasts of burden are virtually a thing of the past, and man is waited upon by a host of electrical servants.

We need not belabor the point, but the past hundred years or so have brought about an increase in knowledge unsurpassed in all human history. Whether we use it wisely or not, these accomplishments are truly amazing.

What does it all mean?

Why is all this happening now? In all the thousands of years of human civilization, there were many great men of genius. Why could they not bring about the revolution of knowledge that we are now experiencing? Why did it have to wait until this century?

And what is it all leading to?

And in the midst of this, why do we suddenly find a generation that will no longer tolerate war, injustice, inequality, the poisoning of our environment, or any of the other evils that we once felt were inevitable? Why this sudden global change of conscience that seems to be shaking the very roots of our civilization? Why are more and more people coming to the conclusion that the evils of society are not merely the natural consequences of civilization, but are diseases that call for a cure?

Is there any relationship between the information explosion and man's increased awareness of social justice?

We might seek sociological reasons connecting the two. We might dismiss it as mere coincidence. However, there is a third ingredient, one that already affects the entire world, but is uniquely related to us as Jews.

After 2000 years of suffering and prayer, we are once again in control of our ancient homeland.

Again, the relationship between this and the other two could be dismissed as mere coincidence except for one thing.

It has already been foretold.

If one looks with an unprejudiced eye at the world today, he will see that we are living in an age where almost all the Jewish prophecies regarding the prelude to the Messianic Age are coming to pass. Even the most doubtful skeptic cannot help wondering how this could be mere coincidence. The man with clear vision can truly see the hand of G-d at work.

We who believe in G-d know that He controls the final destiny of mankind. Although each individual has free will, G-d guides the general course of history towards His ends.[1] The collective wills of societies are therefore often determined by G-d. Inventions and discoveries come about as a result of the divine will.[2] Governments are guided by G-d to work toward His ends. This is what the scripture means when it says (Prov. 21:1), "The king's heart is in the hand of G-d . . . He turns it wherever He wills."[3]

The ultimate goal of the historic process is the perfection of society. Since everything was created by G-d, all must eventually be perfected.[4] This is even true of man's mundane world, which was created as an arena for our service toward G-d.[5]

This ultimate goal is what we call the Messianic Age. It is the focus of the entire historical process. The coming of the Messiah is a basic belief of Judaism.[6] This yearning and expectation gives Jews great optimism concerning the ultimate future of mankind.

However, if you have ever gone through the many passages in the Bible, the Talmud, the Midrash, and the Zohar that speak of this Messianic Age, you might become somewhat confused. Some traditions seem to contradict others, while the line between prediction and allegory often seems very thin. For many of us, any attempt to find rhyme or reason in these teachings seems fraught with frustration.

One of the basic points of contradiction is whether or not the onset of the Messianic age will come through miracles. Many teachings seem to support the view of the miraculous, such as (Dan. 7:13), "Behold, one like the son of man came with the clouds of heaven." On the other hand, others seem to support a more prosaic view, such as (Zech. 9:9), "Behold, your king comes to you . . . lowly, and riding on a donkey."

The Talmud was aware of this contradiction, and answered it

by stating that there are two basic ways that the Messianic age can commence. If we are worthy of miracles, it will indeed be miraculous. If we are not, the Messianic Age will arrive in a natural manner.[7]

Whether or not we are worthy of miracles, G-d will guide the forces of history to eventually bring about the Messianic Age. If, however, we merit miracles, we can bring it about before the historical process has paved the way.[8]

Miracles are not something to be taken lightly. Man's free will is one of the prime ingredients of creation. If man would lose his free will to act or believe then he obviously could not be held responsible for his actions or beliefs. That responsibility is the vital *human* ingredient of man and it is essential that his free will be at all times preserved.

Witnessing a miracle can destroy one's freedom to believe. Therefore, miracles almost always occur under such circumstances where faith is so strong that they do not affect it at all.[9] In order to merit a miracle, man must have such great faith in G-d that it will in no way be affected by witnessing the miracle.

Although some of our sages tried to bring about the miraculous coming of the Messiah,[10] many were resigned to wait for G-d's own time, when the forces of history would bring about this Age without recourse to miracles. Thus, the *Amorah* Sh'muel taught, "There is no difference between now and the time of the Messiah, except with respect to our servitude."[11] We also find many places where our sages teach us that the redemption will not come all at once, but gradually, in a natural manner.[12]

Of course, many of the traditions that we find regarding the Messianic Age are either allegorical or contingent on factors known only to G-d. Therefore, not all are necessary conditions for the redemption.[13] For this reason, the Messiah can come at any time, totally without warning.[14]

In order for a perfect society to exist, such things as disease will have to be eliminated. Thus, it has been predicted (Isa. 35:5), "The eyes of the blind will be opened, the ears of the deaf shall be unstopped; then shall the lame man leap as a hart, and the tongue of the dumb shall sing."[15]

Similarly, other forms of work will be eliminated in order that man devote himself totally toward his ultimate goal.[16] Many such miracles are predicted, such as grapes as large as hen's eggs, and grains of wheat as big as a fist.[17] As we now know, all this can be possible with a technology not too far removed from that of today. Indeed, when Rabban Gamliel spoke of these predicted miracles, he stated that they would not involve any change in the laws of nature, but are allusions to a highly advanced technology. Thus, so little labor will be needed to process agricultural products, that clothing and loaves of bread will seem to grow on trees. Similarly, as we learn the secrets of life processes, it will become possible to make trees bear fruit continually.[18]

When we think of the miracles of the Messianic Age as being technological rather than manifest, then we have no trouble understanding traditions that predict such things as space flight[19] and interstellar colonization[20] in the Messianic Age, even according to those who believe that it will not be a time of manifest miracles.

Of course all of this would be mere conjecture and even forced interpretation if it were not for the fact that our present technological revolution has also been predicted, with an approximate date as to its inception.

Almost 2000 years ago, the Zohar[21] predicted, "In the 600th year of the sixth thousand, the gates of wisdom on high and the wellsprings of lower wisdom will be opened. This will prepare the world to enter the seventh thousand, just as a man prepares himself toward sunset on Friday for the Sabbath. It is the same here. And a mnemonic for this is (Gen. 7:11), 'In the 600th year . . . all the foundations of the great deep were split.' "

Here we see a clear prediction that in the Jewish year 5600 (or 1840), the wellsprings of lower wisdom would be opened and there would be a sudden expansion of secular knowledge. Although the year 1840 did not yield any major scientific breakthrough, the date corresponds with almost uncanny accuracy to the onset of our present scientific revolution.

The tradition may have even anticipated the tremendous destructive powers of our modern technology. Thus, we have the teaching of Rabbi Elazar that the Messianic Age will begin in a generation with the power to destroy itself.[22]

If the technological miracles of the Messianic Age will be dramatic, the social revolution will be all the more profound. On an international scale, it will mean the total end of all war, as the prophet Isaiah predicted (Isa. 2:4), "Nation shall not lift up sword against nation, neither shall they practice war anymore."[23] According to many commentaries, the allegory (ibid. 11:6), "The wolf shall dwell with the lamb, and the leopard shall lie down with the kid," also refers to the peace and harmony between nations.[24] Rabbi Nachman of Breslov states that man will realize the foolishness of war, just as he has already realized that of pagan idolatry.[25]

On an individual level, the changes will be even greater. When nations "beat their swords into plowshares," the hundreds of billions of dollars now used for war and "defense" will be diverted to the perfection of society. There will be a standard of social justice exemplified by the prophecy (Isa. 62:8), "The Lord has sworn . . . Surely I will no more give your corn to be food for your enemies, and strangers will not drink your wine for which they have not labored."[26] This is also the spirit of the prophecy (ibid. 61:1), "To bind up the broken hearted, to proclaim liberty to the captives, and untie those who are bound."[27]

Some of the most radical changes will be a result of the nullification of the curse of Adam.[28] The technological revolution will largely eliminate the curse (Gen. 3:19), "With the sweat of your brow you shall eat bread . . ." But this change will be even more far reaching with respect to woman. Many of woman's disadvantages are a result of Eve's curse (ibid. 3:16), "In pain you shall bear children, and you shall desire your man, and he shall rule over you."[29] Woman's status will change profoundly when this curse is eliminated, and this may well be the meaning of the prophecy (Jer. 31:21), "For G-d will create a new thing, a woman shall court a man."[30]

The rapid changes on both a technological and sociological level will result in great social upheaval. The cataclysmic changes will result in considerable suffering, often referred to as the *Chevley Moshiach* or Birthpangs of the Messiah.[31] If the Messiah comes with miracles, these may be avoided, but the great changes involved in his coming in a natural manner may make these birthpangs inevitable.[32]

Since in a period of such accelerated change parents and children will grow up in literally different worlds, traditions handed from father to son will be among the major casualties. This will be especially true of the values of religion — in such a rapidly changing world, people will naturally be enamored with the new and dissatisfied with the old. Thus, our sages teach us that neither parents nor the aged will be respected, the old will have to seek favors from the young, and a man's household will become his enemies. Insolence will increase, people will no longer have respect, and none will offer reproof. Religious studies will be despised and used by nonbelievers to strengthen their cause; the government will become godless, academies places of immorality, and the religious will be denigrated.[33]

Judaism will suffer greatly because of these upheavals. There is a tradition that the Jews will split up into various groups, each laying claim to the truth, making it almost impossible to discern true Judaism from the false. This is the meaning of the prophecy (Isa. 59:15), "truth will fail."[34]

It has also been predicted that many will leave the fold of Judaism completely. This is how our sages interpret the prophecy (Dan. 12:10), "The wicked shall do wickedly, and not understand."[35]

Of course, there will be some Jews who remain true to their traditions. They will realize that they are witnessing the death throes of a degenerate old order and will not be drawn into it. But they will suffer all the more for this, and be dubbed fools for not conforming to the debased ways of the pre-Messianic Age. This is the meaning of the prophecy (Isa. 59:15), "He who departs from evil will be considered a fool."[36]

One of the most important traditions regarding the Messianic Age concerns the ingathering of the Diaspora and the resettlement of the Land of Israel. It will begin with a measure of political independence,[37] and, according to some, with the permission of the other nations.[38] There are numerous traditions that Jews will begin to return to the Land of Israel as a prelude to the Messiah.[39] There is also a tradition that the land will be cultivated at that time, based on the prophecy (Ezekiel 36:8), "But you mountains of Israel, you shall shoot forth your branches and yield your fruit to My people of Israel, for they are at hand to come."[40] There is also a tradition that the Messiah will reveal himself in the Land of Israel.[41]

There is even evidence that the majority of the Jews will have to return to their homeland before the Messiah comes in a non-miraculous manner. One of our important traditions regarding the advent of the Messiah is that it will mark the return of prophecy.[42] Furthermore, according to many traditions, the Messiah will be preceded by the prophet Elijah,[43] and furthermore, he himself will be a prophet.[44] However, there is a basic teaching that prophecy can only exist in the Land of Israel,[45] and then, only when the majority of Jews live there.[46] Thus, unless we assume that this rule is to be broken, the majority of Jews will have to live in the Land of Israel before the Messianic Age commences.

Another important consideration is the tradition that the *Bais HaMikdash* or Holy Temple will be rebuilt before the onset of the Messianic Age.[47] However, there is also a tradition that Jerusalem cannot be rebuilt before the ingathering of the diaspora.[48] This would also seem to indicate that Israel will be settled before the Messianic Age. However, it is possible that the Messiah himself will accomplish these things before he is actually recognized for what he is.[49] We will discuss this point later.[50]

Into a world prepared to receive him, the Messiah will then be born.

He will be a mortal human being, born normally of human parents.[51] Tradition states that he will be a direct descendant of King David,[52] and indeed, there are numerous Jewish families today that can claim such lineage.[53]

We all know of leaders who have literally changed the course of history. We have seen, for example, how an evil genius like Hitler literally hypnotized an entire nation, bringing it to do things that normally would be unthinkable in a civilized society. If such power exists for evil, it must certainly exist for good.

Now, imagine a charismatic leader greater than any other in man's history. Imagine a political genius surpassing all others. With the vast communication networks now at our disposal, he could spread his message to the entire world and change the very fabric of our society.

Now imagine that he is a religious Jew, a Tzadik. It may have once seemed far-fetched for a Tzadik to assume a role in world leadership, but the world is becoming increasingly more accustomed to accepting leaders of all races, religions, and ethnic groups. We may soon have reached the stage where it is not far-fetched to picture a Tzadik in such a role.

One possible scenario could involve the Middle East situation. This is a problem that involves all the world powers. Now imagine a Jew, a Tzadik, solving this thorny problem.[54] It would not be inconceivable that such a demonstration of statesmanship and political genius would place him in a position of world leadership. The major powers would listen to such an individual.

Let us go a step further. With peace established in the Land of Israel, he could induce many more Jews to immigrate to Israel. Perhaps he would negotiate with the Russian government to allow all of its Jews to leave. Things might by then have become uncomfortable enough for American Jews to induce them to emigrate as well. Witness the decay of the large cities where the majority of Jews live and work. In such an unassuming manner, the ingathering of the exiles could take place.

The Jewish people have always had a profound respect for those who assume roles of world leadership. This Tzadik would naturally be a most respected leader in all Jewish circles. He might even make religion respectable.

It is just possible that all Jewish leaders would agree to name him their leader and confer upon him the Mosaic ordination.[55] The chain of this ordination was broken some sixteen hundred years ago[56] and must be renewed before the Sanhedrin, the religious supreme court and legislature of the Jews, can be re-established.[57] If this Tzadik was so ordained by the entire community, he could then re-establish the Sanhedrin. This is a necessary condition for the rebuilding of the Temple, as we find (Isa. 1:26), "And I will restore your judges as at first, and your counselors as at the beginning, afterward you shall be called the city of righteousness, the faithful city."[58] Such a Sanhedrin would also be able to formally recognize the Messiah.[59]

In his position of leadership, through direct negotiation and perhaps with the concurrence of the world powers,[60] this Tzadik might just be able to regain the Temple Mount for the Jewish people. With a Sanhedrin to iron out the many halachic questions, it might then be possible to rebuild the *Bais HaMikdash,* the Holy Temple.

However, if this is accomplished, we will already have fulfilled the essential part of the Messianic promise.

Thus, the Rambam (Maimonides) writes, "If there arises a ruler from the House of David, who is immersed in Torah and *Mitzvos* like David his ancestor, following both the Written and Oral Law, who leads Israel back to the Torah, strengthening its laws and fighting G-d's battles, then we may assume that he is the Messiah. If he is further successful in rebuilding the Temple on its original site and gathering the dispersed of Israel, then his identity as the Messiah is a certainty."[61]

It is very important to note that these accomplishments are a minimum for our acceptance of an individual as the Messiah. There have been numerous people who have claimed to be the Messiah, but the fact that they did not achieve these minimal goals proved them to be false.

Of course, none of this precludes a miraculous advent of the Messiah or any other scenario. It is a foundation of our faith that the Messianic Age can miraculously begin any day.[62] When Rabbi Yehoshua ben Levi asked Elijah when would the Messiah come, he answered with the verse (Ps. 95:7), "Today — if you hearken to His voice."[63]

As both a genius and Tzadik, the Messiah will see through the sham and hypocrisy of this world. Thus, the prophet foretold (Isa. 11:3), "He will sense the fear of the Lord, and he shall not judge after the sight of his eyes, nor decide after the hearing of his ears."[64]

As the Messiah's powers develop, so will his fame. The world will begin to recognize his profound wisdom and come to seek his advice. As a Tzadik, he will teach all mankind to live in peace and follow G-d's teachings. Thus the prophet foretold (Isa. 2:2-4):

> And it shall come to pass in the end of days
> that the mountain of G-d's house
> shall be set over all other mountains
> and lifted high above the hills
> and all nations shall come streaming to it.
> And many people shall come and say:
> Come let us go up to the mountain of G-d
> to the house of the G-d of Jacob
> and He (the Messiah) will teach us His ways
> and we will walk in His paths.
> For out of Zion shall go forth the Torah
> and G-d's word from Jerusalem.
> And He (the Messiah) will judge between nations
> and decide between peoples.
> And they shall beat their swords into plowshares
> and their spears into pruning hooks;
> Nation shall not lift up sword against nation
> neither shall they practice war any more. [65]

Although the Messiah will influence and teach all mankind, his main mission will be to bring the Jews back to G-d. Thus, the prophet said (Hosea 3:4-5), "For the children of Israel shall sit many days without king or prince . . . Afterward shall the children of Israel return and seek the L-rd their G-d and David their king . . . in the end of days." Similarly (Ezek. 37:24), "And My servant David shall be king over them, and they shall have one shepherd, and they shall also walk in My ordinances and observe My laws."

As society reaches toward perfection and the world becomes increasingly G-dly, men will begin to explore the transcendental more and more. As the prophet said (Isa. 11:9), "For the earth shall be full of the knowledge of G-d, as the waters cover the sea." More and more people will achieve the mystical union of prophecy, as foretold (Joel 3:1), "And it shall come to pass afterward, that I will pour out My spirit on all flesh and your sons and your daughters shall prophesy . . ."[66]

Although man will still have free will in the Messianic Age, he will have every inducement to do good and follow G-d's teachings. It will be as if the power of evil were totally annihilated.[67] And as man approaches this lofty level, he will also become worthy of a divine providence not limited by the laws of nature. What is now manifestly miraculous will ultimately become part of the nature of things.[68]This, wedded to man's newly gained powers to bring forth the best that untainted nature has to offer, will bring man to his ultimate destiny, which is the World to Come.[69]

Living on the threshold of the Messianic age as we do should be a most exciting experience for any Jew. Other generations have expected the Messiah's imminent appearance on the basis of the forced interpretation of one or two prophecies, whereas we are living through the entire range of Messianic tradition, often coming to pass with uncanny literalness. If you keep your eyes open, you can almost see every headline bringing us a step closer to this goal.

But as also predicted, it is a time of great challenge. We live in a time of snares and temptations lying in wait for the unwary, drawing them away from the Truth. As one great Rebbe said, "It is very easy to be a Jew, but difficult to *want* to be a true Jew."

But imagine a time during which the Messiah has already come. The truth has been revealed. The entire world recognizes what Judaism really is, and the Torah is acknowledged as G-d's true teaching to the world. Those who have followed G-d's way are now the teachers and leaders of a generation desperately trying to make up for lives wasted on vanity and foolishness.

There are two groups. Those who have lived by the truth of Torah, and those who have not, now desperately wishing to become a part of it.

To which group will you belong?

NOTES

1. Cf. *Yad, Tshuvah* 6:5; *Moreh Nevuchim* 2:48.
2. *Sichos HaRan* No. 5.
3. See *Ralbag, Metzudos David, Malbim ad loc., Yalkut* 2:959. Cf. *Berachos* 55a Rashi *ad loc.*, "*Terichim,*" *Yalkut* 1:860, 2:306; *Emunos VeDeyos* 4:7 end; Maharatz Chayos, *Megillah* 11a; *Radak* on Jer. 10:23.
4. Rabbi Moshe Chaim Lutzatto, *KaLaCh Pischey Chochmah* No. 2.
5. *Idem, Derech HaShem* 2:1:1.
6. 13 Principles of Faith No. 12; *Ikkarim* 4:42.
7. *Sanhedrin* 98a, *Or HaChaim* on Num. 24:17.
8. *Pesachim* 54b, *Emunos VeDeyos* 8:2.
9. *Menoras HaMaor* 3:end (237), quoting *Shaar HaShamayim; Tosefos Yom Tov* on *Avodah Zarah* 4:7. Cf. *Berachos* 20a.
10. Cf. *Baba Metzia* 85b.
11. *Sanhedrin* 99a, *Shabbos* 63a, Maharsha, Rashash *ad loc. Yad, Tshuvah* 9:2, *Melachim* 11:3. See *Kesef Mishneh, Lechem Mishneh, Tshuvah* 8:7. Also see Abarbanel, *Yeshuos Meshicho* (Koenigsberg, 5621) 3:7 (56b); Maharal, *Netzach Yisroel* 50.
12. *Yerushalmi, Berachos* 1:1, *Yoma* 3:2; *Shir HaShirim Rabbah* 6:16, *Etz Yosef ad loc., Midrash Tehillim* 18, *Zohar* 1:170a. Also see *Shnei Luchos HaBris* (Jerusalem 5720), *Bais David,* 1:37b; Rabbi Tzvi Hirsch Kalisher, *Derishas Tzion* (Jerusalem, 5724) 1:1. p. 88.
13. *Yad Melachim* 11:3, 12:2.
14. Rav Zeral, *Sanhedrin* 97a. Cf. *Tosefos, Eruvin* 43b "*VeAssur,*" *Emunos VeDeyos* 8:6.
15. *Bereshis Rabbah* 95:1; *Tanchuma, Metzora* 2, *Zohar* 2:82b.
16. *Sifri* (315) on Deut. 32:12.
17. *Kesubos* 111b.
18. *Shabbos* 30b, according to interpretation of Rambam on *Sanhedrin* 10:1. Cf. *Yerushalmi, Shekalim* 6:2.
19. *Zohar* 1:12b on Isa. 40: 31. Cf. *Sanhedrin* 92b.
20. *Tikuney Zohar* 14b, on Cant. 6:8. See my article on "On Extraterrestrial Life," in the Cheshvan 5733 issue of *Intercom*.
21. *Zohar* 1:117a.
22. *Pesikta Rabosi,* end of No. 1. Cf. *Shir HaShirim Rabbah* 2:29.
23. *Shabbos* 63a, *Emunos VeDeyos* 8:8; Rambam, *Milchamos HaShem* No. 49.
24. *Radak ad loc., Yad, Melachim* 12:1.
25. *Sichos Moharan, Avodas HaShem* No. 99.
26. *Emunos VeDeyos ibid.* Cf. *VaYikra Rabbah* 25:8.
27. Cf. *Malbim ad loc.* See also *Yad, Melachim* 12:5.
28. *Milchamos HaShem* No. 45. *Berashis Rabbah* 20:10, from Isa. 65:25. See also *Berashis Rabbah* 12:15, *Yeshuos Meshicho* 3:6 (55b), Rabbi Meir Ibn Gabbai, *Avodas HaKodesh* 2:38.
29. Cf. *Gur Aryeh* (Maharal) *ad loc.*
30. Or "a woman shall turn into a man." See Rashi *ad loc., Midrash Tehillim* 73:4, *Zohar* 1:257a. Also see *Midrash Tehillim* 146:6, *Yeshuos Meshicho* 4:3 (70a).

31. *Netzach Yisroel* No. 36. Cf. *Sanhedrin* 98b.
32. Cf. *Emunos VeDeyos* 8:6.
33. *Sotah* 49b, *Sanhedrin* 97a, *Derech Eretz Zuta,* 10, *Shir HaShirim Rabbah* 2:29, *Pirkey Rabbi Eliezer* 32, Zohar 3:67b, 125b.
34. Or "truth shall be divided into flocks." *Sanhedrin* 97a.
35. Rambam, *Igeres Taimon* (Jerusalem, 5721) p. 5; *Sichos HaRan* 35. Cf. *Zohar* 3:124b, 153a.
36. *Sanhedrin* 97a.
37. *Ibid.* 98, Maharsha *ad loc.* "And SheTichla."
38. *Ramban* on Cant. 8:12, *Radak* on Ps. 146:3; *Derishas Tzion* 1:2 (p.90). For an alternative interpretation, see *VaYoel Moshe* 1:68.
39. See Midrash quoted in *Shevelei Emunah* 10:1.
40. *Sanhedrin* 98a. However, see *VaYoel Moshe* 1:66 for another interpretation.
41. Midrash quoted in note 39. Also see *Igeres Taimon* p. 32.
42. *Ibid.* p. 30.
43. Malachi 3:25, *Radak ad loc.*; *Eruvin* 43b, *Eduyos* 8:7, *Targum J.* on Deut. 30:4, *Pirkey Rabbi Eliezer* 43. See *Yad, Melachim* 10:2, *Keresei U'Pleisei,* end of *Bais HaSafak; VaYoel Moshe* 1:52.
44. *Yad, Tshuvah* 9:2.
45. *Mechilta* on Ex. 12:1, *Tanchuma Bo* 5, *Rashi, Radak* on Jonah 1:3, *Zohar* 1:85a, 121a, 2:170b, *Emunos VeDeyos* 3:5 end, *Kuzari,* 2:14, *Ibn Ezra* on Joel 3:1, *Tshuvos Radbaz* 2:842; *Sifri, Ramban, Yalkut* (919) on Deut. 18:15.
46. *Yoma* 9b, *Kuzari* 2:24 (40a). Also see *Avodas HaKodesh* 4:25.
47. *Yerushalmi, Maaser Sheni* 5:2 (29b), *Tosefos Yom Tov,* Rashash, *Maleches Shlomo, ibid.* *Shnei Luchos HaBris, Bais David* 1:37b. Cf. *Megillah* 17b end. In *Yalkut* 2:499, we find that the Messiah will reveal himself on the Temple roof. See also *VaYoel Moshe* 55f, Rabbi Yehudah Gershoni, *Mishpat HaMelucha* 11:1.
48. *Berachos* 49a, *Yalkut* 2:888 from Ps. 147:2.
49. *Yad, Melachim* 11:4.
50. There is, however, another opinion stating that it is forbidden for the Jews to emigrate en masse before the actual coming of the Messiah. This is based on an oath to that effect, cf. *Kesubos* 111a, *Shir HaShirim Rabbah* 2:18, *VaYoel Moshe* 1:10. This is the opinion of the Satmar Chassidim and others who oppose the resettlement of Israel. However, a complete discussion of this issue is beyond the scope of this article.
51. *Yad, Melachim* 11:3, *Yeshuos Meshicho* No. 3, p. 45 ff., *Lekutey Tshuvos Chasam Sofer* No. 98.
52. Cf. Isa. 11:1.
53. Thus, for example, the Maharal of Prague was able to trace his lineage to the Gaonic line of Rav Ha'ai and Rav Sherira, who in turn traditionally were descendants of King David. There are numerous families that still trace their lineage to the Maharal.
54. *Pirkey Rabbi Eliezer* 29, as quoted in beginning of *Yeshuos Meshicho* (our editions lack the critical part); *Igeres Taimon* p. 34, from Ps. 120:5, cf. *Radak ad loc.*
55. *Rambam* on *Sanhedrin* 1:3; *Yad, Sanhedrin* 4:11. Rabbi Yaakov Berab

temporarily restored this ordination in 1538, ordained several Safed scholars, including Rabbi Yosef Karo, author of the *Shulchan Aruch*.

56. Cf. *Bereshis Rabbah* 31:12.
57. *Sanhedrin* 4:4 (37a), *Yad, Sanhedrin* 4:1.
58. *Rambam, loc. cit.* Also see *Megillah* 17b, Rashi *ad loc. "VeKeven"; Eruvin* 43b, Maharatz Chayos *ad loc.*; Rashash, *Sanhedrin* 13b.
59. Cf. *Tosefta Sanhedrin* 3:2, *Yad Sanhedrin* 5:1, *Melachim* 1:3.
60. See Midrash quoted in *Bachaya* on Lev. 11:4.
61. *Yad, Melachim* 11:4.
62. *Eruvin* 43a end.
63. *Sanhedrin* 98a.
64. Cf. *Radak ad loc., Sanhedrin* 93b, *Yad Melachim* 11:3.
65. See *Yad, Tshuvah* 9:2.
66. *Radak, Metzudos ad loc., BaMidbar Rabbah* 15:19 end; Rabbi Moshe Chaim Lutzatto, *Likutey Yedios HaEmes, Maamar HaIkkarim* (New York, 5706) p. 230.
67. *Succah* 52a, *Zohar* 1:109a, 128b, 137a, 2:41a, 136a, 3:54a.
68. *Sh'nei Luchos HaBris, Bais David,* 1:32a; *Yeshuos Meshicho* 3:7 (p. 56b).
69. *Avodas HaKodesh* 2:38, *Netzach Yisrael* 50.

Many times, the missionary attraction has more dimensions than just theology. Young people, in particular, are susceptible to proselytizing movements which are well organized, using charismatic figures to lure them into their fold. This story, as told to Aryeh Kaplan, is a typical example of the way the missionaries actually work, and how their influence can be counteracted.

My Way Back—
A Girl's Story

Let me begin by saying that I had always been turned off by Judaism as a child. I didn't come from a religious family, and whatever I learned in Hebrew School didn't have anything to do with the real world. In general, I got the impression that everyone was merely going through the motions, but that no one was really interested in Judaism. Even my Hebrew teachers did not seem to be convinced of what they were teaching.

Most of the Jewish girls in my school went out with non-Jewish boys, and I was no exception. These boys seemed a lot nicer, and besides, most of the Jewish boys were too busy taking out gentile girls. I was no different than most of my friends, and by the time I was sixteen, I had experienced everything — and I do mean everything.

Even though my parents weren't religious, they tried to shove Judaism down my throat. They got very uptight when I went out with gentile boys, but they could never really give me a good reason. All they could do was hassle me. They didn't like the way I dressed, and blew up when I stayed out all night.

Then one day something happened that changed my life. I met a boy by the name of Greg. As soon as I met him, I realized that he was different. Most boys were only interested in one thing, but Greg wasn't. He treated me like a person and understood my problems.

It wasn't long before I found out the reason why he was different. He told me that he was a Christian — that he had discovered Christ.

I thought that Greg was the most fascinating guy that I had ever met. We talked about religion, and for the first time in my life, it made sense. He told me about G-d and sin, and how one can reach G-d by believing in Christ. He spoke about religion in a very different manner than my rabbi and teachers had. This was the first time that I had ever heard anyone talk like that, and it really turned me on.

I spent many long nights talking to Greg. It seemed like a whole new world was opening for me. I wanted to learn more, and Greg introduced me to the "Jews for Jesus." It was my greatest trip ever.

Soon I was busy attending their meetings and handing out literature. They sent me to a camp to learn how to organize and convince other Jews. When I went to college the next year, I became one of the organizers of "Jews for Jesus" on my campus. We had around a dozen members, but some forty kids usually came to our meetings.

Then, one day, a Jewish organization on campus had a program directed against us. We learned that two rabbis were supposed to be speaking against us. Several of our top men came down and briefed us on how to respond to these rabbis. They gave us the points that they were likely to bring up, and taught us how to answer them. I knew all the Biblical verses by heart, and was aware of what "false" explanations these rabbis were sure to give.

I'll never forget the day of that program. The other Jewish Christians and myself sat in the front row, ready to "do battle for Christ."

One of the things that surprised me about the two rabbis was that they were both young and with it. They were also very bright. During the question and answer period, I found them demolishing all of our well-prepared arguments. All the smooth answers that I had learned didn't seem so smooth any more.

One of the rabbis really put my friend, another "Jew for Jesus," down. The rabbi drew him into a discussion about salvation, and my friend replied that no one could be saved unless he believed in Christ. The rabbi asked if this meant that anyone who did not believe in Christ would go to hell. When my friend answered yes, the rabbi asked, "Does this even include me?" My friend was prepared for this and he boldly answered, "Yes, you too." But the rabbi was not finished. He then threw the punch line: "And how about the six million Jews who died in Nazi concentration camps? Are they in heaven or in hell?"

My friend was taken aback. He mumbled something about them accepting Christ at the last moment, but I could tell that he was shook. To tell the truth, so was I.

The other rabbi was much more pleasant. He had a smile in his voice, and when he spoke to me, he really made me feel as if he cared for me as a person.

After the program, I sought out this rabbi and tried to continue our argument. He would not argue. He told me that he was tired of debating these Biblical passages, and that most of our Christian "proofs" had been refuted centuries ago. He said that if I was interested in returning to true Judaism, he would spend all the time in the world with me, but that for dusty debates, he had no time. Just before I left, he said something that burned in my mind for the next few weeks. They were words that I have never really forgotten.

He told me, "Don't you owe it to three thousand years of Jewish history to learn about your own religion before you try others? Don't you owe it to the millions who gave their lives rather than accept Christianity? Don't you owe it to yourself to try to meet a real turned-on Jew?"

The meeting left me in a state of shock. I couldn't get the rabbi's words out of my mind. What did I owe to our history and our martyrs? He said that he would teach me. I had to speak to him again.

I tried to find out about the rabbi, but no one seemed to know him. Finally, I got up enough courage and asked the boy who had organized the program. His name was Danny, and he was one of the few religious Jewish boys in our school.

Danny explained that the rabbi had just been visiting, and lived in a far-away city. I was downcast. I had to speak to someone, and Danny seemed very understanding.

We began to talk, and I found Danny every bit as fascinating as Greg, but in an entirely different way. He told me how he had come from a nonreligious family just like mine, and how he had finally discovered Judaism. I could really respect the way he was religious. He told me how hard it was, and how he had to explain to his friends why he couldn't eat with them or do anything on Friday night and Saturday afternoon. Danny also spoke about G-d, and his words seemed wiser and deeper than anything I had ever heard from my Christian friends.

I found myself caught in the middle. All my best friends were into Jesus, yet I felt that I wanted out. Somehow, the Jesus trip no longer turned me on. I was starting to really feel Jewish and felt myself being pulled closer and closer to it. It wasn't the dry stuff that I had learned in Hebrew School, or the hypocrisy of my parents. What Danny was telling me about was a kind of turned-on Judaism that I never even dreamed existed. I recalled the rabbi's words, "Don't you owe it to yourself to try to meet a real turned-on Jew?"

Finally, I made my decision. I told my Jesus friends that I was leaving them. They told me that the Devil had gotten me, and that I would be damned in hell. All the love that they had talked about no longer seemed to matter. They were trying to frighten me into staying — but they only succeeded in turning me off completely. I had made up my mind and would give Judaism a chance.

I spoke to Danny a great deal, and he tried to explain the true meaning of Judaism to me. He also told me about a youth group that he was active with, and invited me to spend a "Shabbaton" weekend with them.

I went to the Shabbaton, and I must admit that I had never seen anything like it. The whole weekend seemed to be filled with singing and dancing — a real festival of life. Their prayers were full of life and meaning — nothing like the dry services at my Temple.

Just before the Friday night service some rabbi was supposed to be giving a class. I decided to go, and imagine my surprise when I found that it was the same rabbi who had debated me several months earlier. I don't think he recognized me and I was too embarrassed to say anything about our previous encounter. But somehow, it made me feel that I had come back.

The class began with a discussion about drugs and getting high. The rabbi said that it was possible to get high from davening — praying to G-d. I couldn't quite believe that. But then, at the Friday evening prayers, a young boy led the services. He was only around sixteen, but he sang so beautifully that each word seemed to come straight from his heart. It seemed as if he was flying. It wasn't very long before I felt myself flying along with everyone else.

I must say that this Shabbaton was one of the best experiences that I ever had. I learned so much, and felt even more. When I came back to school, I started saying the *Sh'ma* every morning and night. I even began to try to say some blessings before I ate. It wasn't long before I joined the kosher dining club at school, and I even tried to begin to keep Shabbos.

This might sound corny, but I really think that I'm enlightened. I am happier now than I've ever been before. I don't know how to put it exactly, but I really feel that I have found the true way to G-d.